Creativity is a topic that has traditionally interested psychologists, historians, and biographers. In recent years, developments in cognitive science and artificial intelligence have provided a powerful computational framework in which creativity can be studied and the creative process can be described and explained.

In this book, creativity in technology is discussed within such a computational framework. Using an important historical episode in computer technology as a case study, namely, the invention of microprogramming by Maurice Wilkes in 1951, the author presents a plausible explanation of the process by which Wilkes may have arrived at his invention.

Based on this case study, the author has also proposed some very general hypotheses concerning creativity that appear to corroborate the findings of some psychologists and historians and that suggest that creative thinking is not significantly different in nature from everyday thinking and reasoning.

This book should be of interest to all those interested in creativity, including cognitive scientists, historians and philosophers of science, historians and philosophers of technology, and artificial intelligence researchers. It should also appeal to the general reader.

CREATIVITY IN INVENTION AND DESIGN

CREATIVITY IN
INVENTION AND DESIGN

Computational and Cognitive Explorations of
Technological Originality

SUBRATA DASGUPTA

CAMBRIDGE
UNIVERSITY PRESS

CAMBRIDGE UNIVERSITY PRESS
Cambridge, New York, Melbourne, Madrid, Cape Town, Singapore, São Paulo

Cambridge University Press
The Edinburgh Building, Cambridge CB2 8RU, UK

Published in the United States of America by Cambridge University Press, New York

www.cambridge.org
Information on this title: www.cambridge.org/9780521430685

© Cambridge University Press 1994

First published 1994
This digitally printed version 2008

A catalogue record for this publication is available from the British Library

Library of Congress Cataloguing in Publication data
Dasgupta, Subrata.
Creativity in invention and design : computational and cognitive
explorations of technological originality / Subrata Dasgupta.
p. cm.
Includes bibliographical references and index.
ISBN 0–521–43068–2 (hc)
1. Creative ability in technology. 2. Creative thinking.
3. Microprogramming. I. Title.
T49.5.D38   1994
608'.019–dc20   93–28650
                                                      CIP

ISBN 978-0-521-43068-5 hardback
ISBN 978-0-521-06889-5 paperback

To
My Father-in-Law
Professor Rabindra Kumar Das Gupta
With Affection and Regard

Contents

Preface   *page* xi
Acknowledgments   xiv

Part I: Creativity in invention and design: issues and ingredients

1 *Creativity, invention, and the computational metaphor*   3
   The significance of philosophy of science   4
   Creativity in the sciences of the artificial   6
   The relevance of computer science   9
   The case study approach   11
   The invention of microprogramming: as a case study   12
   The concept of creativity   15
   The relevance of nonpsychological factors   22
   The invention of microprogramming: as a creative act   24
   Metaphors as explanatory models   27
   Metaphors as explanations of creativity   33
   Computation as metaphor for the explanation of creativity   35
   On the testability of a theory of creativity   39
   The broad picture: a summary   43
   Notes   44

2 *A computational theory of scientific creativity*   51
   Multiple description levels   51
   The knowledge level   55
   A computational theory of scientific creativity: the hypothesis   60
   The explanatory nature of the computational theory   62
   The testability of the computational theory   62
   Notes   63

Contents

3   *Maurice Wilkes and the origins of microprogramming: the*
    historical setting   65
    The EDSAC and its control circuits   66
    On the conceptual nature of Wilkes's problem   69
    Representing knowledge: networks and rules   71
    The EDSAC and its diode matrix   75
    The Whirlwind and its control matrix   78
    The emergence of the microprogramming principle   80
    The immediate aftermath   83
    Notes   84

Part II: The invention of microprogramming: a cognitive explanation

4   *Prolegomenon*   91
    A miniexample of a knowledge-level process   94
    Spreading activation   100
    Summary   101
    Notes   102

5   *The genesis of an idea: creating the initial sketch*   103
    Problem recognition and formulation   103
    The idea of a diode matrix   111
    Identifying a stored program computer-like form   117
    Deriving the broad principle of microprogramming   119
    Notes   123

6   *The evolution of an idea: from initial sketch to mature form* 125
    Relating the microprogram and diode matrix ideas   125
    A diode matrix representation of the microprogram   136
    Diode matrix representation of next micro-order addresses   156
    Coupling the diode matrices   168
    The problem of alternative successor addresses   173
    Notes   181

PART III: Reflections on the nature of inventing

7   *Eight hypotheses about the nature of inventing*   189
    Invention as a goal-directed endeavor   190
    Goals as working hypotheses in inventive design   191
    The gradualistic nature of an insight   192

On the mechanics of "bisociation" or the combining of ideas   194
The role of logic and reasoning in acts of creation   196
On the richness and quality of the knowledge body   201
On an assumption concerning the retrieval of knowledge   206
The eight hypotheses   208
Notes   211

8 *Epilogue*   213

Appendix   217
Table A: Inference rules   217
Table B: Facts   219
Table C: Noninference rules   222
Table D: Goals   230

References   233

Index   243

What I am talking about is the theme that historians call "contingency," the notion that given the inordinate complexities of the thousands of unpredictable steps inherent in any complex historical story, and given the large dollop of randomness and irreducible complexity that does exist in the world, you would never get the same thing twice. Whatever happens makes sense after the facts, it is not random and chaotic but it is utterly unpredictable before. If you could rewind the tape . . . you would never know what to predict nor would you ever get again anything like what we got.

Stephen Jay Gould
The Individual in Darwin's World

Preface

The subject matter of this book is creativity in the realm of invention and design. More specifically, it addresses the issues of how significantly original technological ideas or concepts may be produced by individuals. Questions such as this about the nature of the creative process are, of course, far from new. As Brewster Ghiselin pointed out in his introduction to *The Creative Process,* an anthology of writings on the topic, interest in creativity can certainly be traced back to the Greeks. It has continued to be thought about and written on ever since.

The premise of this book, however, is a relatively modern idea. It is the belief that it is possible to construct plausible, detailed, testable explanatory accounts of the cognitive processes underlying specific past acts of creation – acts such as the discovery of physical laws, the elucidation of biochemical pathways, or the invention of artifactual forms. The basic intellectual tool to be used in such explanations originates in the modern disciplines of cognitive science and artificial intelligence: It is the idea that computation-like processes of a certain, rather abstract kind can serve as a powerful *metaphor* with which to probe creativity and that, consequently, it is possible to obtain insight into the nature of specific acts of creation in a way and at a level of detail that has hitherto proved infeasible.

The means by which technological creativity is examined in this book is, in fact, a confluence of three distinct strands. One is the *case study* approach in which a specific episode from the history of computer technology, widely recognized as a highly original landmark, is singled out for study. The episode in question is the invention, in 1951, of a technique called microprogramming and its use in the design of a new form of the control unit in digital computers. The inventor in this case was Maurice Wilkes, one of the handful of computer pioneers in the heady years of the 1940s.

The second strand is, as already mentioned, the adoption of a *computational metaphor* as the basis for explaining creative acts. The third strand in this inquiry is the use of published and other forms of documentary records as the "data" around which a plausible explanation of this particular act of creation is built.

The crucial word here is "plausible"; for every specific process of creation is of a contingent nature. To paraphrase Stephen Jay Gould, if we had the luxury of placing the scientist, inventor, or engineer in exactly the same "initial conditions" as those that led to the relevant act of creation of interest to us, there is no guarantee whatsoever that the same process or even an approximately close process would unfold. Plausible explanations are the best we can hope to achieve.

Plausibility, of course, is a matter of degree. If an explanation of a particular creative act relies on certain assumptions about the creator's background, education, experience, intellectual ethos, and knowledge, then the plausibility (and, incidentally, the testability) of the explanation will largely be determined by the extent to which these assumptions are supported by the historical evidence. Thus, the account given in this book of how Wilkes might have been led to the idea of microprogramming will be judged plausible to the extent that the supportive evidence is thought to be consistent with the documentary records. The extent to which I have succeeded in this regard is a matter for the reader to judge.

The book is organized in three parts. Part I presents general backgrounds to the three main aspects of this work – the notion of creativity itself and the problem of how one may try to understand it, the computational metaphor as it is employed here, and the historical background to Maurice Wilkes's invention of microprogramming.

Part II begins by describing briefly the general manner in which the computational explanation is constructed (Chapter 4). Chapters 5 and 6 constitute the actual computational account of the invention process. These two chapters are unavoidably long and detailed since they aim to provide as complete, comprehensive, and unambiguous an explanation as possible. (The reader may choose to simply dip into some of the sections in these two chapters to get a flavor of the explanations rather than wade through the gory details. By doing this he or she would not lose the main thread of the argument).

Finally, Part III returns to the general issue of creativity and continues the discussion initiated in Part I but with the benefit of the case study in hand. At the heart of this discussion is a set of eight general hypotheses about the nature of the creative process especially as it pertains to invention. Although these hypotheses are the direct fruits of this one particular case study, they appear to be well supported by other studies of the creative process, conducted both within and outside the computational framework. The penultimate hypothesis may be viewed as the single most important philosophical conclusion of this book. It asserts that the process of technical invention is cognitively indistinguishable from the process of scientific discovery.

Manchester, U.K.
March 1993

Acknowledgments

The central figure in this book is, of course, Maurice Wilkes, whom I first met in 1977. Since then, I have had the pleasure and benefit of innumerable conversations with him, in such varied places as Cambridge, Vancouver, Palo Alto (California), Lafayette (Louisiana), and Stockholm, on the early development of computer technology. In the course of this work, he has responded readily to my rather specific queries on the genesis of microprogramming. He also gave me access to his diaries for the relevant period. I thank him for his cooperation in these matters and also for his comments on Chapter 3 of this book.

I also thank the following individuals: James Fetzer, philosopher and cognitive scientist, who reviewed the manuscript both at the very early stage when it was just a proposal and in its completed form, and whose detailed comments have been invaluable; Burton Raffel, eclectic scholar in the humanities, who, having recently written his own book on creativity, offered many insightful comments on an early version of Chapter 1 from his special vantage point; Tony Maida, computer scientist and member of the "artificial intelligentsia," for his very careful reading of, and thoughtful comments on, an early version of Chapter 1; three anonymous publisher's reviewers, for their (mostly) constructive comments on the work both in the proposal stage and after completion; Alan Harvey, my editor at Cambridge University Press, for his constant and friendly support in the course of this project; and Shermain James, my secretary at the University of Manchester Institute of Science and Technology, who, with ever-present equanimity, typed several versions of the manuscript and helped in innumerable other ways.

The initial part of this work was done during a rather idyllic summer spent in 1991 as a visiting scientist at the Indian Institute of Science and the Centre for Development of Advanced Computing, both in Bangalore, India. I thank the United Nations Development Programme for their generous support of this visit and my friends and colleagues in Bangalore for making the stay there so congenial.

I thank the many publishers and authors who permitted me to quote excerpts from their publications. The quotations are taken from the following sources:

M. V. Wilkes, *Memoirs of a Computer Pioneer,* copyright © 1985, MIT Press, Cambridge, MA. Reprinted by permission.

M. V. Wilkes, D. J. Wheeler and S. Gill, *The Preparation of Programs for an Electronic Digital Computer,* copyright © 1951, Addison-Wesley Publishing Company. Reprinted by permission of Addison-Wesley Publishing Company, Inc., Reading, MA.

S. J. Gould, *The Individual in Darwin's World,* Edinburgh University Press, copyright © 1990, S. J. Gould. Reprinted by permission.

D. N. Perkins, *The Mind's Best Work,* copyright © 1981, Harvard University Press, Cambridge, MA. Reprinted by permission.

P. N. Johnson-Laird, *The Computer and the Mind,* copyright © 1988, Harvard University Press, Cambridge, MA. Reprinted by permission.

M. V. Wilkes, *Automatic Digital Computers,* copyright © 1956, Methuen & Co., London. Reprinted by permission of the publisher.

M. V. Wilkes, "The Best Way to Design an Automatic Calculating Machine," Report of the Manchester University Computer Inaugural Conference, 1951, copyright © 1951, Ferranti. Reprinted by permission of Ferranti International plc.

A. Koestler, *The Act of Creation,* copyright © 1964, Hutchinson & Co., London. Reprinted by permission of the publisher.

M. V. Wilkes and W. Renwick, "The E.D.S.A.C.," Report of Conference on High Speed Automatic Calculating Machines, January 22–5, 1949, University Math Laboratory, Cambridge. Reprinted by permission of M. V. Wilkes and the Cambridge University Computer Laboratory.

R. Arnheim, *Picasso's Guernica: The Genesis of a Painting,* 2d Edition copyright © 1972, The Regents of the University of California. Reprinted by permission.

M. V. Wilkes and J. B. Stringer, "Microprogramming and the Design of the Control Circuits in an Electronic Digital Computer," *Proceedings of the Cambridge Philosophical Society,* pt. 2, 49, April 1953, 230–8, copyright © 1953, Cambridge University Press. Reprinted by permission.

M. V. Wilkes, "The Design of a Control Unit – Reflections on Reading Babbage's Notebooks," *Annals of the History of Computing,* 3, 2 (April 1981), 116–20, copyright © 1981, AFIPS (now IEEE). Reprinted by permission.

M. V. Wilkes, "The Genesis of Microprogramming," *Annals of the History of Computing,* 8, 2 (April 1986), 116–18, copyright © 1986, AFIPS (now IEEE). Reprinted by permission.

M. V. Wilkes, "EDSAC 2," *IEEE Annals of the History of Computing,* 14, 4 (1992), 49, copyright © 1992, IEEE. Reprinted by permission.

Finally, and most importantly, I thank my wife Sarmistha and my sons Jaideep and Monish (alias Shome) for providing the support, encouragement, and domestic congeniality without which work such as this is hardly possible. This book is dedicated to a scholar extraordinary whose learning, wisdom, and intellectual integrity has sustained and inspired me for two decades and more.

Part I

Creativity in invention and design:
issues and ingredients

1

Creativity, invention, and the computational metaphor

Among the many features of the mind that humans have chosen to speculate on, few evoke a greater sense of enigma than creativity. Believing that as a cognitive act it stands well beyond the humdrum, we pay special homage to those whose occupations are thought to be intrinsically creative: artists, scientists, writers, musicians, and inventors. Recognizing further that even among them there are a few whose works are so very special and so far transcend the achievements of the rest, we accord them extra reverence; we often bestow on them the appellation "genius"; we wonder, sometimes in awe and not without a tinge of envy, about their mental makeup; and we ponder the nature of the process their minds have enacted in arriving at a particular poem, symphony, theory, or artifact.

We see evidence of this compelling interest in creativity in many distinct forms. The very best type of biography, for instance, embodies an engagement on the part of the biographer with his or her subject's life and work. The biographer's task is to comprehend how childhood, social background, world-view, intellectual influences, personal relationships, and so on may have affected, perhaps even serve as an explanation of, the subject's particular acts of creation. In Richard Ellman's (1982) biography of James Joyce, there is a chapter titled "The Backgrounds [sic] to 'The Dead'" in which the main elements of this short story – its characters, the setting, even the basic plot – are explained or elucidated by Ellman in terms of Joyce's own background and experience. If one wants to know or understand how Joyce came to create "The Dead," then Ellman's account is at least a partial account of that process.

We see a similar though more explicit preoccupation with creativity in the work of historians of science as, using documentary evidence, they strive to trace in detail how particular scientists were led to the formulations of particular theories or laws. A notable illustration of this is Conant's (1950a) account of how Antoine Lavoisier's chemical researches in the eighteenth century led

conclusively to the refutation of the theory of phlogiston and effectively
brought about the chemical revolution. Another example along the same lines
is Holmes's (1980) reconstruction of Hans Krebs's discovery of the ornithine
cycle for urea synthesis in the 1930s. Historians such as Conant and Holmes
are satisfied neither with mere descriptions of events in the annals of science
nor with dispassionate explanations of the causal structure among "objective
scientific facts." They attempt to comprehend the very thought processes
whereby particular scientists – Lavoisier in one case, Krebs in the other – came
to realize particular hypotheses. Such histories are nothing less than inquiries
into the creative process.

On a few occasions, as documented by Ghiselin (1952), the creators themselves have conducted such inquiries. So we have on record, as celebrated
examples of introspection, the account by the nineteenth-century chemist
Friedrich August Kekulé of how he came to discover the ring structure of
benzene, the poet Coleridge's statement as to the genesis of his fragmentary
poem "Kubla Khan,"[1] Mozart's and Tchaikovsky's letters on the methods of
their composition, and the description by the mathematician Henri Poincaré of
the background to his discovery of a particular class of mathematical functions.

Finally, there are the studies of those whom (in the absence of a better term)
we may call the systematists. They are the ones who attempt to study creativity
more objectively and systematically, in the hope that general accounts or
theories of the creative process might emerge. For the nonspecialist, the classic
work in this regard is the novelist and student of scientific thought Arthur
Koestler's stupendous study *The Act of Creation* (1964). As we shall see, the
systematists include cognitive psychologists, philosophers of science, and
most recently, computer scientists.

The significance of philosophy of science

For many, the making of a scientific discovery – especially a major one –
epitomizes the highest plateau of creativity. Thus, one might expect that
philosophy of science – the academic discipline concerned centrally with the
structure of science and scientific thought – will have interesting things to say
about the nature of creativity. Quite the contrary, at least until very recent
times! Philosophy of science in fact has shown itself to be remarkably and
stubbornly tardy when it comes to the question of creativity; for, until scarcely
three decades ago, philosophers concerned with science had chosen more or
less to ignore the problem of how scientific discoveries are made.

The chief culprit for this state of affairs is generally thought to be Hans Reichenbach, who in his *Experience and Prediction* (1938) made the explicit distinction between what he called the "context of discovery" and the "context of justification." The former term refers to the actual process whereby discoveries are made, while the latter refers to the means or the logic by which the fruits of discoveries – theories, laws, models – can be validated or justified.

According to Reichenbach, the act of discovery pertains to psychology. Justification, being a construction of the logical grounds of why a given theory or law is (or is not) considered "correct," belongs, properly, to epistemology (to use Reichenbach's word). In other words, philosophy of science is, properly, to be concerned with the context of justification, leaving the context of discovery to the psychologist.[2]

In fact, this notion – that the discovery process itself falls outside the proper concern of philosophy of science – actually predates Reichenbach. In his highly influential *Logic of Scientific Discovery* (1968), originally published in Vienna in 1934 as *Logic der Forschung*, Karl Popper, after noting that the aim of the logic of scientific discovery is to provide an analysis – a logical analysis – of the procedure whereby scientists both construct hypotheses and test them, goes rapidly on to ignore his own advice and, indeed, to refute the very title of his book.

Popper makes the distinction between the *psychology of knowledge* and the *logic of knowledge*. The act or procedure by which a theory is invented or a new idea formulated (or, for that matter, a musical theme is conceived) belongs to psychology, he says, and is of no interest or relevance to the logical analysis of scientific knowledge, that is, to philosophy of science. The latter, according to Popper, is concerned only with the question of validity or justification, that is, with such matters as whether a scientific statement can be justified and, if so, on what grounds. Thus, Popper, even before Reichenbach, consigned the discovery process to the scrapheap of psychology, claiming that there is no logical method for having new ideas and that no one can logically reconstruct such a process.

Thus, for an entire generation, scientific discovery – and, consequently, the creative aspect of the scientific enterprise – remained firmly excluded from the philosopher's domain of inquiry. It remained so until the appearance of Norwood Russell Hanson's *Patterns of Discovery* (1958). Hanson argued that contrary to the received wisdom as expounded by Popper and Reichenbach, there is indeed a logic of discovery that allows one to infer an explanatory hypothesis for some given phenomenon. In contrast to induction – famously rejected by Popper, following David Hume's (1748/1977) argument – or deductive logic, however, the logic of discovery takes the form of *abductive* inference, which is characterized by the schema

(1) Some problem-phenomenon Ψ is observed or needs to be explained.

(2) Ψ would be explicable if hypothesis or theory T were to be true.

(3) There is reason to think that T is true.

Here, the statements above the horizontal line signify the premises (or *antecedents*) of the inference and the statement below the line denotes its conclusions (or *consequence*).[3]

The main problem with this proposal, as pointed out by Nickels (1980b), is that while Hanson provides a rich discussion in support of his argument for abduction as the logic of discovery, he sidesteps the actual issue of how T came to be constructed in the first place. This construction is treated by Hanson as largely a gestalt-like perception, an instantaneous act.

An important characteristic of Hanson's approach is his use of actual historical evidence – as, for instance, when he discusses the birth of Kepler's laws (1958, pp. 73–85). Hanson's philosophy of science may, thus, be viewed as more *empirical* in flavor than those of his celebrated predecessors Popper, Reichenbach, and Carnap.[4] Following Hanson, some of the most impressive insights into the process of scientific discovery (and justification), from a philosophical perspective, have emerged from scholars who either have themselves conducted actual historical studies of specific scientific episodes or have drawn on the evidence provided by historians of science as the empirical basis for their work in much the same spirit that theoretical scientists connect data or other empirical findings to their theory constructions. Thomas Kuhn's seminal monograph *The Structure of Scientific Revolutions* (1962) – possibly the most widely read and discussed tract on the methodology of science after Popper's *Logic* – as well as the more recent writings of Laudan (1977, 1984), Lakatos (1976), Feyerabend (1978), and Ruse (1988), are deeply informed by their familiarity with the relevant historical literature. As we shall see later, historical evidence and, in particular, the case study approach will play a central role in this book when we address the problem of creativity in invention and design.

Creativity in the sciences of the artificial

This brings us to the heart of the matter. The focus of this book is not creativity in general, but creativity in particular (with the hope that light shed on the latter will also illuminate the former) – and, rather specifically, creativity as manifested in the invention and design of artifacts, in the realm of what Herbert Simon (1981) first termed the "sciences of the artificial."

If philosophy of science prior to Hanson proved to be disappointing in the context of discovery – the very stuff of scientific creativity – then philosophy of science both before and after Hanson has remained devastatingly silent when it comes to the sciences of the artificial. To philosophy of science, "science" means the *natural* sciences and the question of how theories about nature came about.[5] It has virtually nothing to say about how theories *about artifacts* are framed.

In *The Sciences of the Artificial* (1981) – first published in 1969 and, in many ways, as profound and original a work as Kuhn's *Structure* (though, perhaps, less well known) – Simon pointed out that the main characteristic of artifacts is that they come into existence with a *purpose* and that, as a consequence, the sciences of the artificial (or more simply for our convenience, the *artificial sciences*), while obviously relying on and founded on the natural sciences must, in a very definite sense, transcend the latter. The natural sciences are concerned entirely with the structure and behavior of things as they *are,* whereas the artificial sciences must necessarily describe objects from the perspective of what purposes they are or were intended to serve – that is, in the context of how things *ought to be.*

It is because of this that an artifact such as the computer can never be "explained" *solely* in terms of semiconductor physics. A computer is intended to serve some purpose, and physics has nothing to say about purpose. A science of computer design must embody principles, laws, theories, and so on that allow an explanation of how computer structure and behavior are related to intended functions or goals. Such laws or theories cannot be restricted to physical laws, though the latter play obviously important roles. Additional principles pertaining to such concepts as organization, system, hierarchy, rationality, and even aesthetics are equally crucial. A science of the artificial is, therefore, a complex compendium of both laws of nature and what might be called *artificial laws.*

It may also be noted at this point that the concept of artifact in Simon's sense (and in the sense used in this book) is broad enough to embrace not only physical artifacts such as computers, aircraft, and buildings, but also symbolic or abstract entities. These include computer programs, economic or social plans, the diagnosis of illnesses, and the organizational structures of corporations.

The artificial sciences thus include not only the hard or classical engineering disciplines – civil and mechanical engineering, chemical technology, metallurgy, and the like – but also computer science, agriculture, management science, and architecture.

Clearly, until we have established a reasonably precise characterization of creativity we can scarcely speak with any authority about what counts as "being creative" in the artificial sciences. This issue is addressed later in the chapter. For the present, we can assert, however, that just as creativity in the natural sciences relates, intuitively, to scientific discovery, so also, as far as the artificial sciences are concerned, creativity must (according to our intuition) relate to the *invention of forms that are to satisfy some requirements or purpose.*

The activity of inventing the *form* of an artifact – in contrast to the act of building or making or physically *realizing* the artifact – is also called *design.*[6] Hence, a major issue pertaining to creativity in the artificial sciences is the issue of how the act of creation occurs during the activity of design. Thus, the central concern of this book is the creativity entailed in the act of *designing or inventing new forms of artifacts.*

One may protest that not every act of design counts as a creative act – no more, that is, than does every instance of scientific problem solving. The engineer, it may be said, very often – perhaps for the larger part of his or her professional career – practices what Brown and Chandrasekaran (1989) referred to as "routine" design and that hardly deserves the appellation "creative." The validity of such observations will, of course, depend on what exactly we mean by creativity or to be creative – issues yet to be addressed. Yet, if we view creativity as characterizing some kind of a cognitive *process,* we suspect that the boundary between routine and creative design – between the concoction of any old form and the invention of new form – may be as problematic to establish formally as that between Kuhn's (1962) celebrated normal science – during which, according to Kuhn, the scientist solves puzzles within the framework or confines of a given paradigm – and revolutionary science, during which an entire paradigm may be supplanted by another.[7]

On the other hand, even though the processes underlying creative and the more humdrum intellectual acts may be difficult to distinguish, scientists – whether in the natural or the artificial domain – usually reach agreement at some point of time as to whether a particular entity in their domain (a theory, an idea, a design) is *important* or *influential* in advancing the "state of the art" of that domain. Accordingly, I shall first identify a particular invention from the domain of computer design that is unequivocally acknowledged by theorists and practitioners alike as a major contribution in computer design. I shall then use this act of invention as the vehicle for examining the nature of creativity in the artificial sciences. Of course, in order to proceed with this latter plan, we shall also have to see in what ways and the extent to which the selected case study exhibits the characteristic symptoms associated with the outcomes of creative acts.

It has already been noted that philosophy of science has had little to say about the artificial sciences, and though the discipline of *history of technology* is rich in its contribution to our knowledge of various aspects of the technological past (Pacey 1992) and has even made some interesting contributions to our understanding of how artifacts and their forms evolve over time (Basalla 1988), there is scarcely any philosophy of the artificial sciences that, one may claim, has originated from the realm of traditional professional philosophy.

In fact, if one were to ask such questions as What is the structure of knowledge in a particular artificial science and how does such knowledge change? What kind of reasoning underlies the design process? If the artificial sciences are indeed governed by laws, theories, or principles that are distinct from those of the natural sciences, what are these differences? Do practitioners in the artificial sciences frame "hypotheses" in the sense this word is understood in the natural sciences? The most interesting, illuminating, and useful answers will most likely emerge from the artificial sciences themselves.[8]

Certainly, Herbert Simon himself, possessed of a catholicity rare in these times, both in his *Sciences of the Artificial* and by his many contributions to artificial intelligence, cognitive psychology, administrative decision making, the theory of economic rationality, and human problem solving, must be regarded as a major figure – perhaps *the* foremost figure – in this arena.[9] However, other important contributions have been made by architects, metallurgists, civil, mechanical, and aeronautical engineers, artificial intelligence researchers, social scientists, and computer scientists.[10]

The relevance of computer science

Computer science plays two central, distinct, yet complementary roles in this discussion. Both stem from the nature of the discipline itself and from the fact that computer science is, in its own right, a science of the artificial.

Broadly stated, computer science is the study of computers and the diverse phenomena surrounding them. In its very essence, the discipline (and the profession it has given rise to) is concerned with the design of artifacts that perform computation, process information, and solve problems. Computational artifacts are of three kinds: They can be *material* objects subject to physical laws – such as the complex electronic circuitry constituting an actual physical computer. They can be *quasi-abstract* in the sense that although, on the one hand, they themselves are not tangible, on the other hand, their existence, usefulness, and "life" depend on an underlying material artifact. All computer programs – "software" – belong to this second category. Finally, computational artifacts may be purely abstract or *formal* entities, existing merely as strings of symbols on paper (or on the terminal screen) and devoid of any physical meaning: Algorithms and the purely mathematical computers called Turing machines are examples of this category.

Regardless of whether they are material or formal, the artifacts of computer science are, almost universally, *complex* in form and *hierarchical* in structure. They are complex in that a given artifact is typically composed of a large number of parts that interact in nontrivial ways. They are hierarchical in that a given whole consists of a number of loosely interacting subsystems; the latter in turn consist of sets of still smaller subsystems, and so on.[11]

Computational artifacts thus provide a rich source of examples for any investigation of the nature of artificial sciences. This is, then, one way in which computer science contributes to this work. As I shall describe in the next section, for our particular purposes – namely, the study of the nature of creativity in invention and design – an aspect of computer design called *microprogramming* will be the focus of investigation.

The other facet of computer science of fundamental relevance to this book originates in the fact that the scope of computer science extends beyond the boundaries of artifacts considered strictly as products of human thought and action to the realm of the natural; for, computer science – and, in particular, the branch of it called *artificial intelligence* (AI) – provides a powerful *language* by means of which cognitive processes can be modeled or described effectively and precisely. Those who conduct research in AI are largely interested in designing artifacts – computer systems – that mimic such aspects of cognition as visual information processing, language understanding, game playing, and so on. The cognitive scientist, on the other hand, uses the theories, tools, and the language of computer science (and AI in particular) to *model* cognitive phenomena and to construct *computational explanations* of such phenomena (Boden 1989).

It is in this latter sense that computer science is particularly relevant to this book. Creativity is manifestly a cognitive process. As we shall see later in this chapter (and in considerably more detail in those to follow), the language of computation allows us to provide *plausible accounts of how creativity may come about in a given situation*.

The case study approach

It was noted earlier that the use of historical material by certain contemporary philosophers of science has added greatly to the plausibility of their accounts of the nature of the scientific enterprise. Likewise, some psychologists, notably Howard Gruber, have also advocated strongly the *case study approach* for investigating the psychology of creativity (Gruber 1981, Wallace and Gruber 1989).

Gruber's argument is persuasive. The systematic study of creativity (if the meaning of creativity is not to be utterly trivialized) must deal "not with the predictable and repeatable – the stuff of normal science – but with the unique and unrepeatable" (1989, p. 3). Insisting that each creative person is a coherent and unique knowing system, a unique ensemble of an entire network of knowledge, beliefs, and values, Gruber is interested in comprehending the specific process and circumstances whereby a particular person gives birth to a particular act of creation. For the observer and student of creativity, it is this inimitability of the creative process that is of central concern – hence the case study approach, one that Gruber used so effectively in his *Darwin on Man: A Psychological Study of Scientific Creativity* (1981) and exemplified further by the studies of Wordsworth, Lavoisier, Faraday, Einstein, William James, and others that appear in the volume edited by Wallace and Gruber (1989). Other discussions along the same lines include F. L. Holmes's masterly studies of Antoine Lavoisier's biochemical discoveries (Holmes 1985, 1989) and of Hans Krebs's elucidation of the mechanics of urea synthesis (Holmes 1980, 1989, 1991), and Arthur Miller's (1986) detailed analysis of the role of imagery in scientific thinking – as observed, in particular, in Einstein, Boltzmann, Bohr, and the gestalt psychologist Max Wertheimer.

In this book we shall follow Gruber's lead. We shall, like Gruber, use a single case study – though from the domain of the artificial rather than the natural sciences. However, the point of departure or divergence from Gruber's approach lies in the purposes that the chosen case study is to serve, as will be explained.

To recall Karl Popper's well-known aphorism, all observations are "theory-laden" (1968, pp. 106–7): One observes within a particular theoretical framework and interprets one's observations in the light of that framework. In the writings of Thomas Kuhn (1962, 1970a, 1970b, 1977), such a framework is generalized into the concept of a "paradigm" whereas Laudan (1977) refers to it as a "research tradition." The case study pursued in this book will allow us, first, to examine in detail how a particular and unique act of invention or design may have come about. We wish to *explain* this act of inventing. Such an explanation demands a paradigm – a theory of the creative process – to work within. As explained later in this chapter, we shall use a theoretical framework or paradigm that is rooted in the *computational metaphor.* The case study will, accordingly, be conducted and the particular act of inventing be explained in the light of this paradigm.

At the same time, it can be argued that case studies may also serve to *test* a paradigm – or, at least, the testable elements therein. In our particular situation, the chosen case study can provide either corroborative evidence in support of the computation metaphor-based theory of the creative process or evidence that casts doubt on the validity of the paradigm.

The invention of microprogramming: as a case study

Although it is a truism to say that significant moments of creativity continue to happen in all the sciences, computer science is especially distinctive in that the birth of the entire field practically took place within the lifetimes of most of those who are currently active in the field. Several of the pioneers involved in the design and construction of the very first digital computers, the first programming systems, the first programming languages, the very first computer programs, and even the first books on computer design and programming are still alive; some even remain active in research, teaching, and industry. This state of affairs presents the student of creativity with a rather unique opportunity for investigating the circumstances under which an entire new artificial science was born.

In the case of the modern digital computer – technically known as the *stored program computer* – it is quite misleading to talk about its invention as if this was the work of a single person. The matter of its origins is complex, diffuse, and still controversial. Common lore has it that John von Neumann was the inventor of the stored program computer. However, as recorded by Randell (1975, chap. 8) and others, the basic concept had actually emerged from discussions, held at the Moore School of Electrical Engineering in Philadelphia, among the same group of engineers and scientists that had previously been involved in the design and construction of the ENIAC (one of the first electronic – though not stored program – computers ever built) at the time this group was planning the successor to the ENIAC.[12]

The main members of this group happened to be Presper Eckert and John Mauchly (the principal designers of the ENIAC), Arthur Burks, von Neumann, and Herman Goldstine. However, according to Wilkes (1968) and Metropolis and Worlton (1980), Eckert and Mauchly had *conceived* the stored program idea *during* the ENIAC project – that is, before von Neumann became associated with the Moore School group. Burks (1980), on the other hand, has broadly apportioned credit for the hardware and engineering aspects of the EDVAC design to Eckert and Mauchly, while the logical design (or, in current terminology, its "architecture") and programming aspects are attributed to von Neumann.[13]

The point of this minor detour in our discussion is simply to draw attention to the fact that selecting the invention of the modern digital computer as a case study – remarkably fascinating and important though it would be – would entail the examination of *group creativity.*

It would be imprudent to suggest categorically that there are fundamental differences between group and individual creativity. However, it is certainly the case that the activities of individuals within a group that has embarked on a common cause – whether in the shape of a brainstorming problem-solving session or collaborating over a protracted period on, say, a scientific project – occur concurrently in time. That is, such activities, at the very least, overlap in time. And one of the important insights that computer science has revealed over the past three decades is that *parallel* processes – that is, processes occurring concurrently and having the obligation to interact, cooperate, and communicate with one another in order to make any collective progress – are enormously more complex and difficult to comprehend than individual, isolated, or *sequential* processes – which have no such obligations.[14] Thus, as a computer scientist interested in studying creativity within a computational framework, I have placed the enterprise of group creativity beyond the scope or intent of this book on the grounds of complexity alone. My focus, like Gruber's, is on the *creativity of the individual* – recognizing fully, of course, that no individual, even of the most creative variety, is an island of herself.

Fortunately, there are other significant episodes in the annals of computer design that have not only resulted in the invention of genuinely new forms, but are associated quite unequivocally with specific individuals. One of these is the invention of microprogramming. Indeed, if creativity in the artificial sciences pertains to the invention of form, then perhaps no better example can be found. The development of microprogramming led to an entirely new form or architecture for what is known as the *control unit* of a computer. This, as the name suggests, is the part or the component of the computer responsible for activating its internal operations as it executes a program.

A description of the microprogramming concept and the circumstances of its genesis will be presented in some detail in Chapter 3. For the present, it should suffice if only the broad significance of the idea is delineated. This will then allow us to establish its relevance, as a case study, to the question of creativity.

The general history of the origin of microprogramming is well known. In the middle of 1949, the EDSAC computer, designed and constructed by Maurice Wilkes and his collaborators at the Cambridge University Mathematical Laboratory,[15] successfully executed its first few programs (Wilkes and Renwick 1949; Wilkes 1984, p. 142). The EDSAC thus became the first *fully operational* stored program computer, just slightly ahead of its contemporary, the Manchester Mark I, developed by F. C. Williams and his associates (Williams and Kilburn 1948; Kilburn 1949) at the University of Manchester.[16] Both projects were somewhat further ahead than the other efforts under way in the United States and Europe.

Soon after the completion of the EDSAC, Wilkes became occupied with the issues of the *regularity* and *complexity* of computer designs. This concern was largely prompted by the irregularity (and the resulting complexity) of the organization of EDSAC's control unit – a characteristic that contrasted sharply with the ordered structure of its memory unit. Precisely why this concern was important is a matter we shall consider in Chapter 3. For the present, however, we can record the following indubitable facts:

(1) Wilkes *invented or recognized a problem,* which was that of producing a design (or a form) for the control unit that would be as systematic and regular in its structure as two other major components of the computer, namely, the memory and arithmetic units, were then already known to be.

(2) The problem, as identified by Wilkes, was basically of a *conceptual* kind. That is, it pertained to rather abstract, imprecise, and subjective properties or predicates such as "regular," "complex," and "systematic," the satisfaction of which by any particular solution is not (without further elaboration or refinement) testable. Wilkes's problem was, thus, not of an *empirical* nature, which would have been the case had it been characterized by predicates that, on a priori grounds, were known to be empirically testable. Simple examples of the latter are the properties "a maximum throughput that is twice that of computer XYZ" or "cost of manufacture that is no more than 80 percent that of system ABC." These are clearly predicates that are empirically testable in a way that the property "is regular in structure" is not since what constitutes "regularity" is not clearly specified.[17] Conceptual problems in the domain of science are especially interesting in the context of creativity since the *recognition* of such a problem by an individual is frequently prompted by philosophical or aesthetic considerations rather than strictly scientific or technical needs. In the particular case of microprogramming, for instance, Wilkes (1984) remarked that without

a particular philosophical perspective, the problem he identified and investigated would not make sense.

It was largely in response to the problem mentioned in (1) above that the principle of microprogramming (as a method for implementing a computer's control unit) was invented by Wilkes in 1951 and announced in a short and deceptively unassuming paper (Wilkes 1951). In a series of subsequent publications over the next two or three years, Wilkes and his colleagues further elaborated on the basic idea and the first *microprogrammed control unit* was implemented as part of the EDSAC-2. This was commissioned in early 1958 (Wilkes, Renwick, and Wheeler 1958).

Soon after the appearance of the first papers, interest in microprogramming began to spread well beyond Cambridge and the United Kingdom, and several papers were published by scientists from the United States, Italy, Germany, France, Japan, and the Soviet Union between the mid-1950s and the early 1960s (Wilkes 1969; Husson 1970). In the mid-1960s, the microprogramming concept was adopted commercially by IBM and became a crucial factor in the success of their highly influential System/360 series of computers. From then on, the microprogrammed control unit was rapidly espoused by most of the major manufacturers as the standard means for implementing the control units of their computers. This state of affairs prevailed till the late 1980s when new developments in semiconductor technology resulted in a comparative diminishing of the presence and influence of microprogramming in computer design. In addition, the development of the microprogramming concept has spawned a vast field of research both on the architecture of computer systems and on the methodology of computer systems design.[18]

The concept of creativity

What grounds are there to think that Maurice Wilkes's invention of microprogramming was, in fact, a creative act? The question seems rather pertinent, for, if we wish to advance an explanation of how a particular creative event may have come about, we must have an *independent* means of determining that the event in question was indeed creative. Since the aim of this book is to explain how creativity in the artificial sciences may occur and since it is the invention of microprogramming that is the case in question, one must clearly establish an a priori argument in support of the claim that this particular invention was, in fact, a legitimate act of creation – and, therefore, a worthy case study.

What is it we refer to when we apply the word "creative"? The psychologist Calvin Taylor (1988) has referred to one study in which more than fifty definitions were identified; the fecundity with which such definitions have come forth is an obvious indicator of the many interpretations – some differing in only subtle ways – that may be placed on the very *idea* of creativity. Taylor has also recorded that these various interpretations fall broadly into one of several classes:

(1) *Gestalt type:* in which the major emphasis is on the recombination of ideas or the restructuring of a gestalt.
(2) *End product–oriented:* according to which creativity is a process that results in a novel output or work.
(3) *Expressiveness-related:* in which the important factor is self-expression. Whenever one expresses oneself in a unique or individualistic way, one is considered as being creative.
(4) *Psychoanalytic:* in which creativity is defined in terms of the interactions between the id, ego, and the superego.
(5) *Process-oriented:* in which the emphasis is on the thinking process itself. That is, a certain type of process is said to characterize creativity.

Clearly, each of these distinct classes of definitions contribute to and enrich our overall understanding of creativity. Some may emphasize certain kinds of activities more than others – expressiveness, for example, is arguably more relevant to children's play, the composition of music, or the writing of poetry than to scientific research. Furthermore, these classes or categories are not necessarily mutually exclusive: A scientific discovery may be such as to satisfy both the gestalt and end-product–oriented definitions; the focus and attention of psychoanalytic theories are more likely to be on the personality traits of creative persons – that is, persons who may have been judged to be creative according to one of the other criteria.[19]

However, given that the intent of this section is to establish or confirm that the invention of microprogramming was an act of creativity, it seems quite legitimate for our purposes to assert that

(1) The attribute "creativity" is a property of some *cognitive act or process* – in this case, this being the process that produced the idea or the invention or the design concept called microprogramming.[20]
(2) However, the process is deemed to be "creative" only because of, or only as the consequence of, some other set of *independent* attributes or properties attached to the *product* of that process – in this particular instance, the product being the concept of microprogramming.

In other words, *a cognitive process P resulting in a product Π will be said to be creative when Π satisfies certain kinds of properties or exhibits certain kinds of symptoms.*

Note that while Π is the result of P – that is, P temporally precedes Π – the attribute creative is assigned to P only *after* Π is available and one can ascertain whether or not Π exhibits "certain kinds" of properties or symptoms. This definition is incomplete; there remains the question of exactly what these certain kinds of properties or symptoms are that must attach to Π in order for its generating process P to be deemed creative. Our identification of these symptoms relies on the notion of a *knowledge body.* We shall use this term to mean an integrated and organized collection of facts, theories, rules, exemplars, models, beliefs, metaphysical commitments, and values pertaining to a particular subject matter or *domain.* We shall also refer to the individual and discrete elements within a knowledge body (e.g., a specific fact or a rule) as knowledge *tokens.*

For example, in the domain of physics, the laws and theories of classical, relativistic, and quantum mechanics, such metaphysical commitments as Bohr's Complementary Principle and Einstein's belief in determinacy, and the aesthetic principle that, echoing John Keats, relates truth to beauty, constitute fragments of a typical physicist's knowledge body.[21] In the domain we call English literature, the entire corpus of published literary works in the English language, together with critical analyses, theories of literature, techniques of narrative and poetic construction constitute elements of its knowledge body.

In the chapters to follow, the nature and structure of knowledge bodies and the role they play in the creative process will be clarified as we examine the invention of microprogramming. For the present, the preceding characterization will suffice provided the following caveats are attached:

(1) A particular knowledge body K pertaining to a particular domain D that is associated with an individual person or, more generally, *agent A,* will be referred to as A's *personal* knowledge body (about D).

(2) A knowledge body K pertaining to a domain D that is shared by a community C of agents (i.e., K is the personal knowledge body of every agent in C) will be referred to as C's *public* knowledge body (about D).

(3) What constitutes an agent's personal or a community's public knowledge body with respect to a domain is a function of time. That is, knowledge bodies can *change* over time.

Consider now the situation in which a particular thought or cognitive process P conducted by an agent A results in a *thought product* Π relevant to a domain D.

Here, Π may be an idea, a theory, a literary work, a work of art or a musical composition, a useful artifact, a method of doing something, or the like. Then

(1) Π is said to be *psychologically novel* for A if, according to A's personal knowledge body $K_A(D)$ relevant to D, there does not exist any other product Π' that is identical to Π.

(2) Π is said to be *psychologically original* for A if Π is psychologically novel for A and is also believed by A to add significantly to the knowledge body $K_C(D)$ associated with community C relevant to D.

(3) Π is said to be said to be *historically novel* for a community C if, according to C's public knowledge body $K_C(D)$ relevant to D, there does not exist any other product Π' which is identical to Π.

(4) Π is said to be *historically original* for a community C if according to C's public knowledge body $K_C(D)$ relevant to D, Π is historically novel and is also believed by C to add significantly to $K_C(D)$.

Clearly, the completeness of these definitions is limited insofar as such notions as "is identical to" and "add significantly to" are left unspecified. In fact, whether or not a product Π is identical to another product Π', or whether Π adds significantly to a knowledge body, are determined by the particular standards, criteria, and values attending the domain of interest, which, of course, are themselves part of the relevant (personal or public) knowledge body associated with D. The concepts *novel* and *original* are, therefore, functions of – and relative to – specific bodies of knowledge and the agent or the community under consideration. There are no absolute notions of novel or original.

We are now in a position to characterize the concept of creativity:

> A process P conducted by an agent A and giving rise to a product Π relevant to a domain D is said to be *PN-creative* if Π is psychologically novel for A. It is *PO-creative* if Π is psychologically original for A. P is said to be *HN-creative* if Π is historically novel for some community C. It is *HO-creative* if Π is historically original for C.

Several remarks need to be made concerning these definitions. First, the qualifiers "psychological" and "historical" are taken from Boden (1991), who introduced the phrases *psychological* (or P-) *creativity* and *historical* (or H-) *creativity*. In the preceding concept of creativity, these have been further refined to distinguish between mere novelty and true originality, in both the personal-psychological and communal-historical contexts. Second, and somewhat tritely, what is considered novel (or original) by the agent may not be considered novel (or original) by the community to which the agent belongs.

Third, it might appear at first blush that, in the converse situation, an inclusion relationship holds between historical and psychological originality – that what is original for the community is also (or was) original for the individual agent responsible for the product. While this is generally likely to be the case, it need not always be true. For example, a scientist $S1$ may observe some phenomenon *but not recognize* its significance. The thought process incurred in this observation would not, then, constitute a PN-creative or a PO-creative process – by definition.[22] At some later time (by when $S1$ may even be dead), some other scientist $S2$ may come to realize the significance of $S1$'s observation – that it constituted a genuinely new discovery, for instance – in which event $S1$'s process would be deemed to have been HN-creative or HO-creative.

A more probable case is for the individual scientist to recognize the novelty of a discovery he or she has made without attaching much significance to it. It is left to the relevant community to determine its significance. Thus, a discovery process that is deemed HO-creative by the community may have been judged PN-creative by the discoverer. Similarly, a novelist, on completing a work of fiction, may not place too much value on it (insofar as its contribution to literature is concerned); yet critics and scholars may, contemporaneously or later, elevate its status to that of a significantly original work of fiction.

Fourth, because the novelty or originality of a product is determined relative to some specific body of knowledge, the adjudication itself may change over time, since knowledge bodies – their constituent facts, theories, value, standards, and so on – change over time. However, the impact of such a change in the state of a *product* on the state of the *process* that gave rise to it will vary according to whether one is considering a product that was in one of the originality states or in one of its novelty states.

To take an example that, though extreme, is not unknown in the annals of science, consider the situation in which a scientific result or theory T appearing in a journal is recognized at the time of its publication (and for long after) as being significantly original; according to our definitions, the relevant scientist's particular cognitive act that gave rise to T is inferred as HO-creative. Later, it is discovered that, in fact, the data relevant to T was forged. T can no longer be considered original as it was based on false data. There is, consequently, no justification for viewing the original process as having been historically creative.[23]

In contrast, consider the following, not infrequent occurrence: A scientist $S3$ submits a paper to a journal describing a result he or she believes is (psychologically) original. However, the journal's editor rejects the paper, not on the grounds of the work being flawed, but because the same result had, unknown to

S3, been published elsewhere. S3 *now* knows that the work is, in fact, not even (historically) novel. In the context of S3's body of knowledge *at the time the work was done,* the cognitive process can be inferred to be PO-creative. It would be counterintuitive to claim, however, that in the light of S3's *revised* knowledge body, the process that had given rise to the result is *now* no longer PO-creative. That S3 was creative at the time the work was performed (and produced a result that he or she believed at the time to be significantly original) can surely not be denied even though from the point of view of the discipline itself, the work is not original.[24]

Thus, the adjudication, on the part of a community, of an agent's creativity, being determined only by virtue of whatever knowledge, standards, and values attach to the community, can change over time since the communal knowledge body changes over time. However, an agent's perception of his or her own creativity, being determined by the personal knowledge body at the time the process occurs (or soon after) will likely be retained even when the agent no longer believes that the product itself is original or even novel.

Fifth, observe that the four kinds of creativity identified here are essentially a finer resolution of, and in general agreement with, the two types of creativity several other writers – including, as mentioned, Boden (1991) – have discussed: namely, that which is associated with the individual and that which is valued by the relevant community. It turns out that the former kind is preferred by many as the more interesting type of creativity. For example, Johnson-Laird (1988a, 1988b) and Nozick (1989) both adopted what I have referred to as PN-creativity or PO-creativity as a basis for their respective "working" definitions. According to Johnson-Laird:

> *A creative process yields an outcome that is novel for the individual, not merely re-membered or perceived and not constructed by vote or by a single deterministic procedure* [italics in the original] . . . the result [of the creative process] may not be truly original: a mental process can be creative even if other people have had the same idea. Genuine originality matters to society but it is not a purely psychological notion. What is valuable about a creative process is that its results are judged as striking, brilliant and not banal. These judgements depend on the mental processes of many people and they might be explicable in general terms by cognitive science. They do, however, depend on historical, cultural and scientific events. . . . *Hence the immediate goal of cognitive science is to explain how mental processes create ideas that are novel for the creator; a more remote goal is to explain how a critical con-sensus can be reached by society.* (Johnson-Laird 1988a, pp. 255–6; italics added)

A sixth and final comment relates to the question of whether, or in what sense, mere novelty matters in the present context; for, surely (it may be said), it is only when the product of one's cognition is *original* (in the historical or the psychological sense) that the process becomes interesting creativity-wise. However, our taxonomy provides for a more liberal view of the matter. Consider, for instance, the high school student attempting to solve an algebra problem. The student's personal knowledge body does not contain the requisite solution (we may presume), hence any solution that is produced – effectively, a theorem – is unlikely to be identical to any other solution or theorem he or she knows. The output will certainly be psychologically novel, and the student may judge (and we may agree) that the mental process leading to the solution was of a creative sort. However, the same student would not, in all likelihood, believe that the solution adds significantly to mathematical knowledge. More probably, he or she will have assumed that the community's knowledge body contains the solution or that, even if otherwise, the solution is not particularly significant as far as the state of algebraic knowledge is concerned. The student will probably have realized that one's objective is merely to add the result or theorem (or the technique producing it) to one's personal knowledge body. The output will be novel but not original; in producing the theorem, one will have been PN-creative but not PO-creative.

It is worth contrasting this situation with that of the remarkable Indian mathematician Srinivasa Ramanujan (1887–1920). In 1913, as a totally obscure clerk in Madras, India, who had not even passed the most preliminary of college examinations, he had despatched a bundle of mathematical manuscripts to the eminent Cambridge mathematician, G. H. Hardy, requesting his opinion on his work. Many years later, reflecting on Ramanujan's letters, Hardy commented:

Ramanujan's letters to me, which are reprinted in full in the *Papers,* contain the bare statement of about 120 theorems, mostly formal identities extracted from his notebooks. I quote fifteen [here] which are fairly representative. They include two theorems (1.14) and (1.15) which are as interesting as any but of which one is false and the other, as stated, misleading. The rest have all been verified since by somebody . . .
. . . I have proved things rather like (1.7) myself and seem vaguely familiar with (1.8). Actually (1.8) . . . is a formula of Laplace first proved properly by Jacobi; and (1.9) occurs as a paper published by Rogers in 1907 . . .
. . . [The formulae] (1.10) – (1.12) defeated me completely; I had never seen anything in the least like them before. A single look at them is enough to show that they could only be written down by a mathematician of the highest class. They must be true because if they were not true, no one could have had the imagination to invent them. (Hardy 1940, pp. 7–9)

Hardy later went on to say: "It was inevitable that a very large part of Ramanujan's work should prove on examination to have been anticipated. . . . I would estimate that about two-thirds of Ramanujan's best Indian work was rediscovery" (Hardy 1940, p. 10).

Based on these excerpts, it seems reasonable to say that a large part of Ramanujan's work before he was "discovered" by Hardy (Hardy 1940; Snow 1967) involved PO-creativity rather than PN-creativity – for the fact that he had despatched these results to a highly distinguished English mathematician seeking his opinion seems to indicate that, unlike our anonymous high school student, Ramanujan believed (or hoped) that his results constituted original theorems.

As for novelty of the historical sort, at least some part of what Kuhn (1962) termed "normal science" produces results that are historically novel without being historically original. Indeed, the vast majority of scientists – in both the natural and the artificial sciences – conduct professional lives sparked by cognitive episodes that are at best HN-creative.

In conclusion, there is little doubt that creativity of the PN or HN types have, as it were, substantial constituencies. They cannot be dismissed in the general context of understanding creative processes.

The relevance of nonpsychological factors

In discussing the various types of creativity, the point was made that if the output of the cognitive process of some individual is judged original by the relevant community, it will, in general (though not inevitably), also have been thought to be original by that individual. That is, in most cases, a cognitive act thought to be HO-creative will also have been thought to be PO-creative. HO-creativity is, arguably then, the most formidable of the types of creativity I have identified.

I shall argue in the next section that Maurice Wilkes's invention of microprogramming was, in fact, and can be so judged an act of HO-creativity. Before pursuing this argument, however, we need to deal with an argument against the whole notion of historical creativity.

It has been said that, in the historical case, the judgment of novelty or originality of the product is often determined by criteria other than psychological – by social, political or axiological factors, for example;[25] therefore (so the argument goes), historical creativity should not be the focus for understanding the *cognitive* processes underlying creativity. This point is quite explicit in the earlier excerpt from Johnson-Laird (1988a). Nozick (1989) makes a similar point, while Boden (1991), in addressing the question of how originality is at all possible, stressed that it is psychological creativity that is relevant rather than the historical kind.

Yet the historical record belies the claim that nonpsychological factors are of no intrinsic interest when we wish to study the cognitive act of creation; for, the very same criteria, standards, and values exercised by the relevant *community* in judging whether or not a product is novel or original may also be – and, indeed, are in most fields in which creativity is observed – the forces that drive the *individual* toward the generation of products he or she considers novel or original. One cannot meaningfully distinguish between nonpsychological factors and those that are purely psychological, for the former are as intimately the ingredients of the cognitive process as the latter.

This point has been made by both Gruber (1989) and Perkins (1981). A key aspect of Gruber's "evolving systems" theory is that agents become or are creative because they choose to perform tasks that make them so. They *intend* to add to the relevant community's knowledge body; the act of creation, according to Gruber, is driven by the goal of seeking to produce something original – in the historical sense. Thus, it should not be merely that the *agent* believes that his or her product will significantly contribute to the communal knowledge body but that the *community* should think so. Thus, the very same factors or criteria employed by the latter in judging the originality or novelty of a particular thought product will also participate in, or be the ingredients of, the individual's thought process that generated the product. The context of discovery to this extent and in this sense overlaps with the context of justification.

Perkins (1981) in his brilliant and wide-ranging study of creativity comments similarly on the criteria or standards exercised by the creative individual. The agent who brings about a "premature closure" on a problem or task – that is, one whose standards are relatively low – is not likely to generate original products. Again, clearly, such standards are determined by the community of which the agent is a member.[26]

Csikszentmihalyi's (1988) model of the creative process is, like Gruber's, systemic in nature and includes as a critical component the social organization of the domain – or, as he calls it, the "field" (which corresponds to my *community*). The field not only determines which products (of cognitive acts) are admissible into the domain (i.e., into the knowledge body); it also serves as a force in generating processes that lead to novel or original products: "A field . . . may stimulate directly the emergence of new ideas in people who otherwise would never have taken up work in a particular domain" (Csikszentmihalyi 1988, p. 333). Using examples from the art of the Italian Renaissance to illustrate the nature of this influence, he concludes that "it was the tremendous involvement of the entire community in the creative process that made the Renaissance possible . . . an unusually large proportion of the social system became part of the art 'field' ready to recognize and indeed to stimulate new ideas" (Csikszentmihalyi 1988, p. 336).

It seems, then, that the deepest investigations of creativity in any domain should be based on processes that are commonly viewed as HO-creative and were also, at the time of their occurrence, considered PO-creative; for it is in the study of such cases that most of the dimensions that may impinge on the creative act are likely to be rendered visible.

The invention of microprogramming: as a creative act

We now return to the earlier question, What grounds are there to think that Wilkes's invention of microprogramming was, in fact, a creative act? In the light of the foregoing discussions, we may rephrase this question as follows: What grounds are there to think that Wilkes's invention was, in fact, an HO-creative act?

Notice that this revised question pertains to HO-creativity! That is, there is a tacit claim being made here that Wilkes's work represented the highest type of creativity: The invention was not only considered novel by the relevant community; the latter had also come to believe that it contributed *significantly* to the knowledge body relevant to computer design. Clearly, there is an obligation to provide evidence for this claim. In so doing, we shall also see that Wilkes himself was fully aware of the significance of this work. Hence, it may be claimed that his invention of microprogramming was, apropos Wilkes, also PO-creative.

There are several external (i.e., social or historical) criteria that can be used for judging the significance, importance, or originality of scientific work. To begin with, it is widely agreed among scientists and historians and philosophers of science that a discovery or invention that leads (immediately or eventually) to a paradigm shift (Kuhn 1962) or a major change in the conceptual structure of knowledge in that science (Thagard 1990; Thagard and Nowak 1990) must be regarded as highly original, significant, and even revolutionary in nature. It is also widely agreed, certainly among working scientists, that even when falling short of initiating a revolution (in Kuhn's [1962] or Cohen's [1985] terms), a discovery or invention that opens up a new field of study or a new class of research problems constitutes a significant act of originality.

Furthermore, both scientists and those broadly concerned with the sociological aspects of science admit that a publication that is referenced or cited frequently by others is likely to represent work of considerable importance and originality. In other words, while not an inevitable indicator of scientific originality, a high index of citation is, nonetheless, a good measure of the esteem in which the work reported in the pertinent paper is held by members of the relevant community. In the case of the artificial sciences, the purely scientific criteria are augmented by a more practical factor: An invention or design having industrial implications – being adopted by the industrial sector – is widely thought to embody a high level of technical originality.

Wilkes's invention of microprogramming satisfies all these criteria or signposts of HO-creativity. First, it produced a new paradigm for the organization and design of computer control units.[27] On a longer time scale, it has exercised a considerable influence on certain developments in computer design.[28] Both these aspects have contributed to a considerable *change in the conceptual structure* of the knowledge surrounding computer design as well as to the *enrichment* of the knowledge body.[29]

It is obviously of relevance to this discussion to establish the *manner* in which Wilkes's invention constituted a new paradigm, the way, that is, in which it effected a change in the conceptual structure of the pertinent knowledge body. We will consider this matter only briefly at this point but will return to it often in later chapters.

Several thinkers, including Koestler (1964) and Boden (1991), have remarked on the element of *unexpectedness* or *surprise* that frequently attends the act of creation. Indeed, to the psychologist Jerome Bruner (1962), the ability to produce what he called "effective surprise" is a key characteristic of the creative enterprise. G. H. Hardy, in describing his first reactions to the batch of theorems sent to him by Ramanujan in 1913 said, "[The formulas] (1.10)–(1.12) defeated me completely; I had never seen anything in the least like them before. . . . They must be true because if they were not true, no one would have had the imagination to invent them" (1940, p. 9).

In other words, Hardy did not *know* that these particular theorems were, in fact, true. It was their surprisingness that appealed to him. And in *A Mathematician's Apology*, his haunting "defence" of mathematics, also first published in 1940, Hardy wrote, with reference to Euclid's proof of an infinity of primes and Pythagoras's proof of the irrationality of $\sqrt{2}$: "In both theorems (and in the theorems, of course, I include the proofs) there is a very high degree of *unexpectedness* combined with *inevitability* and *economy*. The arguments take so odd and surprising a form" (Hardy 1969, p. 113; italics in the original).

One sees the same element of unexpectedness in the concept of microprogramming. Precisely why this was so will become evident in Chapter 3, where the principle of microprogramming is discussed in detail. For the present, it may be said that in solving the problem he was concerned with – namely, that of producing a form for the computer's control unit that would be as systematic and regular in structure as, say, the memory and arithmetic units (see the section "The invention of microprogramming: as a case study") – Wilkes's solution to what was basically a *hardware circuit* design problem concerning a *component* of the computer relied on principles borrowed or adopted from the *programming* domain and more significantly, took a form that resembled *the form of the whole artifact of which the component happened to be a part.* That is, there was an element of what mathematicians and computer scientists call *recursion* in the solution[30]: The control unit of the stored program computer was, in effect, itself a stored program computer!

Second, Wilkes's invention of the concept of microprogramming led to the birth of a new subarea of the same name within computer science (or more precisely, within computer architecture, the field concerned with the logical design and organization of computers) and later to an offshoot called firmware engineering (Dasgupta and Shriver 1985). The extent or scope of micro-programming as a well-defined subarea can be gauged by the fact that it led to the formation of a special interest group and a technical committee on micro-programming under the respective stewardships of the two major professional societies in the United States devoted to computer science and engineering, as well as to the establishment (in 1967) of an annual conference on micro-programming that still continues to enjoy international participation.[31]

Third, in spite of the vast literature on the subject, Wilkes's original (1951) paper continues to be cited – a remarkable state of affairs considering the rapidity with which older papers usually get dropped from citations in the computing literature.

Fourth, as already noted, the industrial adoption of microprogramming began in the 1960s. It has, till very recently, continued to enjoy wide popularity in almost all classes of computers save those in the highest performance range.[32]

Based on such criteria, Wilkes's invention of microprogramming can clearly be regarded as a creative event of the highest order – that is, as a manifestation of HO-creativity. This, incidentally, is a fact that has been quite explicitly recognized by the computing community at large in the form of the many honors bestowed on him. For example, the Computer Pioneer Award given to Wilkes cited his contribution to microprogramming. The reprint (in Ash-enhurst and Graham 1987) of his 1967 ACM Turing Award Lecture (Wilkes 1968) – considered the most prestigious recognition in computer science – also cited, among his major contributions, the invention of microprogramming.[33]

Metaphors as explanatory models

The question that the student of creativity would *really* like to ask is, What was the cognitive process that led to the emergence of the microprogramming concept? Clearly, this question is futile since it is most unlikely that we can ever know or be able to determine the *actual* thought process underlying any past act of creation. A more tractable problem is the following: Taking into account the available historical and documentary evidence, can we construct a structure of cognitive events that would serve as a plausible explanation of how Maurice Wilkes *might* have been led to his invention? The idea, then, is to construct a *plausible model of creativity* that can *explain* a particular act of creation in the realm of invention and design in a manner that is consistent with the historical record.

What might be the nature of such an explanatory model? And in what sense will such a model explain Wilkes's creativity? These questions are addressed, at least in part, in the upcoming section and then in more detail in Chapter 2. For the moment, consider the more pressing issue: What do we understand by the word "model" in the present context?

As noted at the beginning of this chapter, accounts of one sort or another of the creative process have been advanced from many quarters. A striking aspect of these accounts is the prolificity with which *metaphors* appear as patterns of explanation.

That metaphors play an important role, often a profound one, in thought, speech, and understanding, has been widely recognized by scholars belonging to very diverse fields. In his classic discussion of the topic from a literary perspective – and it is, of course, as a literary device one most commonly thinks of it – the critic and theorist I. A. Richards (1936) referred to the metaphor as the "omnipresent principle of language." The psychologist Julian Jaynes (1976) made the point that understanding is primarily a matter of constructing a metaphor whereby that which we wish to understand (the *metaphrand*) is related to (or mapped onto) something we do understand or are familiar with (the *metaphier*). More recently, Minsky (1985), echoing Richards but dwelling in an intellectual milieu far removed from the one in which the latter resided, has remarked on the inseparability of metaphorical and ordinary thought – that all thought is, to some extent, metaphorical in nature.

What is perhaps less commonly understood or realized is the extent to which metaphors are vehicles of understanding in the more formal, more structured domains of thought as, for example, the sciences. Examples abound.

Howard Gruber (1981) described how Darwin used not one but an ensemble of metaphors along the path that led to his theory of evolution: "branching tree of nature," "war," "artificial selection," and the "free market of Adam Smith." And as Osowski (1989) has documented, the American psychologist William James, like Darwin, also employed a whole range of metaphors in developing his magisterial *Principles of Psychology* (1st edition, 1890). James's theory of consciousness was founded on such notions as "stream of thought," "the flight and perching of birds," and "herdsmen." Of these, one metaphor – "stream of thought" or "stream of consciousness" has traveled far beyond psychological theory building, through the novels of James Joyce and Virginia Woolf into the literary language of this century.

As yet another example, F. L. Holmes in his detailed study of Antoine Lavoisier's discovery of the chemistry of respiration, has described how Lavoisier had shifted from a view of respiration as combustion to one of respiration as a "kind of" burning of a candle (1985, pp. 451–2).

Consider, finally, two of the most celebrated *introspective* reports of the circumstances attending particular acts of creation. First, the nineteenth-century German chemist Friedrich August von Kekulé, discoverer of the ring structure of benzene in 1865, has described how (at the time he was thinking about this problem), dozing at his fireside, he dreamt of "atoms . . . gamboling before my eyes . . . long rows . . . all twining and twirling in snakelike motion"; it was this image of "one of the snakes [that] had seized of its own tail" that, he claimed, suggested the structure of benzene (Findlay 1948, pp. 36–8).

Second, the French mathematician and savant Henri Poincaré had been trying for some time to prove that there could not be any such class of mathematical functions known as the Fuchsian functions. One evening, he drank black coffee and could not sleep: "Ideas rose in crowds: I felt them collide until pairs interlocked, so to speak, making a stable combination" (Poincaré 1913/1946, p. 87). By the following morning, Poincaré was able to demonstrate the existence of a class of Fuchsian functions.[34]

Yet one must make a qualitative distinction between Poincaré's ideas rising in crowds and colliding or Kekulé's snakelike atoms seizing their own tails or James's "stream of consciousness," on the one hand, and those of Darwin's artificial selection or Lavoisier's burning of a candle, on the other. Consider, for example, Kekulé: To begin with, his description of atoms as "twining and twirling in snakelike motion" is not consciously constructed but a recapitulation of an image perceived in a dream. The problem he had been preoccupied with was the structure of the hydrocarbon benzene. In his dream, he "saw" rows of atoms as snakes. The image of the snake seizing its own tail gave Kekulé the clue for the structure of the benzene molecule.

Kekulé had been seeking a *literal picture* for the structure of benzene. The image of molecules as snakes provided him with an analogy between the structure of molecules and the form of snakes. The seizing of its own tail by one of the snakes suggested, in turn, the closing in of the benzene molecule. Thus, the latter is *likened* to a snake. This is the metaphor. It is an instance of what the philosopher Max Black (1962) called "metaphor as comparison" – in this particular case, the comparison is, so to speak, of a visual kind.

The origins of James's most famous and enduring metaphor, "stream of consciousness," lay in the fact that he wanted to convey the idea of consciousness as a continuous, fluid entity – in contrast to the (then prevailing) view of consciousness as a "chain" or "train" (i.e., a linear composition of atomistic, discrete entities). Consciousness, according to James, "flows." Thus, it was the image of the river or stream that suggested itself to him (Osowski 1989).

James's use of the stream concept appears to represent both what Black (1962) called the "substitution" and the "interaction" views of metaphors. It is substitutive in that a term or phrase ("stream") was used to describe a quality of conscious thought because, in fact, there existed no literal term or expression for this quality. It is also representative of Black's interactive model in that consciousness, being viewed as a stream, inherits (selectively) some of the attributes we associate with streams, namely, continuity, flow, change, occasional turbulence or agitation, and so on.

If we now ask whether Kekulé's metaphor of atoms as snakes seizing their own tails served any purpose *other* than that of suggesting the ringlike structure of benzene, the answer must be in the negative. Clearly, no other attributes or properties of snakes were invoked for the purpose of explaining anything further about the benzene molecule. James's metaphor seems somewhat more powerful. Yet here also, if we ask, if the metaphor of consciousness as stream helped in any further elucidation of the nature of consciousness, the response must again be in the negative; for, the concept of a stream and all its associated properties have not, since James, entered into the technical vocabulary of the psychology of consciousness. The subsequent understanding of the latter has not drawn on the science of fluid mechanics. In both cases, then, while there exists *descriptive* power in the metaphors, they fall short of *explanatory* capabilities.

Consider, in contrast, Lavoisier's candle-burning metaphor. On the one hand, this is an instance of Black's metaphor-as-comparison – in that the process of respiration is likened to the burning of a candle – and, on the other, it exemplifies metaphor-as-interaction (between two systems), in that as a result of the comparison, the relevant chemistry of candle burning can be (and was) transferred to the respiration domain.[35]

We may further appreciate the power of this metaphor by probing the matter in more detail. Based on Holmes's (1985, pp. 451–2) description of Lavoisier's thinking, the development and application of the metaphor can be represented as follows:

A. The problem and observations
  1. *The metaphrand:* The chemical nature of respiration
  2. *Observation relevant to the metaphrand:* Respiration of animals results in oxygen being consumed and "carbonic acid" and water being formed.[36]
  3. *Observation relevant to candle burning:* A candle burning in air consumes about half its oxygen and replaces it with carbonic acid and water.
B. Formation of the metaphor
  4. *The metaphor:* Respiration in animals is like a candle burning in air.
  5. *The metaphier:* Candle burning in air.
C. Relevant knowledge about the chemistry of candle burning
  6. Candle is composed of carbon and hydrogen.
  7. Candle burning consumes oxygen and produces carbonic acid and water.
  8. Weight of candle burned + weight of oxygen consumed = weight of carbonic acid + weight of air.
  9. Oxygen can be converted to carbonic acid only by addition of *"charbon."*[37]
  10. Oxygen can be converted to carbonic acid only by addition of hydrogen.
  11. This double combination can take place only with loss of "caloric" from the oxygen.[38]
D. Solution to the original problem
  12. In respiration, carbon and hydrogen are extracted from the blood and replaced by a portion of "caloric."

Two points are worth noting here. First, as we have already observed, once the metaphor was established, the relevant chemical facts surrounding the burning of a candle could be brought to bear on the problem at hand – and to draw appropriate conclusions therefrom. Second, the conclusion, namely, the chemical explanation of respiration, *does not depend on the metaphor itself.* In other words, the metaphor served as a scaffolding that could be discarded once the conclusion has been drawn.[39] Thus, whether the conclusion – the theory of respiration – is correct can be determined regardless of the metaphor that gave rise to it.

Similarly, the idea of artificial selection allows one to draw on facts pertaining to the hybridization of plants and animals through breeding as a suggestive mechanism for how variations of species might occur in nature. Artificial selection formed a central element in the arguments put forth by Darwin in his *Origin of Species*.[40]

As yet another example, we examine a vastly less significant, but nonetheless relevant, metaphor taken from the artificial sciences. Recently, this author, in attempting to explain the basic structure of design processes, suggested that the act of design can be viewed as an evolutionary process (Dasgupta 1989b, 1991). The nature and application of this metaphor can be described in the following terms:

A. The problem and observations
　　1. *The metaphrand:* The structure of the design process.
　　2. *Observations relevant to the metaphrand:*
　　　　a. Because of bounded rationality, a design at any stage of its development is in general, a conjectural or tentative solution to the problem.[41] The adequacy or satisfactoriness of the design is determined solely according to whether it meets the requirements prevailing at that stage of the design process. The design must then be critically tested against the available requirements.
　　　　b. If the test fails, the design must be modified.
　　3. *Observations relevant to Darwinian evolution:* (By the process of natural selection) organisms are constantly tested against the environment and those that survive (and reproduce successfully) are said to be fit relative to the environment.
B. Formation of the metaphor
　　4. *The metaphor:* Design is (like) an evolutionary process.
　　5. *The metaphier:* Darwinian evolution.
C. Relevant knowledge about Darwinian evolution
　　6. Organisms are constantly tested against the environment.
　　7. Those that survive (and reproduce successfully) are said to be fit relative to that environment.
　　8. If the environment changes, then some forms of a given organism may become fit relative to the new environment, while other forms may die out and even become extinct. Thus, organisms appear to constantly adapt to their surroundings.
D. Solution to the original problem
　　9. Design proceeds as a succession of cycles. In each cycle, the design is tested against the requirements.

10. If the design satisfies the requirements, then there is a fit between the two and the former is "adapted" to the latter, otherwise, there is said to be a misfit between design and requirements.
11. Depending on the source of the misfit, the design and/or the requirements are modified to eliminate or reduce the misfit, thus producing a new ⟨design, requirements⟩ pair.
12. The design process halts when adaptation is achieved. However, the process may resume if the requirements are subsequently altered, in which case the previous state of adaptation is disturbed.

Notice, again, that once the metaphor was in place, the salient features of Darwinian evolution (i.e., the testing of organism against environment, the concept of fitness, the appearance of adaptation) were drawn on to construct a general structure of design processes in which Darwinian terms or concepts were suitably adopted. Furthermore, the solution to the original problem, namely, an understanding of the structure of design processes, stands on its own regardless of the metaphor. The latter is discardable. One can test the validity of the proposed structure (as given in section D of the preceding schema) independent of the metaphor.[42]

To summarize the discussion so far, metaphors such as "respiration is like the burning of a candle" or "design is an evolutionary process" are not *merely* evocative in the way that "stream of consciousness," "colliding ideas," or "snakelike molecules" are. They are considerably more; for, as we have seen, they *serve as the bases for explanations*. Such explanations are made feasible by the transfer of certain properties, aspects, attributes, or knowledge belonging to the metaphier domain to the metaphrand domain in a manner that allows certain conclusions to be drawn or explanations to be offered about the latter.

Metaphors of this sort play crucial roles (as the preceding examples illustrate) in discovery and invention. For this reason, I shall refer to them as *metaphorical models* (or, where there is no room for ambiguity, as simply *models*). We now have the answer to the question raised at the beginning of this section ("What do we understand by the word "model" in the present context?"): The kind of model we shall seek for the creative process is that of a metaphorical model.

This characterization of a metaphorical model corresponds almost exactly to Black's (1962) "theoretical model."[43] However, we shall not use Black's term here first because it is important to emphasize and remind ourselves that these models are rooted in metaphors and second because the word "theoretical" is variously interpreted to mean mathematical, formal, or purely hypothetical.

The characteristics of a metaphorical model can now be stated as follows (see also Black 1962, pp. 230–1):

(1) There exists a particular fact or phenomenon or situation in a given domain of inquiry demanding an explanation. Following Hempel (1965), we may refer to this as the *explanandum*. The domain of inquiry is, accordingly, the explanandum domain.

(2) There may exist some body of knowledge concerning the explanandum domain that is insufficient for the immediate purpose of explanation.

(3) A metaphor is proposed relating the explanandum to some facts, observations, or theories from some other *unproblematic* domain for which a coherent, integrated, and systematic body of knowledge exists. The explanandum becomes the metaphrand and the relevant unproblematic facts, theories, observations, and so on, the metaphier.

(4) Implicit or explicit rules are available for translating statements or entities belonging to the unproblematic/metaphier domain to statements or entities belonging to the explanandum/metaphrand domain.

(5) Appropriate elements of the unproblematic/metaphier domain's knowledge body are applied to the explanandum/metaphrand to produce an explanation for the latter.

(6) The metaphor is discarded. The validity of the explanation is tested by means that are independent of the metaphor (i.e., independent of the knowledge body associated with the unproblematic/metaphier domain).

Metaphors as explanations of creativity

As noted at the beginning of the last section, metaphors have frequently been advanced as explanations of creative acts. We saw instances in Kekulé's and Poincaré's descriptions of the birth of their respective discoveries. In more recent times, Arthur Koestler, in his monumental *Act of Creation* (1964), suggested that underlying all creative acts is a mechanism that he called "bisociation," which, he said, "connects previously unconnected matrices of experience" (p. 45).

By "matrices," Koestler meant "any ability, habit or skill, any pattern of ordered behavior governed by a *code* of fixed rules" (p. 38; italics in the original). In spite of this assertion, the diagrams Koestler employed to illustrate bisociation seem to strongly convey to the reader that his proposal is essentially imagistic in nature.[44] The "matrices of experience" are represented by planes, and bisociation is what results when two such planes intersect. The metaphor is, loosely, geometrical.

One of the most influential explorations of creativity is the mathematician Jacques Hadamard's (1945) study of mathematical invention in which he pursued a line of thought due originally to the nineteenth-century German scientist von Helmoltz[45] and further developed by Poincaré (1913/1946) and Graham Wallas (1926). According to Hadamard, the creative process involves four steps:

(1) The *preparation* stage, during which the problem – the explanandum – is consciously studied, investigated, and worried over from all conceivable points of view.
(2) The *incubation* stage, during which the problem moves from the realm of conscious thought into the unconscious. The person does not *consciously* think of the problem; rather, an involuntary or unconscious mental process may take place during this stage.
(3) The *illumination* stage, at which time, still through involuntary or unconscious processes, the solution to the problem – the explanation for the explanandum – is obtained.
(4) The *verification* stage, at which time conscious thought is resumed for the purpose of verifying the solution.

The metaphors inherent in "incubation" and "illumination" are so obvious as to scarcely demand any further comment. It may be added, however, that in describing the illumination stage, Wallas and Hadamard both refer to illumination occurring, possibly, at the *fringe of consciousness* that "surrounds our 'focal' consciousness as the sun's 'corona' surrounds the disk of full luminosity" (Wallas 1926).[46]

It is precisely because the metaphors employed by Kekulé and Poincaré, by Koestler, and by Wallas and Hadamard are *only* evocative that as (even fragmentary) explanations of creativity they will not do. That ideas crowded into Poincaré's mind and appeared to collide may indeed have been the case. That Kekulé saw, in his dream, snakelike images may indeed be true. We may also acknowledge that ideas or problems incubate in our unconscious and that illumination may suddenly occur even when we do not appear to be thinking about the problem. But these belong to what Medawar (1990) referred to as the "phenomenology of creative thought." They constitute metaphors that evoke images not explanations. The knowledge body pertaining to the biological phenomenon of incubation or the physiology of illumination could not be transferred to the domain of creative thinking. The deeper question is whether we can construct *metaphorical models* of the creative process in the sense that the chemistry of candle burning served so fruitfully as a model for respiration.

To reiterate a point made before, scientists frequently use such models as frameworks for the investigation of problems. They serve as powerful and effective problem-solving devices. Indeed, a core element in Kuhn's (1962) concept of paradigm is the commitment to one or more *abstract or physical models* to which the relevant domain is assumed to conform.[47] The "models" Kuhn had in mind include such instances as viewing gas molecules as tiny, elastic billiard balls or electric circuits as hydrodynamic systems (Kuhn 1970a). These are, precisely, instances of metaphorical models.

It is important to emphasize the *heuristic nature* of metaphorical models. For instance, the development of the kinetic theory of gases relies on "seeing" gas molecules as hard, elastic, and spherical – that is, as microscopic billiard balls (Holton 1952). Gas molecules are not really thought to *be* billiard balls. Nor did Lavoisier really think that respiration was a case of candle burning. Metaphorical models are constructed and accepted *as if* they are true because, as we have seen in the preceding section, it is useful or fruitful to do so. Viewing gas molecules *as if* they were hard, elastic, spherical entities allowed classical mechanics to explain the known behavior of gases. The candle burning idea provided the analogy that led Lavoisier to the correct chemistry of respiration. To take another example, this from the artificial sciences – computer science in particular – the notion that computer programs can be viewed as strictly formal entities (i.e., strings of symbols or markings) obeying certain well-understood laws of mathematics and logic became the cornerstone for the development of the formal approach to program design (Gries 1981; Hoare 1986).

Thus, the student of creativity may well, like other scientists, profit from seeking an appropriate, heuristic, metaphorical model that can serve as a framework or paradigm within which creativity can be fruitfully investigated.

Computation as metaphor for the explanation of creativity

When we examine the literature on creativity, we can hardly fail to notice how limited is the language of explanation. Gruber (1981), for instance, in his penetrating examination of Darwin, uses terms such as "structure," "system," "process," and "network" in describing the birth of the theory of evolution by natural selection. Yet he goes no further: Precisely what the *composition* of a system or network or structure is remains unsaid. In the concluding chapter of his brilliant study of Lavoisier, Holmes (1985) – using a phrase drawn from

Gruber – describeŝ Lavoisier's work on respiration as akin to a "growth process." Again, in the absence of a way of characterizing "growth," Holmes admits that the phrase can only serve as an evocative metaphor.

In a similar vein, Hadamard (1945) emphasized the (unconscious) process of *combining ideas* as an essential ingredient of invention and discovery. The notion of ideas combining appears in many other writings on creativity, including Gruber (1981), Koestler (1964), whose bisociation principle rests on the notion of ideas belonging to two different "conceptual matrices" coming together, and in Livingston Lowes's (1927) analysis of the sources of imagery in Coleridge's poetry. Yet the question remains as to *how* ideas can combine. To Hadamard, it happens in the unconscious realm through "illumination." For Koestler, it is through bisociation – the mechanics of which is left undefined.

It is precisely when creativity is admitted to be a *process* (as Gruber and Holmes both see it), involving the change in and growth of structures of knowledge over (possibly long periods of) time, that the language and the concepts of *computer science* can be summoned to advantage. This is because computer science, more than any other discipline, is concerned with ways of describing, modeling, and simulating complex, dynamically interacting processes. A computer is, after all, a symbol processing device that effects transformations of one symbol structure to another. A computation is the process that takes place in the course of manipulating and transforming symbol structures. And computer science is the discipline that allows us not only to define or describe symbol structures precisely but also to characterize the very nature of symbol manipulation processes.

Thus, if we are willing to accept that creativity qua mental activity at some appropriate level of abstraction *involves the processing of symbolic structures* – that is, complex structures of entities composed of symbols such as mathematical entities, texts, pictorial elements, and the like – then computation may well serve as an effective metaphorical model for explaining creative processes. This is because the discipline of computer science appears to possess the appropriate armory of language, notation, and conceptual tools for describing and explaining such symbolic processes – including how ideas may, in fact, combine.

We obtain a glimpse of the promise of the computational metaphor from the following passage:

Gestalt psychologists have described productive thinking as a restructuring of the problem situation. Again, the question arises: What determines the direction the restructuring takes? The answer is that the image of the goal situation – that is, a temporary or definitive notion of what needs to be achieved – provides the tension between what is and what should be and, aroused by this tension, the energy necessary for the effort of thinking; it also provides the direction in which the restructuring presses forward. (Arnheim 1962, p. 8)

To the computer scientist, this passage – taken from the art historian Rudolph Arnheim's study of the development of Picasso's *Guernica* – begs to be translated into computational terms. He or she recognizes immediately, for instance, that the notion of the "image of the goal situation" providing a "tension between what is and what should be" and enforcing "the direction in which the restructuring presses forward" constitute, in essence, what computer scientists would call goal-directed heuristic search.

Arguably, the most precise computational description of a creative process would take the form of a computer program expressed in a programming language. Allen Newell, Cliff Shaw, and Herbert Simon (1962) pointed out that if one could design and build a program that would exhibit behavior similar to that of a human performing some creative act, as well as describe the general principles underlying the construction of the program, then the program itself would constitute a "satisfactory theory of creative thought." This is perhaps too bald a statement, for it trivializes, in some sense, what it is we mean by an explanatory theory. This view is, of course, simply a special case of the general agenda of *artificial intelligence* (AI) – the branch of computer science most concerned with the task of making artifacts exhibit capabilities usually associated with human thought and reasoning.

The debate over whether computers can ever be intelligent is as old as computer science itself. It began with Alan Turing's (1950) seminal paper and continues to this day.[48] However, regardless of theoretical debates, the AI research program continues to flourish, to the extent that computational and information processing models of thought and cognition are among the central strands of current psychology. Indeed, the interdisciplinary subject of cognitive science lies precisely at the interface between cognitive psychology and AI (Anderson 1983; Johnson-Laird 1988a; Boden 1989; Simon and Kaplan 1989; Newell 1990; Fetzer 1991).

We shall not dwell here on the matter of whether a computer can really exhibit intelligence or be creative, since such debates are irrelevant to the present discussion; for, the real point of this chapter – and, indeed, the raison d'être for this book – is the usefulness of computation as a *metaphorical model* of the creative process. More exactly, the focus is on the use and the usefulness of a *particular kind* of computational process as a metaphor for the creative act. What precisely is the nature of this particular kind of computational process will be clarified in Chapter 2. In the rest of this chapter, I shall present, in some detail, the nature of the model itself and the contribution it may possibly make to what Newell, Shaw, and Simon (1962) termed a "satisfactory theory of creative thought."

The thing to be explained – the explanandum – is *the cognitive structure of creativity in the natural and artificial sciences.* Our approach will be to construct and use a model based on the computational metaphor. Following the general characteristics of metaphorical models described earlier, the details of this particular model can be stated as follows:

A. The problem and observations

  1. *The metaphrand:* The cognitive structure of creativity in the (natural and artificial) sciences.

  2. *Relevant observations concerning the metaphrand:*
     a. A creative process involves the change and growth of knowledge structures (Gruber 1981; Holmes 1985).
     b. Creativity involves the combination of known ideas or concepts with the consequent production of novel or original ideas (Hadamard 1945; Koestler 1964; Gruber 1981).
     c. The creative agent is purposeful and goal-seeking; that is, creative work occurs within a purposive, goal-seeking context (Gruber 1981; 1989; Perkins 1981; Root-Bernstein 1989).
     d. The creative process involves small changes from moment to moment (Gruber 1981; Holmes 1989).
     e. The creative process is protracted and evolving. It involves revision of earlier ideas or structures of ideas (Gruber 1981; Ellman 1988; Holmes 1989; Jeffrey 1989).[49]

  3. *Relevant observations concerning computation*
     a. Computation entails the continuous modification of symbol structures wherein the change of structure from moment to moment is small.
     b. Computation begins with a goal and evolves a solution that at all times is directed toward the attainment of the goal.
     c. Computations of a certain kind (called "knowledge-level computation") do not inexorably proceed toward solutions as do computations of the "algorithmic" kind. Rather, they involve searching a space of possible solutions with the aid of heuristics to reduce the search amount.

B. Formation of the metaphor

  4. *The metaphor:* Scientific creativity as a cognitive process is like a knowledge-level computation.

  5. *The metaphier:* Knowledge-level computation.

C. Relevant knowledge about knowledge-level computation
   6. The body of knowledge known as the "AI paradigm"
D. Solution to the problem
   7. A theory of creativity, applicable to the natural and artificial sciences in which the process conducted by an agent with the resultant production of a psychologically original or historically original solution is described solely in terms of (1) symbolic structures that represent goals, solutions, and knowledge and (2) actions or operations that transform one symbolic structure to another such that (3) each transformation that occurs is solely a function of facts, rules, and laws contained in the agent's knowledge body and the goal(s) to be achieved at that particular time.

Henceforth, for convenience, I shall refer to this as the *computational theory of scientific creativity* (CTSC). As a hypothesis about the nature of the creative process, its origins lie in Newell, Shaw, and Simon's (1962) classic paper on creativity and its relationship to computation. It may also be viewed as a special case of Newell and Simon's (1976) "physical symbol system hypothesis" according to which any natural or engineered system that operates on symbol structures and produces, in turn, other symbol structures has the necessary and sufficient means for general intelligent action. And most recently, the hypothesis forms the basis of Thagard's (1988) "computational philosophy of science." In the present discussion, however, it must be remembered that CTSC is grounded in, and informed by, the notion of computation *as a metaphor*. Whether the creative process is "really" computational in nature is unimportant and, more significantly, irrelevant; for the theory itself (which, it will be noted from its brief statement above, makes no explicit reference to computation) must stand or fall on its own merit, regardless and independent of the metaphorical scaffolding.

The precise nature of CTSC is presented in the next chapter. What remains to be considered is the problem of how this theory can be tested. This issue is discussed in the next section.

On the testability of a theory of creativity

Very early in the chapter, I remarked on the failure on the part of, or the deliberate avoidance by, philosophers of science to tackle the context of discovery – that is, the cognitive processes whereby scientific discoveries are made. Notwithstanding this limitation or, for that matter, the general indifference exhibited by most workaday scientists toward it, philosophy of science, in conjunction with its alter ego, history of science, has vastly enriched our understanding of the epistemic nature of science – at least, of the natural sciences. It is hard to imagine any scientist who has taken the trouble to examine the writings of at least some of the philosophers and historians to remain unaffected or uninfluenced by what the latter have uncovered about such issues as the nature of scientific theories, the distinction between science and nonscience, the notion of progress in science, the testability of theories, the interplay of observation and theories, the growth of scientific knowledge, the belief and value systems of scientific disciplines, and the subtleties, anomalies, logical flaws and puzzles that attend the practice of science.[50] Much as the impressionist artists made us look at the visible world in new ways, so also these historians and philosophers provided new modes for understanding the very nature of science.

These reflections are pertinent to the present discussion if only because one who is aware of the issues discussed by the philosophers would hesitate to suggest any sharp, tidy criterion whereby the computational theory of creativity can be unequivocally tested. To understand this, let us consider some of the important factors relevant to the matter.

To begin with, creativity is *not a deterministic phenomenon*. That is, suppose we are able, by some means, to present a detailed account of how a particular act of creation took place – for example, the actual process whereby Maurice Wilkes was led to the idea of microprogramming. If we had the luxury of placing the agent concerned in exactly the same initial conditions, there is no guarantee whatsoever that the same process (or even an approximation to it) would unfold or, indeed, that the same output would result. To borrow a felicitous metaphor due to the evolutionist Stephen Jay Gould (1990), a tape on which a creative process is "recorded" and "played back" when rewound and restarted with the same initial conditions would not necessarily record the same process as before. This is because of the contingent nature of every act of creation.

The most important consequence of this is that *no theory of creativity can be predictive*. Given such a theory and some set of initial conditions postulated for an agent (i.e., a specific knowledge body and a goal), the theory can never predict that the agent will execute or perform or generate a particular process leading to the attainment of the goal. The theory cannot even predict that the goal will be attained. Any theory of creativity will, therefore, like the theory of evolution (Mayr 1988), be nonpredictive. This means that unlike physical theories in the natural or artificial sciences, *a theory of creativity cannot be tested by deducing (predicting) a phenomenon from it and determining, empirically, whether the prediction holds or not.*

If a theory of creativity is not predictive, then what kind of a theory is it? It must, in fact, be an *explanatory* theory in the following sense:[51] Given a proposed theory of creativity T, an agent in some initial condition (consisting, specifically, of a knowledge body K) and a novel or original output Π that the agent is *known* to have produced – all of which are expressed as symbolic structures – an *explanation* of how Π was produced will result if a symbol transformation process P can be described such that (1) P is in accordance with T; (2) P uses only the facts, rules, and laws in K; and (3) P produces Π[52]

The process P is thus an integral part of the explanation, and we can notationally express this as

$$\frac{T,\ K}{P:\ \ \Pi}$$

This notion of explanation can be contrasted to Hempel's (1965) celebrated "deductive-nomological" (ND-) model of explanation. According to Hempel, given an explanandum E, an explanation has the form:

$$\frac{F_1, \ldots, F_k}{L_1, \ldots, L_r}{E}$$

Where $F_1, \ldots, F_k$ describe particular facts and $L_1, \ldots, L_r$ are general laws. That is, E follows from the particular facts $F_1, \ldots, F_k$ in accordance with the laws $L_1, \ldots, L_r$. In our explanatory scheme for creativity, *the process P is a part of the explanation.* Without the process, there is no explanation. Or to state this in another way, a different process P' such that

$$\frac{T,\ K}{P':\ \ \Pi}$$

will result in a different explanation. This concept of explanation is, in fact, strongly influenced by the computational metaphor and is along the lines suggested by Thagard (1988).

In the case of a predictive theory T_p, an observation or phenomenon that is predicted from T_p and yet is not part of the explanandum originally giving rise to T_p can serve as a "test" for T_p. In the case of a purely explanatory theory T_E (i.e., an explanatory theory that is not also predictive), such predicted consequences are unavailable.

However, suppose T_E was originally proposed in order to explain a particular phenomenon Ψ but for which a claim is made that it is valid for an entire domain D of which Ψ is an instance or an element. In that case, one may certainly "predict" that given some other phenomenon Ψ' in D, T_E is a theory that explains Ψ'. An explanation of Ψ' from T_E is, then, a test of T_E's acceptability.

Now, in the case of a theory of creativity T and a given output Π acknowledged as original or novel, we have noted that an explanation of Π can come about that will be of the form

$$\frac{T,\,K}{P:\quad \Pi}$$

A test of T will succeed (i.e., it will *corroborate* T) if, in fact, an explanation of this type can be constructed – that is, if the elements assumed to be in the knowledge body K and appearing in the process P can be empirically shown to be valid. The test will *fail to corroborate* T if either an explanation of this type cannot be constructed or, given such an explanation, it can be shown that (as far as the relevant agent is concerned) one or more elements of K or P are, in fact, falsely assumed to hold.

Finally, it is important to continually remind ourselves that empirical theories and explanations – and a theory of creativity as well as an explanation of Wilkes's invention of microprogramming must be empirical in nature – cannot be meaningfully discussed in terms of being true or false, correct or incorrect. As the history of the empirical sciences eloquently reveals, today's truth often becomes tomorrow's falsehood; and a theory discredited when originally proposed may belatedly be accepted. The reasoning underlying the empirical sciences – both natural and artificial – is inherently *nonmonotonic* in nature. That is, the state of one's belief in the validity of an empirical generalization – a law, hypothesis, theory, or the like – is entirely a function of the state of knowledge or evidence invoked in support of, or against, the generalization. It can be constantly revised over time.[53]

Thus, to echo Laudan (1977), it is more appropriate – indeed, it is *only* appropriate – to ask of a theory or a process based on a theory (as already described) whether it provides *adequate* solutions to problems or whether it provides *better* solutions to problems than other alternatives than to ask whether it is true. At best, we can say that a theory is "corroborated" when it provides a satisfactory solution to a problem or is satisfactorily supported by evidence or tests.

We can now see more clearly what this book is really about. The description of Wilkes's invention of microprogramming as a computation-like process is, on the one hand, *an explanation of this particular creative act* within the framework of the computational model; on the other hand, this same description is *a test of the computational theory of scientific creativity.*

The broad picture: a summary

Generally speaking, this book is about the nature of the creative process. The means by which this issue is addressed is itself the confluence of three distinct strands. One is the *case study approach* in which a particular episode acknowledged and widely recognized as a creative act is singled out for examination. The second is that the historical episode is taken from the domain of the *artificial sciences* – the world of technical invention and design. The third strand is the adoption of a *computational metaphor* for the purpose of constructing an explanatory model of the episode in question.

My primary goal is to present a *plausible* explanation of how Maurice Wilkes *might* have been led to his invention of microprogramming using the computational metaphor as the explanatory framework. By "plausible," I mean that the elements of the explanation (the facts, rules, laws, etc.) can be justified on empirical grounds (i.e., there is empirical evidence as to the validity of these facts, rules, laws, etc.) or that they are based on assumptions for which convincing arguments can be made. The emphasis on *might* is necessary because every specific process of creation is of a contingent nature and under the same initial conditions a different process may be followed.

A secondary goal of this work is to use the Wilkes case study to conduct an experiment for testing CTSC, the theory of scientific creativity based on the computational metaphor. In this sense, this work adds to the corpus of computational experiments conducted in recent years by Langley et al. (1987), Kulkarni and Simon (1988), and Thagard (1988, 1990). However, these earlier studies were from the domain of the natural sciences whereas the experiment described here is from the realm of invention and design – the domain of the artificial sciences.

In sum, we hope to see the history of the origin of a particular invention, the cognitive process of its birth and its logical underpinnings, within a single unified framework. There is, however, a further aim of this work: We hope to secure a glimpse, through this particular case study, of how the more traditional concepts and metaphors through which creativity has been previously described – such as the bisociative matrices of Koestler or the illumination stage of Poincaré, Wallas, and Hadamard – can be "mapped onto" the language of computational thinking. In this regard also, the trail has been blazed by Kulkarni and Simon (1988) and Thagard (1988, 1990). Their influence on this work, as also the influence of the historicopsychological studies of Gruber (1981), Wallace and Gruber (1989), and Holmes (1985, 1989), is deep, pervasive, and will become patently obvious.

Notes

1. It is, however, now well known, as so painstakingly documented by John Livingstone Lowes (1927), that Coleridge's famous account of the circumstances of his composing the poem is largely false. For more on this, see Perkins (1981, chap. 1).
2. For a comprehensive review of the context of discovery versus context of justification issue, see Nickles (1980b).
3. Abduction or, synonymously, *retroduction* was first discussed by the nineteenth-century philosopher C. S. Peirce (1931/1958). For a modern discussion, see Thagard (1988). For a somewhat more elaborate formulation of abduction than the one presented here, see Fetzer (1992).
4. See e.g., Carnap (1966). See also Suppe (1977b) for an excellent survey of twentieth-century philosophy of science. For other more general surveys, see Losee (1980) and Harré (1985).
5. Although, as the evolutionary biologist Ernst Mayr (1988, pp. v–viii) has wryly remarked, much of philosophy of science has even ignored biological thought. To a large extent, philosophy of science has meant the philosophy of *physics!*
6. For an extensive discussion of the concept of design, see Dasgupta (1991). See also Pye (1978), Addis (1990), Rogers (1983), Brown and Chandrasekaran (1989), and the anthology of articles in Cross (1984).
7. According to Kuhn's (1962) well-known theory, "normal" science is the practice of science within a particular paradigm. Precisely what are the characteristics of a paradigm is touched on later in this chapter. (See the section "Metaphors as explanations of creativity.") Stating the matter simply here, the practice of normal science takes for granted the theoretical framework within which a problem is to be studied. The framework itself is not questioned. Normal science, then, entails solving scientific *puzzles.* In contrast, "revolutionary" science involves the rejection of an entire theoretical framework in favor of another, in a *paradigm shift,* in other words. The names of the most celebrated men and women in science, e.g., Newton, Einstein, Darwin, Curie, Lavoisier, and Bohr, are associated with revolutionary science. According to Kuhn, revolutionary science entails radical, abrupt, or holistic changes in knowledge. This view has been challenged of late. For example, Laudan (1984, chap. 4) has suggested that what may appear to be a radical paradigm shift when seen across a coarse time grain can, in essence, be explained in terms of a gradual series of smaller changes in

one or another component of the original paradigm. And Thagard (1990) has outlined a computational model to demonstrate how one major conceptual or paradigmatic change – the chemical revolution of the eighteenth century – may be explained in gradualistic terms.

8. For recent perspectives on "philosophy of technology," see Ihde (1991) and Bugliarello and Dover (1979, especially pt. 2).

9. For a selection from Simon's oeuvre that has contributed in one way or another to our understanding of the nature of the artificial sciences and the question of creativity, see Simon (1975, 1976, 1981, 1982, 1983, 1989), Newell and Simon (1972), and Langley et al. (1987).

10. See, e.g., Alexander (1964), Alexander, et al. (1987), Lawson (1980), Rowe (1987), March (1976), and Mitchell (1990) among the architects; Smith (1981) among metallurgists; Addis (1990), Billington (1979, 1983), Petroski (1985, 1991), and Blockley and Henderson (1980) among civil engineers; Rogers (1983) and Vincenti (1990) from aeronautics; Gero and his associates (Coyne et al. 1989), Brown and Chandrasekaran (1989), and Winograd and Flores (1987) from the domain of artificial intelligence; Schön (1983) among the social scientists; and Dasgupta (1991) from computer science.

11. For discussions of complexity and hierarchy in nature and artifacts, see, e.g., Simon (1981), Whyte, Wilson, and Wilson (1969), Pattee (1973), and Smith (1981). For discussions of the complex, hierarchical nature of computers, see Siewiorek, Bell, and Newell (1982, chap. 2) and Dasgupta (1984, chap. 1).

12. In fact, even the question of who invented the first *electronic* computer is engulfed in controversy. The standard version credits Presper Eckert and John Mauchly because of their development of the ENIAC. Of late, this view has been challenged vigorously, for it has been claimed (and judged correct in the law court) that many of the ideas used in the ENIAC were due to John Atanasoff, who, with Clifford Berry, developed the Atanasoff–Berry computer at Iowa State University. For more on this, see Burks and Burks (1981), Atanasoff (1984), and Berry (1986).

13. For more on the debate on the origins of the stored program computer, see Randell (1975, chap. 8), Goldstine (1972, pt. 2), Metropolis and Worlton (1980), Stern (1980, 1981), and Burks (1980). The most recent contribution to this issue is Aspray (1991).

14. For general discussions of parallel processing systems within a computational setting, see, e.g., Hwang and Briggs (1984) or Stone (1990). For an advanced and more formal treatment of the nature of parallel processes, see Hoare (1985).

15. In the early 1970s, this was renamed the University Computer Laboratory.

16. According to Wilkes, the Mark I began to execute programs at about the same time as the EDSAC, but it was somewhat later that the former had regular input and output devices. An earlier version of the Manchester machine was actually demonstrated in June 1948, but this had only rudimentary arithmetical capabilities (M. V. Wilkes, personal communication, January 29, 1986).

17. The distinction between conceptual and empirical problems in the artificial sciences and in the natural sciences is discussed extensively in chaps. 3 and 12, respectively, of Dasgupta (1991). Stated briefly, an *empirical* problem in design is one related to some specific requirements such that whether or not the design solution meets the requirements can be determined through empirical tests. Empirical problems are also said to be "well-structured" (Simon 1973). Requirements pertaining to well-defined functions, cost, performance, and reliability are typical of empirical design problems. A *conceptual* problem in design is posed by requirements of an abstract, often subjective nature. Require-

ments pertaining to aesthetics or some psychological need or conformation to a philosophical idea typify conceptual problems. In the natural sciences, an empirical problem is posed by the observation or detection of some phenomenon in the natural world that demands an explanation. A conceptual problem in the natural sciences arises in the context of a previously established or proposed theory where the latter is perceived to be unsatisfactory on philosophic or aesthetic grounds rather than the empirical. For examples of conceptual and empirical problems in both the artificial and natural sciences, see Dasgupta (1991).

18. For a modern survey of this field, see the collection of articles in Habib (1988a), the anthology of reprints in Milutinovic (1989), and the review by Dasgupta and Shriver (1985). For a discussion of those recent developments in computer design and semiconductor technology that have reduced the ubiquity of the microprogrammed computer, see Dasgupta (1989a, Chap. 5).

19. For a superb discussion, in terms of analytical psychology, of what motivates creativity in artists and scientists, see Storr (1972).

20. In this book, "process" and "act" are used interchangeably. There is no imputation of *instantaneousness* to either of these concepts. It is important to emphasize this point since an act is often construed as something that happens instantaneously or at a particular moment – see, e.g., Gruber's (1989, p. 16) remarks about Arthur Koestler's (1964) *Act of Creation*. The concept of a process will be characterized more precisely in Chapter 2.

21. This is *not* to imply that there is only one knowledge body associated with a domain. In the natural sciences, in particular, what I have termed as "knowledge body" is precisely what Kuhn (1962) first termed "paradigm," modified later by Lakatos (1978) to "research programme" and then to "research tradition" by Laudan (1977). And as Laudan has pointed out, there may be more than one research tradition or paradigm attached to a domain. "Knowledge body" is intended to serve as a broader term applicable to practically any domain, science or otherwise.

   The facts, laws, theories, and exemplars constituting physics are, of course, available in the usual texts on the subject. For a discussion of how metaphysics and aesthetics play roles in the practice of physics – matters that do *not* appear in conventional textbooks, though they constitute elements of the physicist's knowledge body as much as do facts, theories, and laws – see, e.g., Laudan (1984), Wechsler (1978), Chandrasekhar (1987), and Holton (1952). For a brilliant, detailed, and unusual discussion of the artistic traits found in some of the most distinguished scientists and engineers of the nineteenth and twentieth centuries and the influence of these traits on the scientific creativity of these men and women, see Root-Bernstein (1989, pp. 312–40).

22. Of course, more than an agent's thought process may be involved in the observation act – microscopes, telescopes, particle accelerators, or computers, for example. However, the attribute of creativity in this discussion is solely associated with *cognitive* agents. Furthermore, while we may allow for the possibility that a cognitive agent may, in fact, be a machine, our concern here is with *human* cognitive agents only.

23. A celebrated case closely paralleling this situation is that of Sir Cyril Burt (1883–1971), in his lifetime, the doyen of British psychology, whose work on the hereditary nature of intelligence – one of the cornerstones of his scientific reputation – has been strongly discredited on the charge of forged data. For a brilliant discussion of the Burt case, see Gould (1981, chap. 6).

24. A striking example of this sort of situation, cited by Boden (1991), is that of the preeminently distinguished logician, mathematician, and computer scientist Alan

Turing whose fellowship dissertation submitted to King's College, Cambridge, presented results that, it turned out, had been anticipated by a Scandinavian mathematician – a fact that Turing had apparently not known. That Turing was not HO-creative was obvious. Nonetheless, recognizing his inherent creativity in arriving at his result – that is, recognizing and acknowledging his PO-creativity – King's College awarded him the fellowship.

25. In his magisterial book *Revolution in Science* (1985), for example, the historian of science Bernard Cohen uses several "tests" to determine whether some scientific theory is revolutionary or not. Of these, one is the opinion of (later) historians of science; another is the opinion of contemporary working scientists.

26. Consider the following practical example as evidence of this view. In the scientific professions, certain journals are considered to be the most prestigious in their relevant domains. A paper accepted by the editor of such a journal for publication therein is *typically* deemed to be of a higher standard than one *typically* published in other, less well-regarded journals. The more stringent the standards of acceptance, the higher is the prestige of the journal and, consequently, the higher is the expectation or belief (on the part of the community) as to the originality of the works reported therein. A scientist whose aim is to publish in such journals will also set out to tackle problems or generate solutions of a standard high enough for acceptance by these select journals. Of course, whether one is successful or not in attaining one's aim is another matter. The point is that communal standards, criteria, and values participate as profoundly in the cognitive act of scientific problem solving as in the adjudication of papers communicated to the journals. A similar observation can be made with respect to scholarly works of larger scope submitted to book publishers.

27. In Kuhn's (1962) theory of scientific paradigms, a scientific revolution occurs when one paradigm is *replaced* by another and the entire community of relevant scientists transfers its allegiance to the newcomer. This view has been challenged forcefully by Laudan (1977, especially chap. 4), who pointed out that "research traditions" (Laudan's modified version of the paradigm concept) do not necessarily replace one another but may well *coexist* for considerable periods of time. This is certainly the case in the artificial sciences. As I have pointed out elsewhere (Dasgupta 1989c, p. 59), an artificial science or a design discipline may comprise several, coexisting, alternative paradigms at any given time. For example, in structural engineering, it is reasonable to claim that designing steel and concrete structures involve separate paradigms (though they may obviously share common elements – e.g., the theory of the strength of materials). Similarly, in the case of computer design, microprogrammed implementation and hardwired implementation of computers are two alternative, coexisting paradigms. A hallmark of the highest form of originality in the artificial sciences is the generation of a paradigm that is subsequently assimilated into the overall knowledge structure of the discipline without necessarily replacing others.

28. Just what these influences are and precisely how they are exercised are issues that lie far beyond the scope of this book. Stated briefly and for the benefit of those familiar with computer architecture, they pertain to such concepts as emulation, universal host machines, function migration, and reduced instruction set computers. The interested reader may refer to Dasgupta (1989a, chaps. 5 and 7) for discussions of these issues. An early and rather classic account of the significance of microprogramming is Rosin (1969).

29. The nature of the conceptual structure of knowledge (in a particular domain) will be clarified, by way of examples, in Chapter 3.

30. *Recursion* is the principle whereby the definition or computation of a function
relies on the definition itself! For example, the "factorial" of a positive integer N
is conventionally (i.e., without using recursion) defined as

$$\text{Factorial } (N) = (N) \times (N - 1) \times (N - 2) \ldots \times (3) \times (2) \times (1)$$

A recursive definition is

$$\text{Factorial } (N) = 1 \text{ when } N = 1$$
$$= (N) \times \text{Factorial } (N - 1) \text{ when } N > 1$$

31. The Special Interest Group on Microprogramming (SIGMICRO) was formed
under the auspices of the Association for Computing Machinery (ACM). The
Technical Committee on Microprogramming (TC MICRO) is part of the
Institute of Electrical and Electronic Engineers (IEEE) Computer Society. The
Annual Microprogramming Workshop is jointly sponsored by SIGMICRO and
TC MICRO. As of the time of this writing (1992), twenty-four such conferences
have been held. Recently, reflecting the change in emphasis and interest within
the field, the workshop has been renamed the Annual Workshop of
Microprogramming and Microarchitecture. For its history, see Habib (1988b).
For surveys of the state of microprogramming circa the mid-1980s, see Habib
(1988a) and Dasgupta and Shriver (1985). For anthologies of papers on various
aspects of microprogramming, see Mallech and Sondak (1983) and Milutinovic
(1989).
    A rather unique institutional aspect of microprogramming is the
establishment, in the Dupré Library of the University of Southwestern Louisiana
in Lafayette, of an International Archive on Microprogramming containing over
a thousand documents pertaining to the topic. This archive was inaugurated in
1984.

32. The reasons for the exceptions are certain technical issues that are irrelevant to
this discussion.

33. Wilkes's other honors include several doctorate degrees *honoris causa,* election
to the Royal Society in 1956 (at the relatively early age of 43), and elections to
the U.S. National Academy of Engineering in 1977 and the U.S. National
Academy of Science in 1980.

34. For a compendium of views on metaphors in relation to linguistics, science,
psychology, and other aspects of thought, see also Ortony (1979).

35. See Minsky (1985) for a view, along these lines, of what constitutes a good
metaphor.

36. "Carbonic acid" was one of the terms used by Lavoisier to denote carbon
dioxide – also known, then, as "fixed air" (Partington 1960; Holmes 1985).

37. According to Holmes (1985, pp. xxiii), "charbon" was the traditional name for
charcoal. However, Lavoisier used it somewhat inconsistently to mean, at times,
the "pure principle" (i.e., carbon) in charcoal and at other times charcoal itself.

38. "Caloric" was the term used in the eighteenth century to denote the
imponderable "matter of heat" contained in bodies that is released (in the form
of heat) during the process of combustion (Partington 1960, pp. 88–9, 130–1).

39. The reader may note that one metaphor is being used here to describe the
workings of another!

40. According to Gruber (1981), it did *not* play a significant role in the way Darwin
arrived at this theory – contrary to what Koestler (1964) thought.

41. The concept of *bounded rationality* was developed by Simon in the 1940s in the
context of administrative decision making (Simon 1976). It was subsequently

elaborated into a general theory of rationality as much applicable to game playing and design as it is to organizational and economic behavior (Simon 1981, 1982). The crux of the concept is that in a decision-making situation, there are two components, the decision-making *agent* and the *environment* in which decisions are made. In models of perfect rationality, all the constraints attending the decision-making situation are assumed to be contained in the environment. The agent is assumed to have perfect or complete knowledge of these constraints and be able to perform all the computations necessary to arrive at a decision. In contrast, the model of bounded rationality takes for granted that there are constraints on the cognitive and information-processing capabilities of the agent. Consequently, there are limits to the extent to which an agent can arrive at a correct decision. Bounded rationality is further discussed in Chapter 2.

42. In Dasgupta (1991), independent corroborating evidence for this evolutionary structure of design processes is presented by way of several empirical examples.
43. One of the most lucid discussions of the concept of model (and of the concept of metaphor) that has come to this writer's attention is due to Black (1962). As he points out, the word "model" has many different meanings – as in "scale model" or as a reference to a type of design or as in "analogue model" or "mathematical model" or as in what Black termed "theoretical model." The richness of the model concept can be seen in its full splendor by consulting the Second Edition of the *Oxford English Dictionary* (Oxford University Press, 1989).
44. See, e.g., pp. 35–6 and pp. 106–7.
45. Von Helmoltz apparently outlined this during a banquet speech commemorating his seventieth birthday (Wallas 1926).
46. This quotation is taken from the excerpts from Wallas (1926, pp. 79–96) appearing in Vernon (1970, p. 96). Wallas, in fact, acknowledges his debt to William James's *Principles of Psychology* for the "fringe" metaphor.
47. As is well known, in his original (1962) monograph, Kuhn employed the paradigm concept to mean a number of different though loosely related things. In a paper that acquired almost as much fame as Kuhn's book, Masterman (1970) listed no less than twenty-one different ways in which "paradigm" appears in Kuhn (1962). Largely in response to this and other criticisms of his work (see, e.g., Shapere 1964; Lakatos and Musgrave 1970; Suppe 1977a, 1977b; and Laudan 1977, 1984), in a later series of publications Kuhn (1970a, 1970b, 1977) attempted to clarify and distill his notion of a paradigm.
48. For highly critical views of AI, see Dreyfus (1979), Weizenbaum (1976), Searle (1984), and Winograd and Flores (1987). It is a curious fact that both Weizenbaum and Winograd made important early contributions to the subject. For an endorsement of AI from one outside the AI discipline itself, see Boden (1977). For a truly extraordinary, original, and exhilarating discussion of AI (and much else), see Hofstadter (1979, especially chaps. 17–20). A recent discussion of the relationship between AI, cognitive science, and philosophy is Fetzer (1991).
49. Although these observations are all made in the specific context of scientific or technical creativity, they are also mostly applicable to the domains of literature and the arts. *Apropos* this specific characteristic (i.e., revision of earlier ideas), it is worth noting, for instance, that in his essay "He Do the Police in Different Voices," the literary scholar and biographer Richard Ellman (1988) described the interaction between T. S. Eliot and Ezra Pound during the development of Eliot's *The Waste Land*. As revealed by Ellman, Eliot would submit versions of

50 *Creativity in invention and design*

various parts of the poem to Pound and would then revise it on the basis of Pound's criticisms. Similarly, Jeffrey's (1989) account of the development of Wordsworth's autobiographical poem *The Prelude* describes the constant process of rewriting and revision that it entailed, spanning half a century. Finally, there is perhaps no more fascinating a description of this kind of process in action than Arnheim's (1962) study of the steps that led to Picasso's *Guernica*.

50. For modern views on these issues, see, e.g., Carnap (1966), Hempel (1965), Popper (1965, 1934/1968, 1972), Hanson (1958), Kuhn (1962, 1970a, 1970b, 1977), Lakatos (1978), Feyerabend (1978), Ruse (1986), Laudan (1977, 1984) on philosophical matters. See also Suppe (1977a), Losee (1980), and Hareé (1985) for valuable surveys. As outstanding instances of historical studies, see Conant (1950a, 1950b), Roller (1950), Holton (1973), Butterfield (1968), and Cohen (1985). For a very recent discussion of many of the philosophical issues from a variety of ontological perspectives, see Laudan (1990). For a magisterial study of the philosophical issues of science from the Victorian era, see Whewell (1847/1967). An important – and still influential – discussion from the early part of this century is Duheim (1914/1954)

51. I owe this distinction between predictive and explanatory theories to Mayr (1988, pp. 31–2). See also Scriven (1959).

52. The notion of explanation is further elaborated in Chapter 2, in the context of CTSC.

53. For a discussion of the logic of nonmonotonic reasoning, see Reiter (1987). Nonmonotonic reasoning in the context of design is discussed by Dasgupta (1991) and, in greater detail, by Patel and Dasgupta (1991).

2

A computational theory of scientific creativity

Recall from the past chapter (specifically, the section "Computation as metaphor for the exploration of creativity") that what has been named the computational theory of scientific creativity or CTSC is a hypothesis about the nature of creativity (in the natural and the artificial sciences). This hypothesis is, furthermore, firmly rooted in the computational metaphor – more precisely, it relies on the formation of a metaphorical model connecting creative and computational processes.

It also bears repeating that this theory goes back to Newell, Shaw, and Simon (1962) and, in effect, is a special case of a broader theory of thinking known concisely as the physical symbol system hypothesis (Newell and Simon 1976). The theory also serves as the basis for some recent explanations, by Kulkarni and Simon (1988), Thagard and Nowak (1990), and Thagard (1988, 1990), of certain historically important discoveries in the natural sciences. Thus, the general nature of CTSC is well known and has been so for some time. The task of the present chapter is to articulate and state CTSC in a sufficiently precise form such that (1) the reader understands and can anticipate, at least in general terms, the direction along which the explanation of Wilkes's creativity will proceed in the chapters to follow (especially, in Chapters 4–6) and (2) it is posed as a genuinely testable (i.e., in principle, falsifiable) hypothesis for which the Wilkes case study constitutes a nontrivial test. The extent to which CTSC is, in fact, corroborated or refuted by this test, and the general lessons learned from the case study, are matters discussed in the final part of this book.

Multiple description levels

As described in Chapter 1, the computational metaphor relates the creative process to a certain kind of process called knowledge-level computation. The concept of the knowledge level is, thus, central to the discussion to follow and to the theory of creativity presented in this chapter. Its description, however, necessitates an introduction to the general notion of *description levels* – for, as we shall see, the knowledge level happens to be one such description level for cognitive systems, and CTSC is operative at, and relevant to, precisely this description level.

Systems (both natural and artificial) of any reasonable degree of complexity can be designed or explained at any one of a number of different description levels. In fact, multiple description levels constitute a general (indeed, defining) characteristic of all complex systems.[1] As first pointed out in the context of computers by Bell and Newell (1971), these levels are not equivalent in the sense that anything said one way can as well be said another. On the contrary, each description level performs a function that cannot be performed adequately by another. Each description level is *functionally autonomous* in that the structure and behavior of a relevant system can be completely specified, in some particular sense or for some particular purpose, at that level. At the same time, the description levels are *hierarchically organized* in that, given two such levels, the components constituting one level (say L_j) can be defined in terms of, reduced to, or implemented by components constituting the other (say L_i). L_j is then said to be at a *higher* level than L_i.

Figure 2.1 shows, as an example, five of the common description levels for computers. A given computer can be characterized at any one of these levels. The appropriateness of the level at which to describe the computer is entirely determined by the use to which the description is to be put. For example, if the aim is to characterize the "functionality" of the system as a whole (say, for the benefit of programmers who are to build the "operating system" for the computer), then what is variously called the "instruction set processor level," "architecture," or "exoarchitecture" is the appropriate description level. The features of the computer relevant to this level include the instruction set, the data types, and the various kinds of storage (main memory, registers, etc.) in which data and programs can be held and referenced directly by instructions. At this level, many other features of the computer – for example, the technology used to implement the actual circuits or the way in which signals are distributed throughout the computer during the execution of individual instructions – are irrelevant and, therefore, excluded.

Clearly, such details *are* important in other contexts. For example, the computer designer must have knowledge of all the storage elements, the pathways or *buses* through which data is transferred and the various *units* responsible for the actual performance of arithmetic, logical, and decision operations in order to be able to design the control unit that will issue the

Level identifier	Level descriptor(s)
L4	Instruction set processor/architecture/external (exo-) architecture
L3	Organization/internal (endo-) architecture
L2	Microprogram/microarchitecture/register-transfer
L1	Logic/gate
L0	Circuit/transister

Figure 2.1. Common description levels for computers.

control signals to these various components at the right moment of time for the purpose of executing individual instructions. The appropriate level for such purposes is not L4, not even L3, but L2, known variously as the "micropro- gram," "microarchitecture," or "register-transfer" level.

Similarly, when the time comes to design the actual circuits or to fabricate the integrated circuit chips, description level L2 is wholly inappropriate. In- deed, it would be those very components of the microarchitecture that are required to be implemented. In such circumstances, the designer may need to view the computer at what engineers call the "logic" or "gate" level (L1) wherein computers lose their computer-like properties – that is, those proper- ties whereby computers are distinguishable from other digital systems. At level L1, computers are merely digital systems; they are, simply, networks of rather primitive devices called logic gates through which binary (i.e., two-valued) signals flow. Alternatively, the designer may need to view the computer not even as a digital system but as an electronic circuit. At this description level (L0), the laws of physics become *explicitly* relevant – that is, physical laws determine directly the behavior of the system, in contrast, say, to the logic level at which system behavior is defined by the mathematical laws of Boolean algebra. At the circuit level, computers are viewed as networks of transistors and resistors; the properties of interest are current, power, voltage, and heat dissipation.[2]

The functional autonomy of each of these description levels – the fact that computers can be specified completely, in some particular sense, at each of these levels – should be clear from the foregoing paragraphs. Such levels also collectively exhibit the property of hierarchical organization. Thus, the fea- tures constituting the exoarchitectural level can be defined in terms of, or be realized by, a description that refers to features taken from the endoarchitectural level. Consider, for instance, a particular instruction for a particular computer. At the exoarchitectural level, the instruction would be characterized in terms of what it does (i.e., its function or meaning) and how the user may specify it within a program (its form). What actually happens when the instruction is executed or how such an instruction has been implemented will be described in terms of features that are only visible at the next (endoarchitecture) level or, if considerable details are to be revealed, in terms of features visible only at the microarchitectural level.

It is worth noting that a system can have several descriptions without the latter being hierarchically organized in this sense. Consider, as a specific instance, the *Visitors' A–Z London Map*[3] and the celebrated London underground map. The former highlights certain major thoroughfares, parks, museums, theaters, cathedrals, railway stations, the underground stations, and other major historical buildings of London. The latter shows only the various underground stations and the lines that connect them. The two maps clearly constitute two distinct modes of description of Britain's capital. Each is functionally autonomous – each describes London completely in some respect; one can use the underground map to negotiate passage between the underground stations and the *Visitors A–Z* to move aboveground from one landmark to another. They are not, however, hierarchically related: One cannot define any one of the underground lines in terms of features present in the *Visitors' A–Z;* nor, for that matter, is it possible to define most of the features shown in the *Visitors' A–Z* in terms of what is shown on the underground map. There will exist, of course, other maps of London to which both *are* hierarchically related. But considered by themselves, the *Visitors' A–Z* and the underground map constitute two descriptions that are hierarchically unrelated.

The important point to note about multiple description *levels,* then, is their complementary nature: On the one hand, each level is functionally autonomous; on the other, the levels are hierarchically organized. This means, in particular, that *it is entirely meaningful to describe or discuss a system at one level without any reference to levels that are lower in the hierarchy.* To take the computer example, typically, the "architectual handbook" or "principles of operation" manual supplied by a computer manufacturer describes the system solely at the exoarchitectural level (L4 in Figure 2.1) so that its reader can understand the structure and behavior of the computer in some particular sense (i.e., in the context of its usability) without having knowledge of its internal design, the nature of the circuits, or the physical technology involved in the building of the computer. It is sufficient to know that lower levels of descriptions exist and that the exoarchitectural level of description can be defined in terms of these lower description levels. Moreover, if one wishes to explain how the computer behaves while it is computing a particular function (such as determining the factorial of a number), it is not only the case that a complete explanation *can* be provided in terms of the computer's features at the exoarchitectural level (i.e., in terms of memory, registers, instructions, data types, ways of addressing data, and so on); it is also likely to be the *best possible* level at which such an explanation can be provided.[4] Given a particular task to be performed – computing the factorial of a number, sorting an array of integers, formating a page of text – it is the highest possible level at which the behavior of computers in performing such tasks can be specified. Such a description will be less complex, more spare, and more understandable than descriptions at lower levels.

In fact, an explanation of computer behavior in performing some task will take the form of a *program* composed of instructions taken from the instruction set of the relevant computer. This is clearly a *sufficient* explanation since, given the multiple-description-leveled nature of computers, there will always exist explanations of how each individual instruction in the program causes still more primitive behavior within the computer – say, at the microarchitectural level. From the perspective of clarity, simplicity, and abstractness, it will also be the *best possible* explanation since it is at the highest available, relevant description level. This is the great advantage of hierarchically structured systems.

The knowledge level

The relevance of this protracted discussion of description levels to the problem of creativity lies in the notion that the *cognitive system* – the mind–brain complex – is also describable at several levels. In particular, the following have been widely recognized (Newell, Rosenbloom, and Laird 1989; Pylyshyn 1989; Newell 1990):

(1) *The knowledge level* – wherein, cognition is described or explained in terms of goals, actions, knowledge, and intendedly rational behavior.
(2) *The symbol level* – in which cognitive processes are described or explained in terms of symbols (and symbol structures), memory (in which symbols are held), operations (on symbols), and interpretations (of the operations).
(3) *The biological level* – wherein cognition is described or explained in terms of biological structures or structures that are abstractions of biological systems, for example, neural networks.

Both empirical and theoretical arguments have been advanced in support of these levels (see, e.g., Pylyshyn 1980, 1984; Newell 1990), and indeed, specific architectures have been proposed for cognition at each of these levels. These include, for instance, the symbol-level theories ACT due to Anderson (1983) and SOAR, proposed by Newell and his colleagues (Laird, Newell, and Rosenbloom 1987; Newell, Rosenbloom, and Laird 1989; Newell 1990), and the various neural network-based theories such as the "parallel distributed processing" model developed by Rumelhart and McClelland (1986).

Our concern here, however, is with the knowledge level – for it is at this level that computational accounts of scientific creativity have all been presented by, for example, Thagard (1988, 1990), Thagard and Nowak (1990), Langley et al. (1987), and Kulkarni and Simon (1988). CTSC, which will provide the explanatory framework for Wilkes's invention of microprogramming, is, quite explicitly, a knowledge-level theory. One should note, however – and this will be quite obvious from the discussion that follows – that the knowledge and symbol levels are not entirely separable; they share some common characteristics.

While a substantial part of what may be called the "classical" artificial intelligence (AI) paradigm has traditionally been operative at the knowledge level[5] – and, hence, the latter has always been tacitly recognized in both the AI literature and the literature of (computationally influenced) cognitive science – the term "knowledge level" was actually coined (and a systematic treatment of its characteristics first presented) by Allen Newell (1982).[6]

A cognitive system at the knowledge level will be referred to as an *agent*.[7] The main entities with which an agent is concerned are *goals, actions,* and *knowledge* (which includes *facts, beliefs, rules, laws, theories,* and *values*). As Newell puts it, "To treat a system at the knowledge level is to treat it as having some knowledge and some goals, and believing it will do whatever is within its power to attain its goals insofar as its knowledge indicates." (Newell 1982, p. 98). In Newell's formulation, the connection between knowledge, goals, and the choice of which action to take (in order to achieve the goals) is established by a behavioral principle that he termed

> *The Principle of Rationality* (PR): If an agent has knowledge that one of its actions will lead to one of its goals then the agent will select that action.

A problem with PR is that it tells us nothing about what the agent might do if it does not possess the requisite knowledge. Nor is it very helpful in the situation where we observe an agent making a choice in response to a goal. Are we, for instance, to infer *abductively* that the agent possesses the requisite knowledge that that particular action will lead to the desired goal?[8]

Such a conclusion may be wholly unwarranted. In general, an agent may possess *incomplete or partial* knowledge concerning the appropriate action to take in response to a goal. Or the determination of which action to select from a set of alternatives may be *computationally so complex* as to be beyond the agent's capacity. In other words, in addition to the rationality principle PR, it is assumed that an agent is characterized by

> *The Principle of Bounded Rationality* (PBR): Given a goal, an agent may not possess perfect or complete knowledge of, or be able to economically compute or access, the correct action (or sequence of actions) that will lead to the attainment of the goal.

The concept of *bounded* (as opposed to "perfect") rationality is due to Simon (see, in particular, Simon 1976, 1982). Its consequence for the theory of the knowledge-level agent presented here is that, given a goal, there is no guarantee that in selecting an action (or a sequence of actions), the goal will, in fact, be attained.

Ideally, then, an agent's behavior at the knowledge level is governed or driven by PR. In actuality, it is constrained by PBR. We conclude, then, that *any action(s) the agent chooses in order to attain a goal represents, in general, a hypothesis (on the part of the agent) that the action(s) will lead to the goal.*

Thus far, agents have been referred to as conducting actions or sequences of actions. Each individual action *does* something. It has an *input* to it and it produces an *output*. In general, both input and the resulting output may be in the form of matter, energy, or symbols. In particular, in the context of scientific creativity in invention, discovery, and design, we will be concerned only with *symbol processing actions* in which the input and output are both symbol structures.

In general, symbols or structures composed out of symbols may be formal or physical. *Formal* symbols do not designate anything other than themselves. Mathematical expressions such as $y = x^2 + 2$ or logical formulas such as $(\forall y)$ $(\exists x)$ $(y > x)$ are instances of formal symbol structures wherein the marks "y," "x," "$=$," "2," "(," ")," "$\forall$," and "$\exists$" are the individual symbols. The symbols themselves have no intrinsic meaning; the structures are interpreted solely according to the rules of composition associated with a particular system of symbols.

On the other hand, symbol structures may stand for, represent, designate, or be about entities in some external universe, and, so, the meaning of such symbol structures are interpreted with reference to that universe. Such symbol structures will be referred to as *physical* symbol structures. For example, the statement "In the front row of the Odeon theatre on King's Street at the matinee show on October 18, 1988, all the men were sitting on one side and all the women were sitting on the other side" is a physical symbol structure insofar as it is about some particular state of affairs in the real world.[9] We shall use the term general symbol structure to refer to both formal and physical symbol structures.

As noted, the actions of interest here are symbol-processing actions. In fact, actions may themselves be represented by symbol structures. More generally, *all goals, knowledge, and actions pertaining to an agent are representable at the knowledge level by general symbol structures.*[10]

Every action consumes some amount of time. We are not concerned here with the actual duration of an action. However, it is recognized that an action has a *beginning* point in time and an *end*point in time; consequently, an action may begin (or end) earlier (or later) than another.

Actions can take place in sequence or in parallel. A *sequence* of actions α_1, $\alpha_2, \ldots, \alpha_n$, where α_i ends before α_{i+1} begins ($1 \leq i \leq n - 1$) will, as a whole, have an input I that is the input I_1 to α_1 and an output O that is the output O_n of α_n such that output O_i of α_i is the input I_{i+1} of α_{i+1}. Actions may also be conducted in *parallel* (in order, say, to achieve cooperatively one of several goals) by an individual agent or a team of agents. It is not necessary here to enter into a theory of parallelism insofar as it may apply to actions. For the present purpose, it is sufficient to note that regardless of whether parallel actions are conducted by an individual agent or a team of agents, they satisfy

> *The Principle of Determinacy* (PD): If a set of actions $\alpha_1, \ldots, \alpha_n$ are conducted in parallel and if I is the input to this set then the output O will be identical to the output O' that would be produced if the same actions $\alpha_1, \ldots, \alpha_n$ were to be conducted in some arbitrary sequential order with the same input I.

In other words, the input–output behavior of a set of parallel actions is indistinguishable from the input–output behavior of the same set of actions performed in *any* sequential order.

Henceforth, we may refer to any sequential, parallel, or hybrid set of actions as a *structured set* of actions. Such a set will have one or more actions that are its *earliest*, if no actions outside this subset begin earlier than those within the subset.

Thus far, actions have been linked with *goals;* that is, actions are assumed to be invoked in response to goals; furthermore, given a goal, an action or a structured set of actions will be invoked subject to the behavioral principles PR and PBR. An action may also be initiated *without* the stimulus of a goal: It may be initiated by virtue of an element or *token* in the agent's knowledge body. In that case, such an action is neither guided nor constrained by PR or PBR. We shall therefore distinguish between *rational* actions – actions that are invoked in response to goals – and *nonrational* actions – those that are invoked in response to tokens in the agent's knowledge body.

To summarize, an action and the conditions of its selection can be characterized as follows:

(1) The input to an action is one or more symbol structures representing goals or knowledge tokens. In the event that at least one of the inputs is a goal, the action is termed rational. Otherwise, it is nonrational.
(2) The output of an action is one or more symbol structures representing either a knowledge token or a goal.
(3) Every action entails the retrieval and application of tokens contained in the agent's knowledge body.
(4) The choice of an action in response to a goal is governed by the principle of rationality (PR). That is, if an agent has knowledge (or believes) that one of its actions will lead to the goal being achieved, it will select that action.
(5) Because of bounded rationality (PBR), however, an action so chosen may not be the correct action, or the action may not be economically computable by the agent.
(6) Every action consumes time.
(7) Actions may be performed sequentially or in parallel.
(8) In a structured set of actions, its parallel subsets obey the principle of determinacy (PD).

A *knowledge-level process* (or computation) P(KL) is a structured set of actions conducted by one or more agents in response to a goal (or a conjunction of goals) G such that

(1) The input to P(KL) is a set of symbol structures at least one of which represents G.
(2) The output of P(KL) is a set of symbol structures that represent goals or knowledge tokens, where the latter includes, possibly, *solutions* to G – that is, tokens that represent a solution to, or achievement of, G.
(3) P(KL) terminates when either (1) its output contains a solution to G or (2) its output is such that no further action is (or can be) selected.

We can now appreciate in what sense a knowledge-level process is computation-like. It must begin with a goal. Subject to the behavioral principle of rationality, a goal prompts an action that entails the selection of tokens from the agent's knowledge body. The output of the action may be a symbol structure believed by the agent as representing a solution (or a partial solution) to the original goal. However, because the agent is governed by bounded rationality, no such solution may be produced; instead, a new (possibly more tractable) goal results. This output goal prompts a new action to be invoked, and so the computation proceeds. In general, a given goal may cause several actions to be performed cooperatively and in parallel, the parallelism only being subject to the principle of determinacy. Finally, the process terminates when the original goal is achieved or when no further action can be performed by the agent. It may also be noted that a structured set of actions need *not* constitute a knowledge-level process in the sense that this latter concept has been defined. This would be the case when the actions in the structured set are all nonrational.

A computational theory of scientific creativity: the hypothesis

In the section "the concept of creativity" in Chapter 1, several levels or kinds of creativity were identified. Of particular interest are the notions pertaining to "originality." To recall, let Π be the product (relevant to a domain D) of a particular thought or cognitive process P conducted by an agent A. In general, Π may be an idea, a theory, a method, a literary or an artistic work, an artifact, or the like. Then

(1) Π is said to be *psychologically original* for the agent A if (1) Π is psychologically novel – that is, according to A's personal knowledge body $K_A(D)$ relevant to D there does not exist any other product Π' identical to Π, and (2) Π is believed by A to add significantly to the knowledge body $K_C(D)$ associated with a community C relevant to D.

(2) Π is said to be *historically original* for a community C if according to C's public knowledge body $K_C(D)$ relevant to D, (1) Π is historically novel – that is, according to C's public knowledge body $K_C(D)$, there does not exist any other product Π' identical to Π; and (2) Π is believed by C to add significantly to $K_C(D)$.

The process P is said to be PO-creative if Π is (or was) psychologically original; it is said to be HO-creative if Π is (or was) historically original. We also noted that, generally speaking, a product deemed historically original by the relevant community will likely have been judged psychologically original by the agent.

Let us now restrict the product Π to those from the domain of the (natural and artificial) sciences. More specifically still, let us consider only cognitive processes that solve *problems* in the sciences. In the case of the natural sciences, this means that Π is an *explanation* (i.e., a theory, a law, a hypothesis, or a chain of arguments) of some phenomenon or problem Ψ.[11] And since in the natural sciences both problems or phenomena and their explanations are expressed using a combination of natural language, technical terms, and mathematical notation, both Ψ and Π are, clearly, general symbol structures.

In the case of the artificial sciences, the product Π can also be an explanation in the sense that explanations are produced in the natural sciences (except that the problem/phenomenon Ψ pertains to the domain of artifacts rather than of nature).[12] On the other hand, Π can be a *design* for an artifact such that if the artifact were to be built according to the design, it would meet a given set of requirements (Dasgupta 1991, 1992).[13] In this latter case, the set of requirements to be met constitutes the problem. Such requirements are also expressed using a combination of natural language, technical terms, and mathematical notation. Similarly, a design – which constitutes a solution to the problem – is a representation, in some language (mathematical, diagrammatic, verbal, algorithmic, etc.), of the artifact to be built. Thus, in the case of the artificial sciences, as in the natural sciences, both the problem Ψ and the product Π that explains or solves the problem are symbol structures.

Generalizing, we may call the problem/phenomenon to be explained or the requirements to be met a *scientific goal*, for which the corresponding explanation or the design is a *solution*. We can now state

> *The Computational Theory of Scientific Creativity (CTSC):* Let Ψ_G be a scientific goal for which Π is a solution produced by an agent *A*. Let *P* be the cognitive process that produced Π. Furthermore, let Π be psychologically original with respect to agent *A* and domain *D* or historically original with respect to community *C* and domain *D*. Then the process *P* conducted by *A* can be specified as (or explained in the form of) a knowledge level process *P(KL)* with Ψ_G as input and Π as output.

In other words, given a *thought product* – an explanation or a design – in response to a scientific goal, where the product is acknowledged to be original (either by the agent or by the community), the thought process giving rise to it, according to CTSC, can be specified or explained solely in terms of goals, the agent's knowledge body, a structured set of symbol-processing actions involving the retrieval and application of knowledge tokens, and the principles of rationality, bounded rationality, and determinacy.

The explanatory nature of the computational theory

It was noted in Chapter 1 (see the section "On the testability of a theory of creativity") that because of the contingent nature of cognitive acts, a theory of creativity will be explanatory rather than predictive. That is, given a theory of creativity T, a knowledge body K, and an original or novel output Π, an explanation of how Π was produced would be described by a process P that invokes K and is in accordance with T. Notationally, such an explanation is represented as

$$\frac{T,\ K}{P:\quad \Pi}$$

We now have a particular theory of creativity, namely, CTSC. According to this, any specific, known act of creation in the natural or artificial sciences can be explained in the form of a knowledge level process. In the specific case of Wilkes's invention of microprogramming, if Π_μ signifies the idea of microprogramming and K_{MVW} denotes Wilkes's knowledge body at the onset of his investigation, then an explanation of this particular act of creation can be denoted by

$$\frac{T,\ K_{MVW}}{P(KL):\quad \Pi_\mu}$$

where $P(KL)$ designates a knowledge-level process. Note, in passing, that CTSC is not explicitly stated here above the horizontal line since $P(KL)$, being a knowledge-level process, implies that the theory is CTSC. The task at hand is to postulate a plausible knowledge body K_{MVW} for Wilkes and construct a knowledge-level process $P(KL)$, such that the idea of microprogramming Π_μ can be shown to be derivable by this process on the basis of what is contained in K_{MVW}.

The testability of the computational theory

Clearly, CTSC is testable – in the following sense: If, in fact, for a given creative act we are unable to construct a knowledge-level process that explains it or if certain tokens of knowledge are postulated that can be shown to have not been part of the agent's knowledge body, then we will have *failed to corroborate* CTSC as a theory of creativity. This does not mean that CTSC has been falsified and is to be rejected in its entirety (though if several such failures to corroborate occur, this might indeed be the case). It may, rather, mean that CTSC will have to be modified to an improved theory CTSC′ (say) that continues to conform to the characteristics of the knowledge level. CTSC is, after all, an empirical theory that may, like all such theories, be supplanted by improved theories.

Notes

1. The general "architecture" of complex systems including, importantly, their hierarchical character, was discussed in an influential paper by Simon (1962), later reprinted in Simon (1981). Pattee (1973), Whyte, Wilson, and Wilson (1969), and Smith (1981) contain several articles pertaining to the hierarchical structure of complex systems. Bell and Newell (1971), Tanenbaum (1984), and Dasgupta (1984) contain extensive discussions of computers viewed as hierarchical systems.
2. So markedly distinct are these description levels, they have come to be associated with different subdisciplines of computer science and engineering. Designers and researchers whose domains of interest are L4 and L3 (and sometimes L2) are referred to as "computer architects" and the discipline spanning these levels is called "computer architecture." The domain of level L2 is, in particular, the special turf of microprogrammers. "Hardware design" has come to mean design activities at levels L1 and L0 – but even here a distinction is made between the discipline of "logic design and switching theory" (the domain corresponding to L1) and "integrated circuit design" (the domain corresponding to L0).
3. This is a well-known and widely used guide for visitors to London and is published by Geographers A–Z Map Co., Ltd.
4. Of course, if a "high-level programming language" such as FORTRAN, Pascal, or C is available, then a description of how the computer behaves during the computation of the function of interest is even more appropriately given in such a language. The availability of such a language for the computer simply extends the number of description levels for the computer by one. At this new, higher level (L5), the computer is seen as a "high level language" machine.
5. I use "paradigm" here in the Kuhnian sense. The qualifier "classical" has become necessary, of late, since *connectionism* now offers an alternative, competitive paradigm for the AI discipline. See, e.g., the winter 1988 issue of *Daedalus*, the Journal of the American Academy of Arts and Sciences, and, in particular, Papert's (1988) article in that issue. See also Fodor and Pylyshyn (1988).
6. Pylyshyn (1980) referred to this level by such adjectives as "mentalistic" and "representational," while the philosopher Daniel Dennett (1978) used the phrase "intentional stance" to designate Newell's knowledge level. See also Dennett (1988) and Newell (1990) for more on this.

7. Newell (1982) ascribes the knowledge level to both natural (i.e., cognitive) and artificial (i.e., computational) systems. In his formulation, then, an agent can be a computer as much as a person.
8. Abduction was introduced in Chapter 1. (See the section "The significance of philosophy of science.") To recall briefly, abduction is a rule of inference of the form

$$\frac{\text{If A then B, B}}{\text{A}}$$

Here the clauses or assertions above the horizontal line are the premises that, if valid, allow the inference of the assertion below the line (the consequence) to be drawn.

9. In philosophy, the problem of how symbols are ever 'about' something outside the symbol system itself is referred to as the problem of "intentionality" (Searle 1983, 1984). For a discussion of the issue in the present context of the knowledge level, see Newell (1990, pp. 78–80).
10. In Newell's (1982) formulation, symbol structures are not constituents of the knowledge level. They are, rather, realizations of knowledge at the *symbol level* (see Newell 1990, pp. 72–80). In the present formulation, however, it is fruitful to include symbol structures as means of representing goals, actions, and knowledge. It is in this sense that the boundary between knowledge and symbol levels are not sharp or fixed. This characteristic of "fuzziness" is also manifested when we consider, for example, levels of description for computers (Figure 2.1). Although the details are not important nor can they be stated concisely here, it may be mentioned that in certain situations, some features of the endoarchitectural level (L3 in Figure 2.1) may also surface as features of the exoarchitecture (L4). The interested reader may consult Dasgupta (1989a, p. 4) for examples of such cases.
11. It is not important, in the present context, to explicate in what sense Π is an explanation, since the concern here is, *given* that something is an explanation of a phenomenon or a problem and *given* that that explanation is (psychologically or historically) original, what kind of a mental process may have given rise to the explanation.
12. This corresponds to what is conventionally referred to as the "scientific" aspect of engineering or as "engineering science" (Rogers 1983; Addis 1990). A typical example is when given a particular artifact or a system, the question is asked, What are its performance or reliability characteristics as a function of a specific set of parameters? An answer to this would constitute a solution or an explanation in the natural sciences sense. The artificial sciences, of course, involve considerably more than *this* sort of problem solving. The larger kind of problem is of the form: Given a set of "requirements" demanded of an artifact, what should be the *form* of such an artifact. This class of problems constitutes *design*.
13. A design, then, is a theory of the artifact in the sense that it provides a specification of the form of the artifact so as to satisfy the given set of requirements. This notion of *designs as theories* is discussed in some detail in Dasgupta (1991, chap. 12; further elaborated in 1992).

3

Maurice Wilkes and the origins of microprogramming: the historical setting

In May 1949, the EDSAC computer, designed and constructed by Maurice Wilkes and his co-workers at the Cambridge University Mathematical Laboratory successfully performed its first, fully automatic computation (Wilkes, 1956, p. 39; 1985, p. 142; Wilkes and Renwick 1949).[1] The machine was demonstrated soon after, in June 1949, at a conference entitled "High Speed Automatic Calculating Machines" held in Cambridge during which tables of squares and primes were printed out (Worsley 1949). As noted in chapter 1 (see the section "The invention of microprogramming: as a case study"), the EDSAC was the very first stored program computer to become fully operational.

The EDSAC was a serial machine in that (1) reading from or writing into main memory was done in a "bit-serial" manner – that is, each bit of a memory word was read or written into one at a time,[2] and (2) the arithmetic unit performed its various operations in a bit-by-bit manner.[3]

Soon after the EDSAC's completion, Wilkes became preoccupied with the issues of *regularity* and *complexity* in computer design. This preoccupation is documented not only in his retrospective writings (Wilkes 1985, pp. 184–5, 1986), but also in the early sections of Wilkes (1951), as a preamble to his description of the microprogramming principle. Thus, there is considerable evidence that the development of microprogramming was the outcome of the following problem:

> *To design a control unit that would be systematic and regular in structure in much the same way that the memory unit is regular in structure.*

To understand the real nature of this problem, it is necessary to understand what is entailed by such terms as "regularity" and "complexity" in the context of computer design in the immediate post-EDSAC period. It is necessary, in

Creativity in invention and design

fact, to contrast the organization and design of the "control part" of the EDSAC with its memory unit.

The EDSAC and its control circuits

Figure 3.1 shows the internal organization of the EDSAC. This diagram is, in fact, a description at what in Chapter 2 (Figure 2.1) is referred to as the microarchitectural (L2) level. The rectangles represent the principal components at this description level and are labeled by both current names and (in parentheses) the terms used by Wilkes et al. in their discussions of this machine.

The firm lines indicate the *data paths* connecting the various components, while the dotted lines signify *control paths* – that is, the lines along which *control signals* are sent in order to control (or enable) the transmission of data along data paths or the activation of the *functional units* (such as the arithmetic unit, the input unit, and the output unit). The black circles denote logical gates. Typically, a gate has a control path and a data path as inputs to it and a data path as an output. Normally, a gate is "closed"; when a control signal arrives at the gate, the latter is "opened," and the data at the input side is allowed to pass through to the output side. This is how control signals control the transmission of data along a data path.[4] The various control signals are shown as C_1, C_2, and so on.

As the legend in Figure 3.1 indicates, the control signals emanate from essentially three sources: C_1 through C_5 are issued by the main control unit; C_6 through C_{12} are issued as a result of decoding the contents of the opcode or function register; while C_{13} and C_{14} are issued as a result of decoding the contents of the operand-address or location register.[5] In EDSAC terminology, the function and location registers along with their associated circuitry (including the decoders) constitute its "order interpreter."

Thus, the control circuits – the circuits that issue control signals – are not localized in the EDSAC. There is no single or central control unit. The control capabilities are basically distributed between the main control unit and the order interpreter. This is the *first* source of the irregularity and complexity of EDSAC's control circuits.

This is not, however, the sole factor. Control signals are issued to effect certain events at certain points in time. The design of the EDSAC followed the ideas presented in a seminal report, authored by John von Neumann (1945), that served as the planning document for the EDVAC – developed at first at the

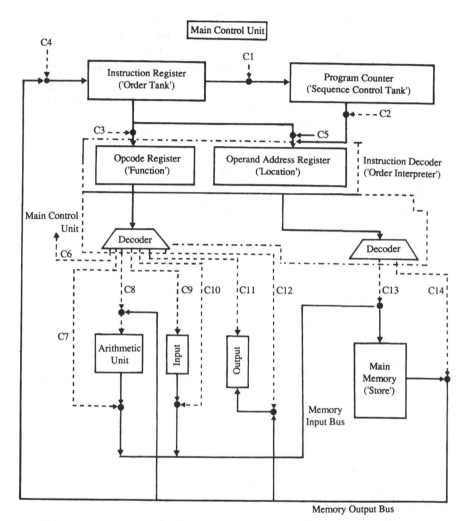

Source of Control Signals:
C1, C2, C3, C4, C5: Main Control Unit
C6, C7, C8, C9, C10, C11, C12: Opcode Register / Decoder
C13, C14: Operand Address Register / Decoder

Figure 3.1. Organization of the EDSAC computer.

University of Pennsylvania and then at the U.S. Ballistic Research Laboratory
between 1946 and 1951 (Randell 1975, pp. 351–2) – and that, more importantly, became the defining document for what came to be known as the stored
program computer.[6]

In the case of the EDSAC, the overall operation of the machine consisted of two stages, and the initiation of these stages were effected by control signals issued by the main control unit. In stage I, an instruction or "order" is transferred from a location in memory – as determined by the location or address stored in the program counter or "sequence control tank" – to the instruction register or "order tank." As suggested by Figure 3.1, this is brought about by the issuance of a set of control signals, namely, C_2, C_{13}, C_{14}, *in the proper sequence,* one of which – C_2 – originates in the main control unit, the others in the order interpreter.

In stage II, control signals are issued causing the instruction in the order tank to be transferred, in part to the opcode/function register and in part to the operand-address/location register. The contents of these registers are decoded, and the outputs of the decoder become control signals that, depending on the precise type of operation stipulated by the opcode/function register, activate transfer of data along data paths or enervate functional units. Thus, in the case of an ADD operation, for example, a control signal (C_{14}) causes main memory to be read and a number (operand) to be transferred to the arithmetic unit, while another control signal (C_8) causes the addition to be performed. In the case of an INPUT operation, control signals C_9, C_{10}, and C_{13} will be invoked. Thus, as in stage I, control signals from one of two different sources have to be issued *in the proper temporal order.* Moreover, the control signal sequences will *vary from one instruction to another.* This is, then, a *second* source of the irregularity and complexity in the control part. Finally, the same control signal may have to be issued *at different points of time.* For instance, as just described, C_{14} is issued in stage I *and* stage II. Herein lies the *third* cause of irregularity and complexity in the control circuits.

In general, then, because of the irregularity and complexity of the control functions, the control circuits in the EDSAC were largely designed in an ad hoc manner. This can be contrasted with the highly regular organization of the main memory, shown schematically in Figure 3.2. The latter was physically organized in terms of thirty-two mercury tanks (see note 2).

In fact, the control circuits were not the only irregular elements in the EDSAC. Wilkes was also initially concerned with the unstructured character of the arithmetic circuits, a property derived from its serial nature. However, in the course of his second visit to the United States, undertaken during the summer and early autumn of 1950 (July 8–September 18) – a visit that, as we shall see, played a key role in the genesis of microprogramming – Wilkes met Julian Bigelow, who was then involved in the development of a computer at the Institute of Advanced Study at Princeton, and came to realize that a parallel

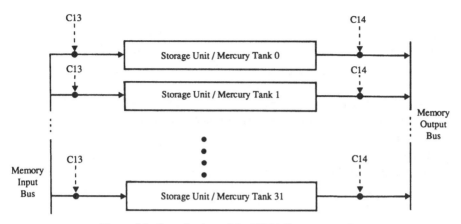

Figure 3.2. Organization of the EDSAC memory unit.

arithmetic unit could attain the same order of regularity as the memory unit (Wilkes 1985, pp. 164–5, 1986).[7]

On the conceptual nature of Wilkes's problem

To repeat, the issue that caught Wilkes's attention and that eventually led to the invention of microprogramming was the irregularity and the ad hoc nature of control circuits – in contrast to the systematic, regular structure of the memory unit and even (subsequent to his meeting with Bigelow) of arithmetic units.

This brings to mind a point made in the section "The invention of micro-programming: as a case study" in Chapter 1, that the issue with which Wilkes concerned himself was essentially of a *conceptual* kind. That is, the problem pertained to such abstract, imprecise, and subjective predicates as regular, systematic, and complex. These are not, inherently, predicates that are testable. That is, whether or not a particular solution (say the design of a control circuit) satisfies such predicates is something that cannot be determined empirically without further refinement of the predicates themselves. Wilkes's problem, at least at the beginning, was not an empirical one.

One of the interesting attributes of conceptual problems is that their recogni-tion or perception by an individual is often, perhaps mostly, motivated by philosophical or aesthetic perspectives rather than strictly scientific or techni-cal considerations. This also seems to have been the case here: In a recorded public lecture, Wilkes (1984) remarked that without a particular philosophical perspective, the problem he investigated and for which microprogramming became the eventual solution would not make too much sense – a point he repeated more recently to the writer. His problem, he remarked, was essentially a *private* problem.[8]

And yet the recognition of irregularity or unstructuredness is *not* the real beginning of this story. At the Manchester conference where he first announced the principle of microprogramming, Wilkes (1951)[9] discussed the paramount importance of "reliability" (of a system or a circuit), which, he noted, depends on the following factors: the amount of equipment (i.e., circuitry), the complexity of the circuit, and the degree of repetition of the subunits constituting the system. By "complexity," Wilkes meant

the extent to which cross-connections between the various units obscure their logical inter-relation . . . A machine is easier to repair if it consists of a number of units connected together in a simple way without cross-connections between them. (Wilkes 1986, p. 118)

In the next paper on the topic – the first devoted entirely to microprogramming – Wilkes and Stringer (1953)[10] began by pointing out that "the sections of an electronic digital computer which are easiest to maintain are those which have simple logical structure" (Wilkes 1986, p. 121). Furthermore, "It is in the control section that the greatest degree of complexity generally arises" (Wilkes 1986; p. 121).

However, they also noted that

for each different order [i.e., instruction] in the code [i.e., program] some special equipment must be provided and *the more complicated the function of the order the more complex this equipment*. In the past, fear of complicating unduly the control circuits of the machine has prevented the designer of electronic machines from providing such facilities as orders for floating point operations. (Wilkes 1986, p. 121; italics added)

It is not absolutely clear whether this latter realization – that the complexity of the function or "order" determines the complexity of the "equipment" in the control section – was a factor that actually preceded the birth of the microprogramming concept or whether it was realized *ex post facto* – for, this point is not discussed by Wilkes (1951). It may, however, be said that the following relationships appear to have been understood quite clearly by Wilkes: Additional functions require additional circuitry and, therefore, entail an increase in the complexity of the control section; and the latter, in turn, diminishes the repairability, maintainability, and reliability of the control unit. Thus, it appears that Wilkes's recogniton of the conceptual (design) problem pertaining to the irregularity and complexity of control circuits was fundamentally motivated by the problem of reliability,[11] and furthermore, it was grounded in a worldview containing at the very least the following:

(1) Empirical knowledge of the ad hoc, unstructured, complex nature of the control circuits in the EDSAC and, most probably, of other contemporary control unit designs (especially that of the Manchester machine).[12]

(2) An understanding of the general relationship between complexity on the one hand and reliability, repairability, and maintainability on the other.

(3) The basic idea that such conceptual desirables as regularity and simplicity were achievable through such means as "replication of identical units," "regular and simple connection patterns," and "modularity of the units" (Wilkes 1951). This idea was at least in part influenced by Wilkes's observation of memory organizations and parallel arithmetic circuits.

(4) The empirical fact that in a computer with a comprehensive order code (i.e., instruction set), each order (i.e., instruction) requires specialized circuitry, and the more complicated the order, the more complex the associated circuitry.

Representing knowledge: networks and rules

As we shall see, knowledge of various kinds will appear ubiquitously in the chapters to follow. That knowledge plays a central role in the kind of computational accounts we shall be concerned with should also be evident from the discussion in Chapter 2 – for CTSC is, after all, a knowledge-level theory.

Scientists in the AI and cognitive psychology domains have developed, over the years, a variety of *knowledge-representation schemes*.[13] Our concern here is not with the relative merits of these various proposals nor with the details of their formal underpinnings. Rather, I have taken an opportunistic approach in selecting those particular representation schemes that seem most appropriate and adapting or tailoring them to suit the specific purposes on hand.

The first of the knowledge-representation schemes we shall use, goes by several names in the AI literature including "associative network" and "semantic network" (Findler 1979; Barr and Feigenbaum 1981; Brachman and Levesque 1985). Following Thagard (1990) we shall refer to the particular form of this scheme adopted here by the term *conceptual network*.

Figures 3.3 and 3.4 are conceptual networks that depict two portions of Wilkes's knowledge body at the time he began to think about the control unit

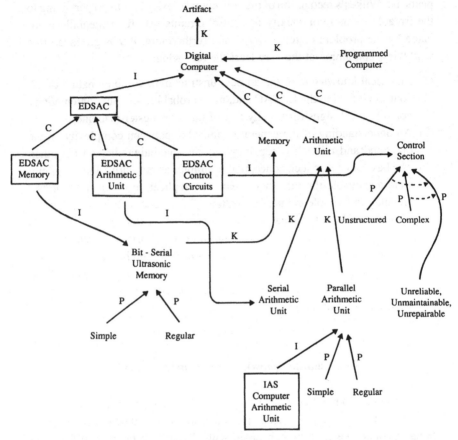

Figure 3.3. A fragment of the conceptual network of knowledge concerning computers circa 1950.

problem. More precisely, one may think of them as two fragments of his conceptual network circa 1950. Here, *concepts* and particular *objects* are denoted by *nodes*, while directed edges or *links* signify connections or relationships between concepts, between concepts and objects, or between objects. In Figures 3.3 and 3.4, objects are enclosed in boxes, while concepts are shown as open nodes. The diagrams also show five kinds of links:[14]

(a) *Kinds of* links – denoted by edges labeled "*K*." These indicate that one *concept* is a kind of another. More specifically, if there is a directed edge to concept C_1 from the concept C_2 with label "*K*," then C_2 is a kind of C_1.

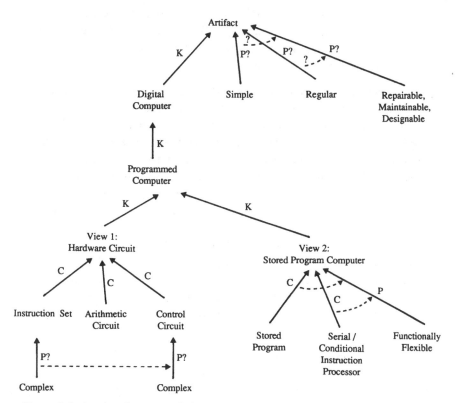

Figure 3.4. Another fragment of the conceptual network of knowledge concerning computers circa 1950.

(b) *Instance-of* links – denoted by edges labeled "*I.*" These indicate that a particular *object* is an instance of a *concept*. A directed edge labeled "*I*" to concept C_1 from object O_2 indicates that O_2 is an instance of C_1.

(c) *Property* links – denoted by edges labeled "*P.*" These indicate that an object or a concept (or, more specifically, any instance of that concept) possesses a property. A directed edge labeled "*P*" to concept or object T from property Y indicates that T has property Y. An edge labeled "*P?*" signifies that an object or a concept may *possibly* (but not necessarily) have the associated property.

(d) *Component* links – denoted by edges labeled "*C.*" These indicate that an object or a concept is a component (or element) of another object or concept, respectively. A directed edge labeled "*C*" to object or concept T_1 from object or concept T_2 indicates that T_2 is a component of T_1 (or T_1 has, as a component, T_2).

(e) *Rule* links – denoted by dotted lines between links. These express general explanatory relations between the propositions signified by the links that they connect. When a rule link is labeled with a "?," this indicates a probable explanatory relationship.

For example, from Figure 3.3 we note that the digital computer concept has, as a component, the control section concept, that (according to Wilkes's knowledge body at that time) any instance of the control section concept has the properties complex, unstructured, and unreliable/unmaintainable/unrepairable and that by virtue of the rule link, there is an explanatory or causal relationship between the former two properties and the latter: Control units are unreliable, unmaintainable, and unrepairable (at least in part) *because* they are unstructured and complex. Figure 3.3 also tells us that the EDSAC is an instance of a digital computer.

From Figure 3.4, it is seen that Wilkes's weltanschauung included the general notion that artifacts can be simple, regular, and repairable/ maintainable/designable (but not necessarily so). The notion by itself means very little. It does become important, however, when the labeled rule links are taken into account. The two labeled rule links are to be interpreted as representing two rules:

> *If* an artifact is simple, *Then* the artifact is repairable/maintainable/designable.
>
> *If* an artifact is regular, *Then* the artifact is repairable/maintainable/designable.

Rules such as these constitute, in fact, the main knowledge representation scheme used in this book. In general, a rule is an entity of the form

> *If* condition, *Then* operation,

which asserts that if the state of affairs in a particular "world" of which an agent has knowledge is such that that "condition" is satisfied, then the corresponding "operation" may be performed. However, in the rules that will appear in this book, the operation to be actually performed may not always be *explicitly* stated in the *Then* part of a rule. It will be understood from the context. For example, in the case of

> *If* an artifact is simple, *Then* the artifact is repairable/maintainable/designable,

the operation is understood to be "assign the properties 'repairable,' 'maintainable,' and 'designable' to that particular artifact that is found to satisfy the property 'is simple.'"[15]

Given Wilkes's knowledge at the time and his identification of the problem, what were the principal factors that led him to the microprogramming concept? The literature provides two important clues relevant to this question. These are considered in the next two sections, respectively.

The EDSAC and its diode matrix

As shown in Figure 3.1, the EDSAC contained a component called the order interpreter. This is a rather specialized control unit that decodes the function (or opcode, in modern terms) part of the order (or instruction) and issues a signal along one of up to thirty-two output lines (corresponding to thirty-two possible functions or opcodes). What is not shown in Figure 3.1 is that there is a further stage within the order interpreter that encodes the decoder output in a different fashion; it is, in fact, the output of the encoder (or, simply, coder) that constitutes the control signals issued to the various parts (i.e., the arithmetic unit, the input unit, etc.).

To understand this issue more clearly, consider a very simple example. Let us suppose that there are only two input lines to the decoder (Figure 3.5). In that case, up to four opcodes can be encoded by these two lines; the decoder output will consist of four lines, and each of these lines will cause *a distinct set* of control signals to be issued in order to execute each of the four opcodes (Figure 3.6).

As Figures 3.5 and 3.6 indicate, the decoder output line O_1 enables control signals C_1, C_2, C_3, and C_6. Similarly, the decoder output line O_2 activates control signals C_3, C_4, and C_5, and so on. Thus, a *particular* control signal may have to be activated from one *or more* decoder outputs – for example, C_3 is shown in Figure 3.6 to be activated by O_1, O_2, and O_4. More precisely, C_3 will be issued if O_1 is active *or* O_2 is active *or* O_4 is active. Similarly, C_1 is issued if O_1 is active or O_3 is active.

Figure 3.7 shows one kind of circuit that enables such behavior to be implemented. It consists of a set of elementary circuits called "OR gates"; the function of each such gate is to perform the "or" operation. The output of an OR gate is set to "1" (i.e., it is activated) if any one of the inputs to that gate is a 1 regardless of the values on the other inputs. Notice also that the circuit of Figure 3.7, when suitably abstracted, is a four-input, six-output encoder that works in series with the two-input, four-output decoder (Figure 3.8).

The irregularity or unstructuredness of the encoder can be easily appreciated from Figure 3.7. If this circuit is scaled up to a more realistic size – if, for

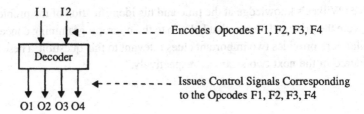

Figure 3.5. A decoder.

Opcode	Decoder Output Line	Control Signals to be Issued
F1	O1	C1, C2, C3, C6
F2	O2	C3, C4, C5
F3	O3	C1, C5, C6
F4	O4	C2, C3

Figure 3.6. Control signals corresponding to decoder output lines.

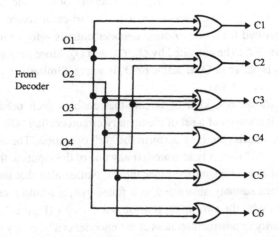

Figure 3.7. Logic circuit for a four-input, six-output encoder.

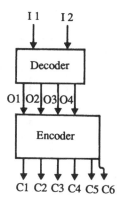

Figure 3.8. The decoder–encoder complex.

example, the number of inputs is increased to thirty-two (corresponding to thirty-two opcodes) and the number of outputs is of the order of a hundred (corresponding to the same order of control signals) – the resulting complexity would be considerable.

There is, however, another equivalent and yet more regular circuit for implementing a set of such functions; and that is by the use of a *diode matrix*. This is an array of intersecting "horizontal" and "vertical" wires – that is, an array of intersecting orthogonal wires – wherein the former serve as inputs to the circuit and the latter serve as the outputs from the circuit. The points of intersection between the horizontal and vertical lines serve as sites for diodes; the presence of such a diode causes the value on the diode input (the corresponding horizontal line) to be "gated" or transmitted to the diode output (the corresponding vertical line). Each vertical line will transmit a signal whenever there is an input signal on any one of the horizontal lines to which it is coupled by means of a diode.

Figure 3.9 shows a four-input, six-output diode matrix that implements the same function as the circuit of Figure 3.7. Recall that C_1 is to be activated whenever there is a signal on O_1 or O_3. In Figure 3.9, diodes (signified by black dots) are appropriately placed at the intersection of the horizontal lines corresponding to O_1 and O_3 with the vertical line corresponding to C_1, and so on.

The point of this whole discussion is that according to Wilkes (1985, p. 178, 1986), the encoding function in the EDSAC was implemented by means of such a diode matrix. And as is evident from Figure 3.9, this circuit is highly regular in form; furthermore, this regularity is preserved even when the circuit is scaled up.

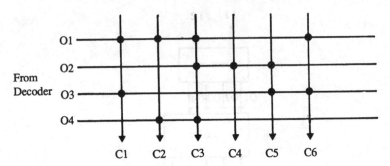

Figure 3.9. A four-input, six-output diode matrix.

The Whirlwind and its control matrix

In several of his writings, Wilkes (1981, 1985, chap. 16, 1986) has recorded details of his second visit to the United States, in the course of which he saw the Whirlwind computer then under construction at the Massachusetts Institute of Technology. In this machine, the duration of each arithmetic operation, except multiplication (for which a separate provision was made), spanned exactly eight pulse intervals. The control signals corresponding to each operation were derived from a diode matrix of the kind just described.

Figure 3.10 shows a simplified version of the Whirlwind type of control unit. Here, it is assumed that there is a set of eight arithmetic operations, denoted as $OP_1, \ldots, OP_8$. The specific sequence of control signals for each operation is shown in the inset at the bottom. The upper part of the diagram shows the diode matrix consisting of eight horizontal lines (each line corresponding to an arithmetic operation) and eight vertical lines (one per control signal of which, in this particular example, there are eight). Diodes are placed at the appropriate intersections.

The outputs of the diode matrix are enabled by means of a "time-pulse distributor," which issues, cyclically, eight pulses so that each control signal is enabled by exactly one pulse of the eight-pulse cycle. For example, C_1 is enabled by pulse 1, C_2 by pulse 2, C_3 by pulse 3, and so on. (The small boxes at the bottom of the diagram denote gates.) This means, for instance, that the execution of arithmetic operation OP_1 involves the issuing of control signal C_1 at pulse time 1, C_2 at pulse time 2, C_4 at pulse time 4, and C_7 at pulse time 7. No control signals are issued at pulse times 3, 5, 6, and 8.

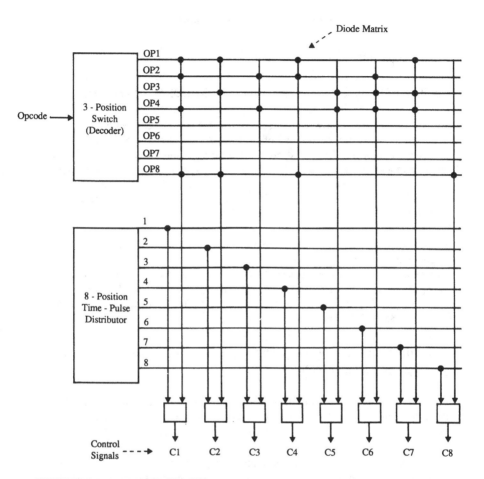

Figure 3.10. Organization of a Whirlwind-type control unit.

The emergence of the microprogramming principle

Wilkes apparently realized that the kind of regularity and simplicity he was seeking for the control unit might be obtained using a diode matrix–like structure of the type used for the encoder in the EDSAC. As he remarks:

All new developments have their antecedents. There was one element of systematic design in the main [*sic*] control unit of the EDSAC. The digits comprising the operation code of an instruction were decoded by means of a diode tree and were then re-encoded in a different manner to provide the static wave forms supplied to the operational units. The re-encoding was done by means of a diode matrix. *It seemed to me that here was a clue. Something similar was needed that would generate sequencing wave forms.* (Wilkes 1986, p. 117; italics added)

We had tried to make the design of the control sections of the EDSAC as systematic as possible, but they contained a great deal of what is now called random logic. I felt that there must be a way of replacing this by something more systematic *perhaps along the lines of the configuration of diodes used for decoding the function digits and subsequently re-encoding them* to drive various gates throughout the computer. (Wilkes 1985, p. 178; italics added)

As for the Whirlwind, the orderliness of its control part appeared to have made a strong impression on Wilkes:

I remember standing in front of the control store – the term was actually used to describe the matrix – of the Whirlwind computer and admiring its elegance and the fact that the control was centralized in one place. (Wilkes, 1981, p. 119)

The elegance of this design appealed to me greatly; it was enhanced by the fact that the diodes were arranged physically, as well as electrically, in the form of a matrix. (Wilkes 1986, p. 117)

It also appeared to confirm, in his mind, the efficacy of using diode matrices for this purpose:

When I saw the Whirlwind computer, I found that it did indeed have a centralized control based on the use of a matrix of diodes. (Wilkes 1985, p. 178)

However, Wilkes wanted far greater flexibility than what either the EDSAC's order interpreter's diode matrix or the Whirlwind's control matrix could provide. In the case of the Whirlwind, for instance, each arithmetic operation required the *same fixed sequence* of control signals to be issued (see Figure 3.10). In general, however, an instruction may demand a *variable* sequence of control signals or "steps," depending on either the data on which the instruction operates or on some condition being generated in the course of instruction execution.

It was only after returning to Cambridge – he left the United States on the *Queen Mary* on September 14, 1950, reaching Britain on September 18 – that "sometime during the winter the ideas fell into shape" (Wilkes 1985, p. 178). Drawing the analogy with programming, he conceived the notion of the control unit as possessing the full flexibility of a programmed computer but in miniature, as it were. In other words, Wilkes likened the sequence of control signals or steps to a sequence of instructions (i.e., a program) and the flexibility of choosing between one sequence of signals and another to the conditional branching within a program.[16]

The notion or conceptualization of *the control unit as a programmed device* in its own right is, in fact, the first major idea one can associate with the invention of microprogramming. However, there still lay the problem of *how* the flexibility of a program could be attained in circuitry in a regular, systematic fashion; the solution lay in the use of one diode matrix to "store" the control signals and a *second* diode matrix that would store the address and control the selection of which control signals to issue over time. The use of *a diode matrix to realize the flexibility of a programming scheme* thus constituted the second major idea to be linked with microprogramming.

Figure 3.11 shows the organization of a centralized *microprogrammed control unit* as finally conceived by Wilkes (1951). An instruction or order is executed in a series of control steps. In each step, one or more control signals are issued. Each vertical line of diode matrix A transmits a particular control signal. Each horizontal line of matrix A stores the control signals to be issued in a given step, in the form of diodes placed at the appropriate intersections. In Wilkes's original description (1951), each such step is referred to as a "micro-operation," although in the next paper on the subject, Wilkes and Stringer (1953) refer to each step as a "micro-order." In modern terminology, the horizontal lines of matrix A are said to represent *microinstructions,* and the elementary operations stored in a microinstruction are called *micro-operations.* The execution of a microinstruction entails the execution of its constituent micro-operations, and the latter results in the appropriate control signals to be issued throughout the computer. Finally, a sequence of microinstructions, or – in the older terminology of Wilkes and Stringer (1953) – micro-orders, is referred to as a *microprogram.*

Each microinstruction has an address. In Figure 3.11, these are denoted as 0, 1, . . . , $n - 1$. For a microinstruction held in address i of matrix A, the corresponding horizontal line of the diode matrix B holds, in an appropriately

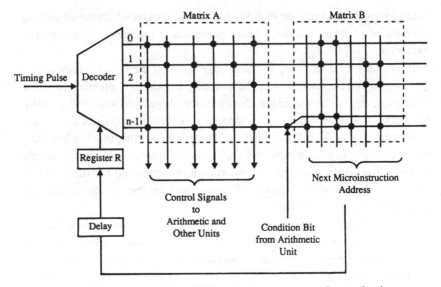

Figure 3.11. Organization of Wilkes's microprogrammed control unit.

coded form, the address of the successor microinstruction to be selected for execution after the microinstruction in address i has completed the execution. For example, suppose line 0 of matrix B holds or encodes the address 20. Then, on completion of the execution of the microinstruction at address 0 (in matrix A), the next microinstruction to be executed is taken from address (line) 20. Strictly speaking, a microinstruction at address i consists of both the contents of line i in matrix A (the contents being the set of micro-operations to be executed) *and* the contents of line i in matrix B (the next address). The two matrices A and B collectively constitute the *control store*.

The operation of the control unit can now be described as follows. Each instruction in the instruction set of a computer is "defined" by a sequence of microinstructions. In modern terms, an instruction is *interpreted* by a particular microinstruction sequence held in the control store. Suppose the address of the first microinstruction in such a sequence is already "loaded" into the register R.[17] The decoder decodes the address and a signal is transmitted along one of the horizontal lines (say, the line corresponding to address i). This signal enters matrix A and gives rise to the execution of the micro-operations held in the microinstruction at that address. Each micro-operation, in turn enables a control signal to be sent to a particular point in the machine.

The signal transmitted along the line corresponding to address i also passes into matrix B and gives rise to signals on those output (vertical) lines of this matrix that are diode-coupled to the horizontal line. Each line i of matrix B stores the address of the successor microinstruction to that executed from address i of matrix A. The output signals from matrix B are transmitted and stored, after a short delay, in register R. R will then contain the address of the next microinstruction to be executed.

As described, the scheme can allow only a fixed cycle of operations to be performed. Its flexibility is considerably enhanced by providing a conditional branching facility in the microprogram, where the condition to be tested to determine whether or not a branch is to be taken is derived from a "flag" or a one-bit register in the arithmetic unit. As Figure 3.11 shows, the status of this bit enables a signal along the horizontal line $n - 1$ of matrix A to be switched along one of two alternative paths in matrix B. One may think of this as an implementation of a "branch microinstruction" along the lines of branch instructions used by programmers.

The immediate aftermath

Wilkes's 1951 paper, delivered at the Manchester Conference held to inaugurate the Ferranti Mark I computer, is now celebrated for its introduction of the concept of microprogramming. In fact, it was more than that – for, in a certain sense, it provided him with an opportunity to present his views on a number of issues pertaining to the "best way to design an automatic computing machine." These issues related primarily to the problem of reliability (see the Section "On the conceptual nature of Wilkes's problem," this chapter). In response to this problem, Wilkes advocated the use of parallel arithmetic units packaged according to what later came to be known as the "bit-slice" principle and, of course, the concept of microprogramming.[18]

As I have recounted in these pages, according to the available documentary evidence, the development of Wilkes's ideas on the control unit began no earlier than the summer of 1949; the solution to the problem was known by the winter of 1950. The Manchester lecture was delivered in July 1951; the first paper devoted wholly to microprogramming was received by the editor of the *Proceedings of the Cambridge Philosophical Society* on November 18, 1952, and published the year after (Wilkes and Stringer, 1953).

At about the end of 1951 or early in 1952, Wilkes and his colleagues – in particular, William Renwick, the chief engineer at the Cambridge Mathematical Laboratory – decided to build a successor to the EDSAC that would incorporate the ideas presented in the Manchester lecture (Wilkes 1991). Of immediate interest to the present discussion is the fact that microprogramming was used to implement practically all aspects of control in this machine – which was named EDSAC-2. As Wilkes put it in a recent paper,

It was accordingly a principle of the design that every gate in the machine that could be driven from the microprogram matrix should be so driven. This goal was achieved to an extraordinary extent. Neither the input and output mechanisms nor the magnetic tape decks had any local sequencing control, but were controlled directly by the microprogram. Even in the memory the reading of a word and its subsequent rewriting were controlled by sequences of micro-operations. (Wilkes 1991, p. 6)

Rather than diode matrices, however, the newly developed technology of magnetic or ferrite cores were used to implement the control store matrices. Ferrite cores had already been used to build the main memory of the Whirlwind I at the Massachusetts Institute of Technology in August 1953 (Wilkes 1956, p. 194).

EDSAC-2 demonstrated beyond doubt to the Cambridge group the practicality of microprogrammed control units. Wilkes recently remarked to this writer that the EDSAC-2 was not intended to be a vehicle for further research on microprogramming.[19] Microprogramming was used because (1) the idea was available and (2), rather more importantly, both Wilkes and Renwick, the engineer responsible for the detailed design of the machine, thought that it was feasible to do so. Had they thought otherwise, the EDSAC-2 project would probably have still gone ahead without the use of microprogramming.

In spite of this caveat, the EDSAC-2 must be regarded, in the history of computer design, as the first empirical test (and a successful one at that) of a new principle of design.[20] The EDSAC-2 became operational in 1958, and a paper describing the design of its control unit was published that same year (Wilkes, Renwick, and Wheeler 1958).

Notes

1. In the early 1970s, the Mathematical Laboratory was renamed the University Computer Laboratory. It is, in effect, the academic department of the University of Cambridge responsible for the university's computer science program.
2. In the stored program computer, the "main memory" is that part of the computer that holds (or can hold) the program being (or to be) executed along with (at least a part of) the data that is either the "input" to the program or is produced as "output" by the program. In the EDSAC literature, the word "store" was used to signify main memory.
   The EDSAC main memory was implemented as an ultrasonic storage device

consisting of a bank of tanks filled with mercury. At one end of each tank, electrical pulses, arriving at fixed time intervals, are converted by quartz crystals into acoustic pulses that traveled along the length of the tank, were converted at the output end into electrical pulses, amplified, and passed back to the input end of the tank. The pulses emerging at the output end could also be "read out" into other parts of the computer. Thus, the train of pulses circulating through each tank represented information "stored" in the device, each pulse (or absence thereof) representing a "bit." In the EDSAC, there were thirty-two such mercury tanks, each capable of storing 576 (32 × 18) bits – i.e., capable of storing thirty-two seventeen-bit numbers (with a space equal to one pulse interval between the numbers). Reading out a particular number (i.e., a particular sequence of seventeen pulses) within a tank would entail a delay until the first bit corresponding to that number (or, in modern terms, the first bit of that particular "word" in a particular "memory address") appeared at the output of a particular tank; and then there would be a further delay until the seventeen pulses (i.e., the remaining bits of the word) appeared one by one. Thus, the address of a "word" in EDSAC memory consisted of a tank number and the relative position of the desired word within the tank.

A bit, of course, signifies a binary digit – i.e., a 1 or a 0. In digital computers, all information processed by the computer (i.e., the instructions and the data on which instructions operate and that are produced by instructions as results) are encoded as patterns or "strings" of bits. For more on ultrasonic memory, see Wilkes (1956).

3. In a serial arithmetic unit, all operations on numbers are done one digit (or a digit pair) at a time. That is, they follow the way humans normally perform arithmetic operations. For example, if two numbers 36 and 26 are added in a serial unit, the digits 6 and 6 would first be fed as input to the circuits; the sum digit (2) would be produced as output and the carry digit (1) fed back, after a suitable delay, as a third input to the adding circuits along with the digits 3 and 2. The resulting sum digit (6) would then be produced. Thus, the positionally corresponding digits of each input number are fed serially, along with the carry from the preceding operation; the addition itself is performed serially; and the digits of the result are obtained serially. (Of course, in digital computers, these numbers are encoded as bit strings so that the actual computations performed by the circuits take 1s and 0s as input and produce 1s and 0s as outputs.) For an early discussion of serial arithmetic units, see Wilkes (1956).

4. "Gate" is, in fact, a technical term in the subdiscipline of computer engineering called *logic design*. It is, clearly, a term that was born of a metaphor, and it is in metaphorical terms that its action has been described here. Obviously, a more formal (or technical) description of gate behavior is provided in the literature on logic design. See, e.g., McCluskey (1986).

5. A decoder is a circuit exhibiting the following kind of property: Suppose there are two input lines I_1, I_2 to a decoder. Then, since one bit of information can appear on each input line and since a bit is a 1 or a 0, four possible binary inputs can appear on the two lines, i.e., 00, 01, 10, 11. The decoder accepts each such value and issues a signal *on exactly one of its output lines*. Thus, given two inputs I_1, I_2 to a decoder, there will be four output lines O_1, O_2, O_3, O_4. If I_1, I_2 = 00, then a signal is issued on a specific output line only, say O_1; if I_1, I_2 = O_1, then O_2 is activated; if I_1, I_2 = 10, then O_3 is activated; and if I_1, I_2 = 11, then a signal is issued on O_4. In general, if there are n input lines to a decoder, then 2^n possible values may serve as inputs – in which case, there should be 2^n distinct output lines exactly one of which will be activated for each of the 2^n input values.

In the case of Figure 3.1, the inputs to each of the two decoders are shown as single lines to reduce clutter in the diagram. Each such line is an abstraction of several lines. In fact, there are five input lines from the function/opcode register to the leftmost decoder so that one of up to $2^5 = 32$ possible output lines may be activated. Only a few of them are shown in the diagram.

A register, like main memory, is a storage device. Typically, however, it is a store (1) for a much smaller amount of information than main memory (e.g., a register may hold a single instruction or a single number), which (2) is characteristically faster – i.e., more rapidly accessible – than main memory.

6. The ideas behind the EDVAC formed the subject of the celebrated series of lectures given by John Mauchly, Presper Eckert, and their associates at the Moore School of Electrical Engineering of the University of Pennsylvania in the summer (July 8–August 31) of 1946 (Randell 1975, p. 351; Wilkes 1985, p. 116). Wilkes attended the second half of this course. However, even before going to the United States for this purpose, he had seen the von Neumann report (Wilkes 1985, pp. 108–9). He began thinking about the EDSAC design soon after attending the Moore School lectures: "I returned to Cambridge with my head full of thoughts for constructing a stored program computer of modest dimensions very much along the lines of the EDVAC proposal. I had spent some time roughing out the design in Philadelphia and on the Queen Mary, and I had formed a preliminary idea – hopelessly optimistic as it turned out – of the number of vacuum tubes that would be required" (Wilkes 1985, p. 127).

7. In a parallel arithmetic unit, the operations are performed in a "bit-parallel" manner. Thus, for example, for performing an ADD operation on two n-bit numbers, there would be n independent and identical adding circuits each of which would have, as inputs, one pair of the positionally corresponding bits of the two numbers. For a discussion of such circuits circa the post-EDSAC period, see Wilkes (1956, pp. 61–5). For a modern discussion, see Hayes (1984, pp. 284–90).

8. M. V. Wilkes, in an interview with the author, December 19, 1991, Olivetti Research Laboratory, Cambridge.

9. This paper appeared in a conference proceedings and is difficult to locate. I shall refer to it as it was reprinted in Wilkes (1986).

10. My references to Wilkes and Stringer (1953) will be to its reprint in Wilkes (1986).

11. In an interview with the author (December 19, 1991, Olivetti Research Laboratory, Cambridge) Wilkes reiterated that the concern for reliability had, in fact, been the prime mover leading to the emergence of microprogramming.

12. Wilkes was, of course, quite familiar with developments in both Manchester and the National Physical Laboratory (NPL), Teddington. At the latter, the Automatic Computing Engine (ACE) was being designed – a project with which Alan Turing was involved in a major capacity in the early stages (Hodges 1983, chap. 6). Wilkes's first-hand familiarity with the Manchester and NPL projects is documented in his *Memoirs* (Wilkes 1985, pp. 134–8, 145). Furthermore, papers discussing both these developments and others then under way in Britain, the United States, and continental Europe were presented at the High Speed Automatic Calculating Machines conference organized by Wilkes and his colleagues and held in Cambridge in June 1949.

13. The interested reader may wish to consult Brachman and Levesque (1985) for articles on various aspects of knowledge representation. This reference also includes an excellent bibliography. For a unified discussion of the topic, see Barr and Feigenbaum (1981).

14. The types of links defined here are based on, and slight modifications of, those suggested by Thagard (1990).

15. The origin of such rules (also called *production rules*) reaches back to the logician Emil Post's 1943 concept of "productions" for the formal (syntactic) manipulation and transformation of symbolic structures (Minsky 1967). This same work may have led to the idea of defining the grammar of a language in terms of "rewriting rules" (Chomsky 1957) or "productions" (Floyd 1961). The use of production rules to represent knowledge in the context of heuristic problem-solving (AI) systems and as a basis for modeling cognitive behavior appears to be due to Newell in the early 1960s. (See Newell and Simon 1972; Anderson 1983).

16. It must be remembered that in the time frame being considered, the EDSAC was operational, and the basic principles of programming a computer were well understood by the Cambridge group. Indeed, the latter was instrumental in pioneering the methodology of programming. One of Wilkes's first research students (and, later, colleague), David Wheeler, was primarily responsible for the programming techniques used on the EDSAC, and his contributions include the invention of the closed subroutine concept (Wheeler 1949, 1951). The use of subroutine libraries was, in fact, a major contribution of the overall EDSAC effort to the development of programming.

    In July 1951, Wilkes, Wheeler, and Stanley Gill – another early research student of Wilkes – published what was in effect the very first book on programming (Wilkes, Wheeler, and Gill 1951). This book described programming techniques for the EDSAC in great detail. The principals of program construction for the EDSAC are also described in (Wilkes 1956, chap. 3), while the early programming experiences of the Cambridge group are recounted in (Wilkes 1985, chap. 14).

17. Since a particular instruction is interpreted by a particular microinstruction sequence, the address of the very first microinstruction to be executed in order to initiate interpretation can be encoded in the opcode (or function) part of the instruction itself. This information when directly "loaded" into the register R will constitute the "starting" address of the microinstruction sequence.

18. Consider a circuit (such as an arithmetic unit or a register) consisting of several identical elements. In a bit-sliced implementation of the circuit, each of the identical elements constitutes a physically distinct unit or "slice," and the circuit as a whole is built from these slices. For example, an N-bit adder can be composed from N one-bit slices each of which contains the circuitry required to add two one-bit digits and a "carry-in" and produce a one-bit result and a "carry-out." For more on bit-sliced devices, the interested reader may consult Dasgupta (1989a, pp. 69–70) or Hayes (1984, sect. 8.2). For a detailed treatment of the topic, see Myers (1980).

19. M. V. Wilkes, in interview with the author, December 19, 1991, Olivetti Research Laboratory, Cambridge.

20. A view with which Wilkes (1991) concurs. The impact of the EDSAC-2 in this regard, went beyond this, however. According to Wilkes (1991), W. S. Elliott, then head of IBM Hurseley Laboratory in the United Kingdom, drew IBM's attention to the EDSAC-2; the consequence was the company's decision to use microprogramming as a key element in the System/360 series of computers marketed in the early 1960s. It was the success of the IBM 360 series in this regard that effectively led to the large-scale commercial adoption of microprogrammed control units.

Part II

The invention of microprogramming: a cognitive explanation

4

Prolegomenon

The main ingredients have now been assembled. We have, first, a computational theory of scientific creativity, CTSC. Its central thesis is that a cognitive act resulting in a scientific product – a solution to a scientific problem – deemed original by the originator or by the relevant scientific community can be specified as, or be explained in the form of, a knowledge-level process.

Second, we have a detailed account of the circumstances attending a particular episode from the arena of computer science: the invention of microprogramming. Since computer science is a science of the artificial, one can regard this invention as signifying the creation of a technological idea, the invention of a new artifactual form that satisfies certain functions or, more prosaically, as an instance of highly original design. In the artificial sciences, these views are virtually indistinguishable.

This historical account is as detailed as the documented evidence will allow. And viewed as a *historical explanation,* it would appear to be satisfactory. That is, to the question What were the circumstances attending Wilkes's invention of microprogramming? the narrative presented in Chapter 3 would constitute an explanation of the sort historians of science ordinarily produce. It identifies the state of affairs that existed regarding computers and computing circa 1950. It then presents the particular problem that exercised Wilkes (i.e., that of regularity and order in the design of the control unit) and describes, in terms of the known state of affairs (specifically with regard to the EDSAC), how or why the problem arose. The narrative then points out that Wilkes was led to the idea of the diode matrix in the EDSAC order interpreter. This idea was lent a firmer shape by his witnessing the Whirlwind I control matrix. However, the latter did not exhibit the kind of flexibility Wilkes demanded of his control unit. The need for such flexibility and his involvement with the development of the stored program computer led to the model of the control unit as a stored program computer in miniature – a computer within a computer; an electronic version of the homunculus, as it were. The final link in the chain was the idea of combining the regularity of diode matrices with the flexibility of the programmed computer by using two diode matrices, one to specify and store the control signals, the other to achieve the flexibility needed to sequence through control steps.

In understanding why or how a certain thing happened in history, a narrative of this kind constitutes an explanation. As Stephen Jay Gould, in the passage quoted at the beginning of this book so eloquently asserts and as I have discussed at some length in the section "On the testability of a theory of creativity" in Chapter 1, a historical explanation – and by this is meant an explanation of how or why a certain event or episode in history took place – is not a predictive explanation. Such explanations are not theories that can be tested or corroborated or falsified by postulating a prediction deduced from the theory and seeing whether the prediction is correct or not. Episodes in history bear the stamp of contingency. Circumstances could have been otherwise; it just so happened that they were not. Thus, historical explanations seek to construct, ex post facto, a plausible, coherent, and consistent causal account of the events that led to the episode in question. Historical explanations can be tested not through predictions but by examining the details of the causal pattern presented and determining whether or not the elements of the pattern are supported by the documentary (or other acceptable forms of) evidence and whether or not the reasoning underlying the causal pattern is valid.[1]

This latter issue is important for it implies that historical explanations, despite their nonpredictive quality, are not atheoretical; they are not "just so" stories. Historical explanations are rendered within a theoretical framework, which, in the large, sets the channels – to borrow another of Gould's (1990) felicitous phrases – within which contingency operates.

In the case of Maurice Wilkes and the invention of microprogramming, the account given in Chapter 3 constitutes an attempt at such a historical explanation. The historian of science can evaluate this account by examining each of its key elements and by enquiring into the validity of the causal chain suggested. In this case, the chain is founded loosely on the common modes of reasoning that humans ordinarily follow and that the historian takes for granted.

As far as *this* book is concerned, however, the matter does not end here. We desire an explanation of how Wilkes arrived at his concept at a deeper level, where the theoretical framework is tighter, more rigorous or formal. More exactly, we seek an explanation at the knowledge level of cognition since we already have a theoretical framework apppropriate to this level, namely, the computational theory set forth in Chapter 2. To appreciate the difference between what might be called the orthodox historical explanation and an explanation at the knowledge level, consider the following example.

The historical account presented in the preceding chapter tells us that given the goal of achieving a systematic and regular control unit, Wilkes's knowledge of the EDSAC order interpreter led him to the idea of using a diode matrix. Clearly, such an explanation appeals to *certain tokens of knowledge* that Wilkes either already possessed (e.g., his knowledge of the EDSAC order interpreter) or were freshly obtained (as when he observed the Whirlwind). But it tells us nothing about what *kinds of mental actions* might be invoked in order to utilize such knowledge and proceed toward a particular goal. Thus, the orthodox historical explanation is, certainly, knowledge based. But it is not a *knowledge-level* explanation – for, as described in Chapter 2, a knowledge-level agent is concerned quite explicitly with knowledge of which actions to take to achieve a given goal. A knowledge-level explanation may thus be viewed as a historical explanation – but of a different kind than the orthodox variety with which historians are usually concerned, since it appeals to precise actions that connect the known events, circumstances, and facts identified in the historical version. An explanation at the knowledge level will be in the form of a *computational process* comprised of goals, knowledge, and sets of actions invoked from within the agent's knowledge body in order to achieve the goals, subject to the principles of rationality and bounded rationality.

It is because of this that an important caveat is in order at this point: The form of the narrative will change slightly in the next two chapters to reflect the fact that they are concerned with the description of a *process* and the manner in which it unfolds.

Since a process – at least as we shall be concerned with – is an entity that (1) captures the nature of *change,* (2) occurs over *time,* and (3) is governed by certain *causal relationships,* its description will take the form of a network of inferences that superficially resembles the network of deductions in a mathematical argument.[2] The resemblance is superficial only, for in mathematics, an inference of a proposition P from a set of propositions $P_1, \ldots, P_n$ is grounded only in the rules of deductive logic. In contrast, the description of a knowledge-level process draws on inferences other than (or, rather, in addition to) deduction.

Furthermore, a mathematical argument is a *formal* entity. It relies on a set of basic premises ("axioms") and a set of rules of deduction. The validity of an argument in mathematics – that is, the validity of the "proof" of a theorem – is determined solely with respect to whether or not the rules of deduction have been applied correctly. The rules and the axioms themselves are not held in doubt. A knowledge-level computational process, however, is an *empirical* entity: Its assumptions and the rules of inference it draws on are themselves open to empirical inquiry. Thus, there is nothing sacrosanct about an inference made in the course of a knowledge-level process (even when a rule of inference is applied correctly). An inference is merely a tentative, testable hypothesis.

A miniexample of a knowledge-level process

Perhaps, it will be useful at this point if we were to move out of the realm of generalities and consider more concretely how, in the forthcoming chapters, the knowledge-level process will be described. This will also facilitate a clearer understanding of the nature of knowledge-level processes. An example should serve these purposes. Suppose an agent is given the following goal:

G.a: The control unit (to be designed) must be functionally
        flexible.

Let us further suppose that the agent's knowledge body contains, inter alia, the knowledge tokens shown in Figure 4.1. Here, F.a is a *fact* that establishes a "kind-of" relationship between the class of entities (or the concept) called "artifact" and the class of entities (or the concept) called "control unit." R.a is a *rule* relevant to both stored program computers and artifacts and is related to the property of functional flexibility. R-Inst is also a rule; however, it has the characteristics of (1) being domain independent – that is, it is relevant to arbitrary classes of entities in general rather than to specific artifacts or organisms – and (2) allowing inferences to be made, thereby generating new tokens of knowledge. This particular rule allows an *instantiation* of a rule to a particular instance based on some known fact. Finally, R-Abd is also a domain-independent rule that enables inferences to be drawn. In this case, however, the rule embodies the reasoning mode called "abduction" to be applied resulting in the establishment of a new goal.[3]

These knowledge tokens are presented here textually and in natural language for convenience. This will be the usual way in which knowledge will be represented in the ensuing chapters. However, it may be recalled from the section "Representing knowledge: networks and rules" in Chapter 3 that relationships between knowledge tokens can also be represented graphically, in terms of conceptual networks. In addition to textual descriptions, then, we shall – when necessary and in the interest of clarity – have occasion to use such conceptual networks as part of the narrative.

F.a:		A control unit is a kind-of artifact.
R.a:	*If*	a device or artifact is in the stored program computer form,
	Then	the device or artifact is functionally flexible.
R.Inst:	*If*	R is a rule about class of entities C_1 *and* entity class C_2 is a kind-of C_1,
	Then	R is a rule about C_2 (after substitution).
R.Abd:	*If*	G is a goal to be met or a problem to be solved *and* G is solved or met if some other goal G′ is solved or met,
	Then	establish G′ as a (sub)goal.

Figure 4.1. Some possible tokens in an agent's knowledge body.

Figure 4.2 shows the network representation of F.a and R.a using the link types introduced in Chapter 3. Recall that a rule is represented by a dotted line or arc as shown in this diagram. For our purposes, however, it is more convenient to denote a rule by a *node* in the network and link the node to other nodes to which it is related. We shall, therefore, use the following:

> Rule links – denoted by edges labeled "R." These indicate that a rule is associated with an object or a concept. Specifically, a directed edge labeled "R" to a concept or object T from a rule E indicates that E is *a rule about T.*

We will also use a link type called *goal links* defined as follows:

> Goal links – denoted by edges labeled "G." These indicate that a goal is associated with an object or a concept. More specifically, a directed edge labeled "G" to a concept or object T from a goal L indicates that L is *a goal about T.*

Using these link types along with those previously introduced, the four knowledge tokens of Figure 4.1 can be represented by the network fragment depicted in Figure 4.3. Note that the network contains nodes signifying two very general concepts, "goal" and "entity"; that G.a is an instance of the goal concept; and

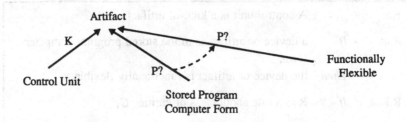

Figure 4.2. Conceptual network representing fact F.a and rule R.a of Figure 4.1.

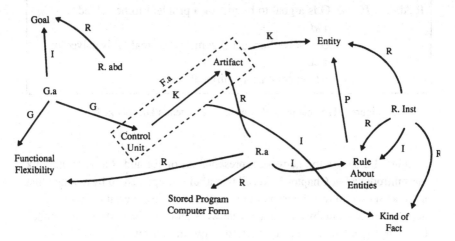

Figure 4.3. Conceptual network representing the knowledge tokens of Figure 4.1.

that R-Abd is a rule about goals. Note also that there is another node that signifies the concept "rule about entities" and that this concept is a property of the concept entity. It can also be seen that R-Inst is an instance of this concept. Finally, the network contains a node signifying the general concept "kind-of fact" – that is, the class of facts of the form "A is a kind-of B." Clearly, F.a is an instance of this concept. This is represented here, first, by the dotted rectangle, which is intended to convey the idea that its contents can be collapsed or abstracted into a single node denoting F.a, and, second, by an instance-of link from this node to the kind-of facts node. R-Inst is also a rule about kind-of facts.

We can now describe a particular knowledge-level *action* as shown in Figure 4.4. Here, the fact that G.a is about control units is used to *retrieve,* from the agent's knowledge body, the fact F.a. The fact that a kind-of fact and a rule

Input	G.a.:	A goal about control units and functional flexibility.
		*
Retrieve	F.a:	A kind-of fact about control units and artifacts.
Retrieve	R.a:	A rule about artifacts, stored program computer forms, and functional flexibility.
Retrieve	R-Inst:	A rule about kind-of facts, entities, and rules about entities.
Apply	R-Inst:	With R.a and F.a as substitutions in the condition and operation parts of the rule.
		*
Output	(as the consequent of applying R-Inst)	
	R.a1: *If*	a control unit is in the stored program computer form,
	Then	the control unit is functionally flexible.

Figure 4.4. A knowledge-level action (A_1) producing a rule R.a1.

about entities have been accessed allows R-Inst in turn to be retrieved. The latter is then *applied* to produce an instantiation inference, which we may depict by the notation

$$\frac{\text{F.a, R.a}}{\text{R.a1}}$$

Here, the entities above the horizontal line are the antecedents of the inference, and the entity below the horizontal line is the consequence. The inference results in a rule R.a1, which is an *instance*-of the more general rule R.a. R.a1 thus becomes an addition to the agent's knowledge body. The stages or steps of retrieval of facts and rules and the application of rules will be referred to as *subactions*.

Figure 4.5 describes another action, which has as input the goal G.a and the new rule R.a1. In this case, the fact that G.a is a goal to achieve a particular property in some entity – specifically, the control unit achieving functional flexibility – and the fact that R.a1 is a rule about how to achieve such a property in the entity concerned are used to retrieve rule R-Abd, which is a rule concerned with goals and rules to achieve such goals. R-Abd is then applied, producing, by *abduction,* the inference

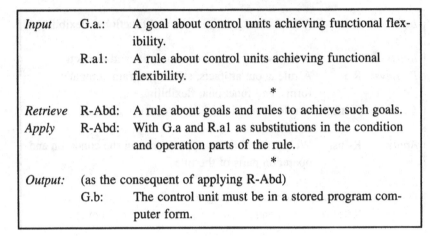

Input	G.a.:	A goal about control units achieving functional flex-ibility.
	R.al:	A rule about control units achieving functional flexibility.
		*
Retrieve	R-Abd:	A rule about goals and rules to achieve such goals.
Apply	R-Abd:	With G.a and R.al as substitutions in the condition and operation parts of the rule.
		*
Output:	(as the consequent of applying R-Abd)	
	G.b:	The control unit must be in a stored program computer form.

Figure 4.5. A knowledge-level action (A_2) producing a new goal G.b.

G.a, R.al

―――――

G.b

the consequence of which is a new goal (or, more precisely, subgoal)

G.b: The control unit must be in a stored program computer
form.

In other words, beginning with the goal (G.a) of making (or designing) the control unit so as to achieve functional flexibility, the agent has produced a new goal (G.b) of designing the control unit in a stored program computer form. The hypothesis implied is that if G.b is achieved, then so will be G.a.

Let us consider, then, the way in which this small example exhibits the general characteristics of the knowledge-level process as defined in Chapter 2. An action, it will be recalled, can be initiated by a goal and produces, as an output, one or more symbol structures. Figure 4.4 depicts one such action – call it A_1 – the input to which is the goal G.a. The performance of A_1 consumes (some unspecified amount of) time and involves the access to and retrieval (by successive associations) of the fact F.a, the rule R.a, and the rule R-Inst from the agent's knowledge body and, then, the application of R-Inst, resulting in an inference. The output is a symbol structure – the rule R.al. This latter rule is clearly an additional token that enters the agent's knowledge body. Its associations or links with other tokens are shown in Figure 4.6. This is the conceptual network shown earlier (Figure 4.3) augmented with the new rule.

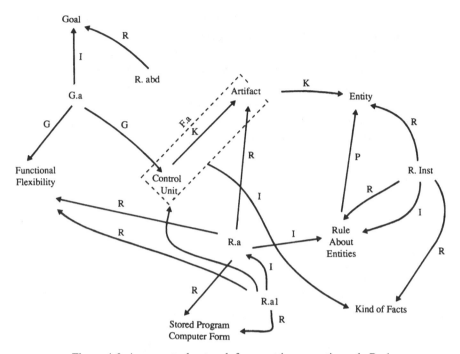

Figure 4.6. A conceptual network fragment incorporating rule R.a1.

Figure 4.5 shows another action – call it A_2 – the inputs to which are the symbol structures referred to as goal G.a and rule R.a1. The performance of A_2 entails the retrieval, by association, of rule R-Abd from the agent's knowledge body, application of this rule, and the consequent production, by abductive inference, of the symbol structure designated as goal G.b.

The *sequence* of actions $\langle A_1, A_2 \rangle$ thus constitutes a knowledge-level process P' invoked in response to the original goal G.a. Its output is another goal G.b such that the achievement of G.b represents a possible solution to, or the achievement of, G.a. G.b is, then, a subgoal of G.a. It will be noted that the first action in this process, A_1, does not actually achieve the goal G.a nor does it produce a subgoal. It generates, rather, a new knowledge token, which then participates in the performance of the second action, A_2. It can also be noted that since G.b has yet to be achieved, the process P' cannot be said to have terminated.

According to the characteristics of knowledge-level systems, the choice of an action in response to a goal is dictated by the principle of rationality. If an agent has knowledge that an action will lead to a goal, then the agent will perform that action. In the present example, given the original goal G.a and that the agent's knowledge body contains the particular tokens listed in Figure 4.1, the performance of A_1 *appears* to satisfy PR, since the resulting rule, R.a1, suggests a precondition for how the goal may be achieved. Likewise, the choice of A_2 *appears* rational insofar as the resulting goal G.b is a direct consequence of the original goal G.a and the knowledge token R.a1. Clearly, though, at this stage there is no *guarantee* that G.b is attainable nor that the achievement of G.b will, in fact, entail the achievement of G.a. This is in accordance with the bounded rationality principle.

Spreading activation

In describing the knowledge level in Chapter 2, nothing was said of how knowledge is accessed. The omission was deliberate since at this level of abstraction all that is admitted about the knowledge body is that *it exists* and that its constituent tokens *are accessible*. This property of the knowledge level – that is, the property that details such as where and how knowledge is held, how it is accessed, the time required for its access, and so on, are abstracted away – constitutes one of the main attractions of the knowledge level as it allows one to focus solely on the knowledge itself as the source of the agent's actions. Details of the kind just mentioned enter the cognitive picture at lower levels of the description hierarchy, notably at the symbol and biological levels (Rumelhart and McClelland 1986; Newell 1990; see also the section "The knowledge level" in Chapter 2).

Nevertheless, the miniexample dealt with here suggests that in the knowledge-level model of cognition, the general nature of access to knowledge tokens is that of *association:* The goal G.a, being a goal involving control units, led to F.a, a fact concerning control units; F.a being also a fact about artifacts, in conjunction with G.a being a goal concerning functional flexibility, led to the retrieval of R.a, a rule about artifacts being functionally flexible; and R-Inst, in turn was retrieved or "activated" by the conjunction of F.a and R.a, since these latter tokens matched the condition part of R-Inst.

In this respect, the (hitherto tacit) assumption of such association-based retrieval of knowledge tokens – and this is an assumption that will be adhered to throughout the chapters to follow – is clearly influenced by the "principle of spreading activation" known in cognitive psychology (Collins and Loftus 1975; Lachman, Lachman, and Butterfield 1979, pp. 324–7; Anderson 1983, chap. 3; Holland et al. 1986, pp. 56–8; Thagard 1989, pp. 19–25).

The main idea of spreading activation is that given a conceptual network,

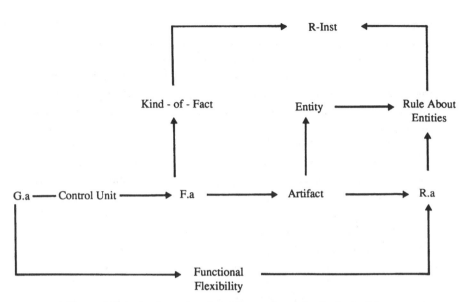

Figure 4.7. Activation network leading to the retrieval of rule R-Inst.

activating a node corresponding to some concept or object activates in turn the adjacent or associated nodes that then cause the activation of *their* adjacent nodes, and so on. Thus, activation spreads throughout the network, though decreasing over time and "distance" from the original node. A knowledge token or concept is activated to the degree it is related to the source of activation.

The spread of activation through the conceptual network leading to the retrieval of R-Inst can be depicted as shown in Figure 4.7. Here, the lines or links suggest the *direction of activation* of a node that is linked to one or more others in the conceptual network. Thus, for example, G.a activates the concept "control unit," which activates F.a, and so on. Networks such as this may be referred to as *activation networks*.

Summary

Through the medium of a small example, we have seen, in this chapter, the form of a knowledge-level process, the kind of notation to be employed, and the modus operandi we shall pursue to explain how Wilkes might have been led to the idea of microprogramming. In general, such an explanation will involve an ordered set of *goals*. We shall see that, of these, one or two will serve as the input to the process as a whole; the others will be generated as subgoals much as G.b was generated from G.a in the preceding example. Given a goal, a set of knowledge tokens in the form of *facts* and *rules* will be postulated, and a structured set of *actions* will be suggested as a means of achieving a goal. Each action will entail, through a spread of activation of associated links, the retrieval of facts and rules from the knowledge body and the application of certain of these rules. The latter results in the *inference* of either a partial solution – that is, a partial form or design of the artifact that satisfies the goal – or new facts, rules, or subgoals. Eventually, a complete solution – a complete form for the control unit – will emerge. The set of actions leading to this final, complete solution will constitute a knowledge-level process that will serve to explain how Wilkes may have been led to his invention.

There remains, finally, the question of the plausibility or validity of this explanation. If the computational theory of scientific creativity (CTSC) is itself accepted as a viable paradigm, the validity issue can be resolved by providing *evidence* in support of the facts and rules postulated as part of Wilkes's knowledge body and invoked in the course of the explanation.

As I shall show, a large part of this knowledge body is supported by *empirical evidence,* drawn either from the historical account presented in Chapter 3 or, more indirectly, from what was known about the states of computing, science, and technology circa 1950. Another part of the knowledge body is supported by our knowledge of Wilkes's personal background as documented in *Memoirs* (1985). There will remain a residue of knowledge tokens for which the justification is not empirical but which, I shall argue, are reasonable assumptions to make for any agent with Wilkes's background.

Notes

1. A classic discussion of historical explanation by one of the preeminent historians of this century is Carr (1961). For discussions of this topic from a philosophical perspective, see Gardiner (1961) and, especially, Popper (1957).
2. I use the word *network* (of inferences or of deductions) instead of the standard descriptor "chain." Both, of course, are used metaphorically. But the metaphor of chain clearly conveys a sense of linearity; that is, a "chain of deductions" carries with it the notion of a single sequence of propositions $P_1, P_2, \ldots, P_n$, where P_2 is deduced from P_1, P_3 from P_2, and so on. In contrast, many mathematical arguments and certainly the kinds of inferences we shall be concerned with here take the form of relationships between propositions that resemble a network – or, more mathematically speaking, a directed graph.
3. See the introductory section of Chapter 1 for more on abduction.

5

The genesis of an idea: creating the initial sketch

Problem recognition and formulation

The reader will recall from the section "The concept of creativity" in Chapter 1, that the criteria whereby a cognitive process P is deemed creative pertains to the nature of the product Π of that process. It is quite easy to be seduced into assuming, when we talk about Π, that we are really referring to a *solution* to some problem. This need not be so. Π may, in fact, itself be a *problem* and P the process of *identifying* it.

That the recognition of a problem and its formulation in a tractable or solvable form is one of the characteristic features of the creative mind – at least in the realm of scientific discovery and invention – is widely acknowledged (Sternberg 1988b; Root-Bernstein 1989). In the case of the invention of microprogramming, we have seen, according to the account in Chapter 3, that Wilkes was not presented with an "open" problem – that is, a problem already identified and acknowledged within the relevant community. He *saw* a problem others had not seen. The problem, it will be recalled, was conceptual in nature, having to do with such attributes as regularity and complexity. And as noted in Chapter 3 (section "On the conceptual nature of Wilkes's problem"), the recognition of such a problem by an individual is frequently inspired by a personal philosophical stance or set of values. This seems to have been the case with Wilkes, for, as he has remarked, it was essentially a "private" problem for him. Thus, at least in the case of microprogramming, problem recognition and formulation may be said to constitute an integral part of the overall concept formation activity.

As described in Chapter 3, problem recognition began with an empirical (i.e., observed) fact:[1]

> F0: Extant control units are difficult to design, maintain,
> and repair because of their complexity.

This, in turn, produced a goal:[2]

> G0: To develop a control unit form that is easy to design,
> maintain, and repair.

G0 is thus an initial statement of the problem. But *how* was G0 generated from F0? A possible sequence of knowledge-level actions, beginning with F0 and ending in G0, may be described as follows. First, the following tokens in Wilkes's knowledge body are postulated:

> F1: A control unit is a kind-of artifact.
> F2: Difficulty of design, maintenance, and repair constitutes
> a negative property of an artifact.

Here, F1 is an obvious empirical fact, while F2 is a conceptual fact pertaining to artifacts in general.[3] F1 and F2 are invoked in the context of (i.e., by association with) F0, and they, in turn, invoke the following rule, which is applicable to and indeed, one might claim, inherent to the whole domain of design and hence of the artificial sciences.[4]

> R0: *If* an artifact demonstrates some negative or disad-
> vantageous character,
> *Then* establish as a goal/problem the elimination of
> that character.

Next, the following knowledge tokens are postulated to be invoked:

> F3: An artifact is a kind-of entity.
> R-Inst1: *If* R is a rule about a class of entities C_1
> *and*
> entity class C_2 is (postulated to be) a kind-of
> C_1,
> *Then* R is (postulated to be) a rule about C_2 (after
> substitution of terms/concepts from C_2 in C_1).

F3 is an obvious empirical fact, while R-Inst1 is a rule applicable to entities in general.

Using fact F1 and applying R-Inst1, the (relatively general) rule R0 is *instantiated* to a control unit–specific rule according to the inference

$$\frac{F1, R0}{I0: \quad R0.1}$$

where the consequence is

R0.1: *If* a control unit demonstrates some negative or disadvantageous character,

Then establish as a goal/problem the design of a control unit in which the negative character is eliminated.

Next, by appealing to a second type of instantiation rule

R-Inst2: *If* R is a rule about entity class C possessing a type of property P_1

and

type-of property P_2 is a kind-of P1,

Then R is a-rule-about entity class C possessing type-of property P_2 (after substitution),

the inference

$$\frac{F2, R0.1}{I1: \quad R0.1.1}$$

produces a new rule,

R0.1.1: *If* a control unit is difficult to design, maintain, and repair,

Then establish as a goal/problem the design (or development) of a control unit (form) that is easy to design, maintain, and repair.

Finally, given F0 – that extant control units are difficult to design, maintain, and repair – and rule R0.1.1, the deductive rule called *modus ponens,*

R-ModusP: *If* a fact or goal or rule *A* is the case

and

there is a rule "*If A* is the case, *Then* the fact or goal or rule *B* is the case,"

Then establish B as a fact or goal or rule

when applied, yields the inference

$$\frac{\text{F0, R0.1.1}}{\text{I2:}\quad \text{G0}}$$

thereby producing goal G0.

Thus, a sequence of three *nonrational actions* (see section "The knowledge level," Chapter 2) as postulated here can lead from fact F0 to goal G0. The details of the individual actions are shown in Figures 5.1, 5.2, and 5.3. The fact that the retrieval steps – the subactions – are textually ordered does not imply that, in fact, they take place in that order. Certain actions may take place in parallel. The nature of the ordering of subactions is more explicitly indicated in the activation networks of Figures 5.4 and 5.5, which depict the spread of activation (see section "Spreading activation," Chapter 4) over concepts leading, respectively, to rules R0.1 and R0.1.1. The labels on the activation edges indicate the *weakest* relative ordering that must prevail in order for this explanation to be valid. For example (referring to Figure 5.4), facts F1 and F2 may be retrieved in parallel; R0 and F3 may also be retrieved in parallel, but they must both follow F1 and F2. The dotted lines in the activation networks signify the "apply" subactions leading to a new rule (as in Figures 5.4, 5.5), goal, or fact.

The literature on creativity has conventionally assigned a prominent role to the *unconscious* as a factor in creative thought. For instance, in the Helmoltz–Poincaré–Wallas four-stage model described in Chapter 1 (section "Metaphors as explanations of creativity"), the incubation and illumination stages are both postulated to operate in the realm of the unconscious (Poincaré 1913/1946; Wallas 1926; Hadamard 1945; Boden 1991). The general idea is that at the level of the unconscious, ideas may combine with a degree of freedom that is denied to the conscious level.

That unconscious thought plays *a* role in creative acts is widely acknowledged. That it plays the *most critical* role is less universally accepted. Both Perkins (1981) and Weisberg (1986), for example, have challenged this notion. Still more significantly, Perkins rejects the assumption that thought conducted unconsciously is inherently unexplainable. This point is pertinent to the present discussion, for I suggest that *a structured set of nonrational actions* – such as the one described to explain how Wilkes may have made the mental transition from an observed fact F0 to a purposeful goal G0 – *is a knowledge-level explanation of an unconscious thought process* of the kind in which, in the absence of a goal or an explicit problem, one proceeds toward and arrives at an idea, a concept, or a problem.

It may be remarked that to make the transition from fact F0 to goal G0 does

Input	FO:	A fact about control units and the difficulty of designing, maintaining, and repairing.
		*
Retrieve	F1:	A kind-of fact about control units and artifacts.
Retrieve	F2:	A fact about artifacts and the difficulty of designing maintaining, and repairing.
Retrieve	R0:	A rule about artifacts and negative properties of artifacts.
Retrieve	F3:	A kind-of fact about artifacts and entities.
Retrieve	R-Inst1:	A rule about kind-of facts, entities, and rules about entities.
Apply	R-Inst1:	With F1 and R0 as substitutions.
		*
Output	R0.1:	A rule about control units and negative properties of control units.

Figure 5.1. An action producing R0.1.

Input	R0.1:	A rule about control units, negative properties, and an entity class possessing a property.
	FO:	A fact about control units and the difficulty of designing, maintaining, and repairing.
		*
Retrieve	F1:	A kind-of fact about control units and artifacts.
Retrieve	F2:	A fact about kind-of relationship between the artifactual properties "difficulty of designing, maintaining, and repairing," and the concept "negative property."
Retrieve	R-Inst2:	A rule about entity class possessing a type of property and a kind-of relationship between property types.
Apply	R-Inst2:	With F2 and R0.1 as substitutions.
		*
Output	R0.1.1:	A rule about units and the property "difficult to design, maintain, and repair."

Figure 5.2. An action producing R0.1.1.

Input	R0.1.1:	A rule about control circuits being difficult to design, maintain, and repair.
	F0:	A fact about control circuits being difficult to design, maintain, and repair.
		*
Retrieve	R-ModusP:	A rule about a fact and a rule about that same fact.
Apply	R-ModusP:	With R0.1.1 and F0 as substitutions.
		*
Output	G0:	A goal about a control unit being easy to design, maintain, and repair.

Figure 5.3. An action producing G0.

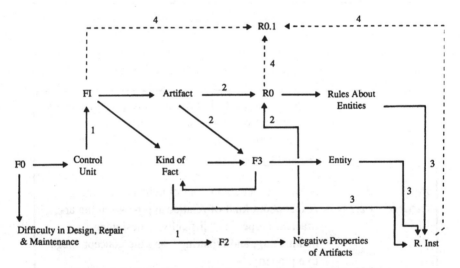

Figure 5.4. Activation network leading to the production of R0.1.

not appear to signify a profound or highly creative act. Yet if we accept that "seeing" a problem that was also not "seen" by others is a hallmark of the imaginative mind, we must admit that the formulation of G0 by Wilkes *is* a matter of some significance. The historical fact is that it was Wilkes who identified this problem and no one else. Perhaps there were others involved in

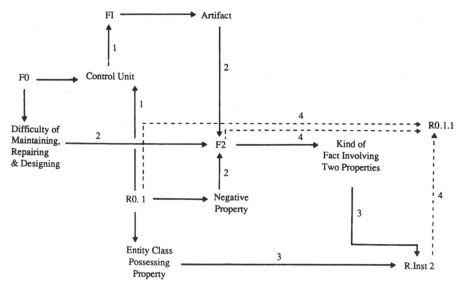

Figure 5.5. Activation network leading to the production of R0.1.1.

designing computers in the 1940s who also possessed F0 as part of their respective knowledge bodies. It was, however, only Wilkes who transformed it into a goal – that is, who perceived it as a problem required to be solved.

There are many ways, no doubt, by which one may attempt to satisfy goal G0. In Wilkes's particular case, given the historical evidence (see Chapter 3, in particular Figure 3.4) we may postulate the following rule from his knowledge body:

R1: *If* an artifact has a simple, repetitive, and regular structure,
Then the artifact is easy to design, maintain, and repair.

R1 is specific to the general domain of artifactual design, which, in the context of G0 and F1, can be *instantiated* according to the inference

$$\frac{F1, R1}{I3: \ R1.1}$$

the consequence of which is a "new" control-unit-specific rule.

Input	G0:	A goal about control units being easy to design, maintain, and repair.
		*
Retrieve	F1:	A kind-of fact about control units and artifacts.
Retrieve	R1:	A rule about artifacts and ease of design, maintenance, and repair.
Retrieve	R-Inst1:	A rule about kind-of facts, entities, and rules about entities.
Apply	R-Inst1:	With F1 and R1 as substitutions.
		*
Output	R1.1:	A rule about control units and ease of design, maintenance, and repair.

- -

Input	G0:	A goal about control units being easy to design, maintain, and repair.
	R1.1:	A rule about achieving ease of design, maintenance, and repair for control units.
		*
Retrieve	R-Abd:	A rule about a rule about achieving the goal.
Apply	R-Abd:	With G0 and R1.1 as substitutions.
		*
Output	G1:	A goal about control units having simple, repetitive, and regular structures

Figure 5.6. Action sequence producing (sub)goal G1 from goal G0.

R1.1:   *If*   a control unit has a simple, repetitive, and regu-
                lar structure,
        Then the control unit is easy to design, maintain, and
                repair.

This rule, in the context of G0, can in turn be used to yield the inference

$$\frac{\text{G0, R1.1}}{\text{I4:}\quad \text{G1}}$$

resulting in a new (sub)goal,

G1:   Design a control unit that has a simple, repetitive, and
      regular structure.

The inference I4 is by *abduction*. It will be recalled (from Chapter 1, section "The significance of philosophy of science") that this is, in general, an inference of the form: Given Ψ, a phenomenon to be explained or a problem to be solved; and given that Ψ will be explained or solved if theory *T* happens to be the case; therefore assume (as a hypothesis) that *T* is the case. In the present specific situation, the *rule of abduction* may be stated as

R-Abd: *If*   P is a problem to be solved/goal to be achieved
         and
         there exists a rule "*If* the proposition *H* is the
         case/the subgoal *H* is achieved, *Then P* is
         solved/achieved,"
      Then (assume) *H* is the case/subgoal.

It may also be recalled from Chapter 1 that one of the objections raised against Norwood Russell Hanson's (1958) suggestion of abduction being the logical basis of discovery was that it was not clear as to how the rule schema "Ψ would be explicable if hypothesis or theory *T* were to be true" came about in the first place. In our present case, the corresponding rule is R1.1, which is simply an instance of the more general rule R1. The latter is postulated to already exist as a token in Wilkes's knowledge body *as a consequence of his prior experience with the EDSAC*. Just how such generalization may come about on the basis of one or a small number of particular empirical cases is discussed later in this chapter. Figure 5.6 summarizes the two-action sequence leading to goal G1. Note that both actions are of the rational kind.

The idea of a diode matrix

The idea of using a diode matrix may be viewed as the first substantial step in the process of achieving the goal G1. As I have described in Chapter 3 (see esp. the sections "The EDSAC and its diode matrix" and "The Whirlwind and its control matrix"), the available evidence (Wilkes 1985, 1986) makes it plausible to suggest that this phase began with two empirical facts known to Wilkes from the EDSAC and other contemporary design projects,

    F4: The EDSAC order interpreter (which issues control sig-
        nals to the arithmetic, input/output, memory unit) is
        (partially) implemented in the form of a diode matrix,

F5:   In the MIT Whirlwind, each arithmetic operation (bar-
      ring multiplication) involves exactly eight pulses issued
      from a control unit implemented in the form of a diode
      matrix,

augmented by two, more abstract conceptual properties of the EDSAC and the
Whirlwind:

F6:   EDSAC's order interpreter is simple, repetitive, and
      regular,

F7:   Whirlwind's control unit is simple, repetitive, and
      regular.

We may also recall that Wilkes (1985, p. 178, 1986, p. 117) had acquired the
general idea of using a diode matrix–like structure for the control unit because
of the regular, repeatable form he had observed in the case of the reencoder part
of the EDSAC order interpreter. His writings suggest that he did not know the
manner in which the diode matrix would serve the desired purpose – just that
the diode matrix form satisfied the properties he was concerned with. Then, on
visiting the United States and seeing the Whirlwind computer at MIT, his
observation of this machine's control matrix seemed both, to *confirm* his initial
"hunch" and to offer further *clues* as to how a diode matrix could be used.

Thus, we can hypothesize that, first, an inductive *generalization* took place
as follows. The inference

$$\frac{\text{F4, F6, F8}}{\text{I5:}\quad\text{R2}}$$

in which, in addition to F4 and F6, the obvious empirical fact

F8:   The EDSAC order interpreter is an instance-of an order
      interpreter

served as an antecedent and produced the rule

R2:   *If*   an order interpreter is (partially) implemented
              using a diode matrix,
      Then (that part of) the order interpreter is simple, re-
              petitive, and regular.

Next, based on R2 and the additional empirical fact obviously known to
Wilkes,

F9:   An order interpreter is a kind-of computer component

the inference

$$\frac{R2, F9}{I6: R2.1}$$

produced, as a further *generalization* of R2, the rule,

R2.1:   *If*   a computer component is implemented using a
diode matrix,

Then   the component is simple, repetitive, and regular.

The question arises as to how a generalization to the rule R2 and then to R2.1 based on the observation of a *single* order interpreter (i.e., the EDSAC's) can be legitimately warranted. More generally, as John Stuart Mill (1843/1974) had asked, what grounds are there for a single instance to be sufficient to make an inductive generalization in some cases but not in others? This issue has been addressed by Holland et al. (1986, chap. 4 and 8) and by Thagard (1988, chap. 2), who noted that the legitimacy of generalizations of the form "All *A* are *B*" or (in the probabilistic situation) "Many *A* are *B*" as a mental act depend on the following factors:

(1) The number of instances of the *co-occurrence* of *A* and *B:* that is, the number of instances in which, when *A* is satisfied, *B* is also found to be satisfied.

(2) The *lack of counterevidence:* that is, whether or not there are no observed instances of *A* being satisfied but not *B*.

(3) *Invariability:* that is, for the type of events or entities being considered, the extent to which the variability of *B* with respect to *A* is known or believed to be low.

This last condition is somewhat more complex than the first two, for the judgment of variability relies on the observer's background knowledge and beliefs about the entities of concern. For example, even if we observe several instances of a new type of car, say, the Lexus, on the road, all of which happen to be white in color, we are unlikely to infer that all Lexuses are white. This is because our background knowledge about cars tells us that they (as manufactured and marketed in this age) come in several colors. In other words, the variability of color with respect to car is sufficiently high to deter us from asserting that "All Lexuses are white."

On the other hand, the generalization to R2 can be warranted on the grounds that (at that time, i.e., circa 1950) the variability of the property "simple, repetitive, and regular" with respect to the artifact type "diode matrix" was practically zero. In fact, the very nature of the concept "diode matrix" was such that "simple, repetitive, and regular" was an attribute inherent to the concept. The generalization of R2 to R2.1, given that the order interpreter is a kind of computer component, is based on the same grounds. In fact, one could have generalized to the yet more universal rule

> *If*   any artifact is implemented using a diode matrix,
> *Then*   the artifact is simple, repetitive and regular

if it were useful to do so. The inference to R2, according to I5, thus, appeals to the following *rule of generalization:*

R-Gen1: *If*   an entity e is an-instance-of or a kind-of entity E
                 and
                 there are predicates A, B such that $A(e)$ and $B(e)$
                 are known to be the case
                 and
                 there is no known entity e' that is an instance-of
                 or a kind-of E such that $A(e')$ and $\neg B(e')$ is
                 known to be the case[5]
                 and
                 the variability of B with respect to A is known to
                 be low,
      Then   assume the rule "*If $A(E)$, Then $B(E)$.*"

Figure 5.7 depicts the details of the relevant action. The generalization of rule R2 to R2.1 according to inference I6 uses a slightly different generalization rule:

R-Gen2: *If*   an entity e is an instance-of or a kind-of entity E
                 and
                 there are predicates A, B such that a rule of the
                 form "*If $A(e)$, Then $B(e)$*" is known to be the
                 case
                 and
                 there is no known entity e' that is an instance-of
                 or a kind-of entity E such that a rule of the form
                 '*If $A(e')$, Then $\neg B(e')$* is known to be the case
                 and
                 the variability of B with respect to A is known to
                 be low
      Then   assume the rule "*If $A(E)$, Then $B(E)$.*"

Input	G1:	A goal about control units possessing a simple, re-petitive, and regular structure.
		*
Retrieve	F6:	A fact about the EDSAC order interpreter being simple, repetitive, and regular.
Retrieve	F4:	A fact about the EDSAC order intepreter being in the form of a diode matrix.
Retrieve	F8:	A kind-of fact about the EDSAC order interpreter and order interpreters.
Retrieve	R-Gen1:	A rule about an entity that is a kind of another "super" entity satisfying two predicates (facts) and about no other entity that is a kind of the same "super" entity satisfying the same two facts and about the low variability of the two facts.
Apply	R-Gen1:	With F4, F6, and F8 as substitutes.
		*
Output	R2:	A rule about order interpreters satisfying the same two predicates.

Figure 5.7. An action producing rule R2.

Figure 5.8 shows the details of this action.

Next, in the context of the goal G1 and the empirically known fact

F10:   A control unit is a kind-of computer component,

an *instantiation* that appeals to the rule of inference R-Inst1 results in the inference

$$\frac{R2.1, F10}{I7: \quad R2.1.1}$$

with the consequence

R2.1.1:   *If*   a control unit is implemented in a diode matrix,
          Then the control unit is simple, repetitive, and regular.

In other words, the rule R2.1.1, which hypothesizes a connection between the properties "simplicity, repetitivity, and regularity" of the control unit and the use of a diode matrix, is based on observations or knowledge of the EDSAC

Input	G1:	A goal about control units possessing a simple, repetitive, and regular structure.
	R2:	A rule about order interpreters satisfying two predicates.
		*
Retrieve	F9:	A kind-of fact about order interpreters being a computer component.
Retrieve	R-Gen2:	A rule about an entity that is a kind of "super" entity satisfying a rule in which it satisfies two predicates and about no other entity that is a kind of the same "super" entity satisfying a contradiction of the rule and about low variability of the two predicates.
Apply	R-Gen2:	With R2 and F9 as substitutions.
		*
Output	R2.1:	A rule about computer components satisfying the two predicates "implemented in diode matrix" and "is simple, repetitive, and regular."

Figure 5.8. An action generalizing rule R2 to rule R2.1.

order interpreter *alone* – that is, before Wilkes visited MIT. This is clearly supported by his remarks (Wilkes 1985, p. 178; 1986, p. 117) about the influence of the diode matrix usage in the EDSAC on his thinking. R2.1.1 may be said to have been *corroborated* through the evidence of the Whirlwind-related facts F5, F7, and F11 where

> F11: The Whirlwind control unit is an instance-of a control
> unit.[6]

For, as he records in his *Memoirs,* "when I saw the Whirlwind computer, I found that it did indeed have a centralized control based on the use of a matrix of diodes" (Wilkes 1985, p. 178).

Finally, by appealing to the rule of *abduction,* R-Abd, the inference

$$\frac{\text{G1, R2.1.1}}{\text{I8:}\quad\text{G2}}$$

generates a new goal

    G2:   Design a control unit to be implemented in terms of a diode matrix.

Identifying a stored program computer-like form

G2 was derived from the original goal G1. But there is another goal inherent in the control unit concept that has not been explicitly stated thus far, and that is the fact that the control unit to be designed must exhibit the *functional flexibility* of previously designed control units (in particular the EDSAC). By "functional flexibility" is meant, in general, that

(1) The entity must be capable of producing, automatically, *variable sequences of operations* depending on the task being performed, and
(2) The entity must be capable of automatically *selecting between alternative sequences of operations* depending on the status of a "flag" register or flip-flop.

That the control unit must satisfy these characteristics would have been known to Wilkes from the EDSAC experience (and other contemporary efforts known to him). That it was central to his thinking about the control unit design is recorded in the retrospective account of his witnessing the Whirlwind:

The elegance of this [i.e., the Whirlwind's] design appealed to me greatly; . . . There was, however, the limitation that the same number of time steps had to be allocated to each instruction. . . . The system could not, therefore, be used for operations such as multiplication and division in which some of the steps must be conditional. (Wilkes 1986, p. 117)

We can, therefore, state the following additional goal

    G3:   The control unit must be functionally flexible.

Now, Wilkes already knew of a class of entities that are inherently functionally flexible, namely, stored program computers. In other words, we may assume, with justification, the existence in his knowledge body of a rule:

    R3:   *If*   a computing device is in the stored program computer form,

             Then the computing device is functionally flexible.[7]

Given the additional fact

   F12:   A computing device is a kind-of device or artifact,

invocation of the rule of *generalization,* R-Gen2 (see the preceding section "The idea of a diode matrix"), enables the inference

$$\frac{F12, R3}{I9: \quad R3.1}$$

the consequence of which is

   R3.1:   *If*   a device or artifact is in the stored program
                   computer form,
            Then   the artifact is functionally flexible.

   On the basis of fact

   F1:   A control unit is a kind-of artifact,

R3.1 can be *instantiated* by appealing to the rule R-Inst1 according to the inference

$$\frac{F1, R3.1}{I10: \quad R.3.1.1}$$

which has the consequence

   R3.1.1:   *If*   a control unit is in the stored program computer
                     form,
              Then   the control unit is functionally flexible.

   Finally, given goal G3 and rule R3.1.1, activation of rule R-Abd allows the *abductive* inference

$$\frac{G3, R3.1.1}{I11: \quad G4}$$

to produce the goal

   G4:   Specify the control unit in a stored program computer
          form.

Deriving the broad principle of microprogramming

The state of affairs at this stage is captured by the two goals

    G2:   Design a control unit to be implemented in terms of a diode matrix,

    G4:   Specify the control unit in a stored program computer form.

The concept of a stored program computer has associated with it a whole complex of notions and ideas, most of which (to the extent they were known at all circa 1950) were obviously known to Wilkes. Of these, two that are immediately relevant may be stated in rule form:

    R4:   *If*   an artifact is a stored program computer,
        Then the task to be performed by the artifact will be specified by a program
              and
              the program is composed of a set of instructions (orders)
              and
              the program will be stored in a memory with each instruction (order) having a distinct memory address.

    R5:   *If*   an artifact is a stored program computer,
        Then on completion of an instruction's (order's) execution, the task of identifying the next instruction [order] normally to execute is specified by a "next instruction" address mechanism.

Given G4 and R4, the following *instantiation* may be postulated

$$\frac{\text{G4, R4}}{\text{I12:}\quad \text{R4.1}}$$

producing the rule

    R4.1:   *If*   a control unit is (to be specified) as a stored program computer,

Then   the task to be performed by the control unit will
be specified by a (micro)program
and
the (micro)program is composed of a set of
(micro)instructions (orders)
and
the (micro)program will be stored in a memory
with each (micro)instruction (order) having a
distinct memory address.

R4.1 is simply a specific instance of R4 except that the prefix "micro" is added
to distinguish the program of a control unit from the ordinary notion of a
program.

By modus ponens, the deductive inference

$$\frac{\text{G4, R4.1}}{\text{I13:}\quad \text{G5}}$$

produces the goal

G5:   The (task to be performed by the) control unit will be
specified by a (micro)program consisting of a set of
(micro)orders each held at a specified address in a
memory.

Figure 5.9 shows, concisely, the sequence of actions leading to goal G5.
Similarly, given goal G4, rule R5 may be *instantiated*, by appealing to R-Inst1,
according to the inference

$$\frac{\text{G4, R5}}{\text{I14:}\quad \text{R5.1}}$$

the consequence of which is the rule

R5.1:   *If*   a control unit is (to be specified as) a stored program computer,
Then   (the control unit is such that) on completion of a
(micro) order's execution the task of identifying
the next (micro)order normally to execute is
specified by a next (micro)order address mechanism.

Input	G4:	A goal about control units and the stored program computer form.
		*
Retrieve	R4:	A rule about artifacts satisfying the properties "stored program computer form" and "task specified as program."
Retrieve	F1:	A kind-of fact about control units and artifacts.
Retrieve	R-Inst1:	A rule about kind-of facts, entities, and rules about entities.
Apply	R-Inst1:	With R4, F1 as substitutions.
Output	R4.1:	A rule about control units satisfying the properties "stored program computer form" and "task specified as microprogram."
Input	G4, R4.1:	
		*
Retrieve	R-ModusP:	A rule about a goal and about a rule about that same goal.
Apply	R-ModusP:	With G4 and R4.1 as substitutions.
		*
Output	G5:	A goal about control unit tasks specified as (micro)programs.

Figure 5.9. Actions producing goal G5 from goal G4.

This, when followed by the inference by modus ponens:

$$\frac{G4,\ R5.1}{I15:\quad G6}$$

results in the goal

 G6: (Design) a control unit in which, on completion of a
    (micro)order's execution, the task of identifying the
    next (micro)order normally to execute is specified by a
    next (micro)order address mechanism.

 The *initial sketch* of the microprogramming idea has thus emerged. Insofar
as we conventionally imagine a design idea as a rough form for the artifact or
as a very abstract representation of the artifact's composition, we may feel

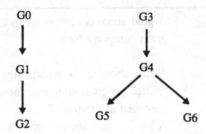

Figure 5.10. First snapshot of the goal graph.

disappointed by the present situation; for the initial sketch as postulated consists really of three ideas expressed in the form:

G2:   Design a control unit to be implemented in a diode matrix.

G5:   The task to be performed by the control unit will be specified by a (micro)program consisting of a set of (micro)orders each held at a specified address in a memory.

G6:   (Design) a control unit in which, on completion of a (micro)order's execution, the task of identifying the next (micro)order normally to execute is specified by a next (micro)order address mechanism.

Of these, G5 and G6 together specify the general idea of using *programming* as a means of realizing the control function – although nothing has yet been established as to how the control function will actually be realized by a program form. It will also be recalled that these two goals are the progenies of the original requirement G3, namely, that the control unit is to be functionally flexible. The goal G2 establishes the idea of implementing the control function in diode matrix form; that is, it establishes a constraint on the *physical form* of the circuit. This is the outcome of the original desire (on Wilkes's part) that the control unit should possess a simple, repetitive, and regular structure; that is, G2 was derived from G1 and constitutes a subgoal of the latter. Figure 5.10 shows a *goal graph* for the goals that have been generated thus far. This is simply a directed acyclic graph wherein the vertices (or nodes) represent goals (and are labeled by the goal identifiers), and an edge from a node Gi to some other node Gj signifies that Gj is a subgoal of Gi or, alternatively, that Gj is directly derived from Gi.

Of the three goals G2, G5, and G6, the most restrictive constraint is probably G2. More precisely, according to the historical evidence, we know that the microprogramming concept was eventually implemented using two diode matrices and some additional circuitry. The question is, starting from the initial sketch – the goals G2, G5, and G6 – what would be a plausible knowledge-level process that could explain how this came about? We consider this issue in the next chapter.

Notes

1. See Table B in the Appendix for a listing of all the facts referred to in this explanation.
2. Table D in the Appendix lists all the goals postulated or generated as part of this explanation.
3. If by *fact* is meant, at the very least, an empirically or logically justified hypothesis about the state of affairs in some world, assertions such as F2 should not be referred to as facts. They are, strictly speaking, subjective beliefs or perceptions held by the agent concerned. We shall, however, collectively refer to all assertions of a declarative kind, regardless of whether they are empirical assertions, logically justified propositions, or beliefs subjectively held in an agent's knowledge body as facts simply to minimize the number of different token types that may be held in an agent's knowledge body. When necessary (as in the case of F2), the term *conceptual fact* will be employed for the sake of clarity.
4. Tables A and C in the Appendix list all the rules postulated or generated in the course of this explanation.

   Several writers on design theory and the methodology of the artificial sciences have noted that, in an ultimate sense, the goal of design or invention is to initiate *change* in some aspect of the world (Jones 1980; Simon 1981; Dasgupta 1991). We perceive an imperfection in the state of affairs in some specific domain, and we conceive or design an artifact that when implemented will, we believe, correct or improve this state of affairs. Thus, R0 is a rule that one may reasonably assume is contained in the knowledge body of most agents concerned with the practice of the artificial sciences and, in particular, with the design of artifacts.

   Basalla (1988, esp. chap. 2) is a rich source of examples from the history of technology of the kinds of imperfections in states of affairs that prompted the invention or the design of artifacts in such domains as stone tools, cotton manufacture, steam technology, and electrical engineering.
5. The symbol "¬" denotes negation or the "not" operation. Thus, ¬$B(e)$ reads as not $B(e)$.
6. An agent's belief in a hypothesis can, of course, be *strengthened* by subsequent *corroborative* evidence – though, from a logical point of view, the hypothesis can never be *confirmed*, no matter how many instances of corroborative or positive evidence one gathers (Popper 1934/1968, esp. chap. 10). However, in the knowledge-level explanatory scheme presented in this book, we do not associate any explicit quantitative measure of the "degree" of corroboration or the strength of (an agent's belief in) a rule with the rule itself. Thus, corroboration of a rule such as R2.1.1 is neither explicitly recorded nor a factor in this discussion.

7. It must be kept in mind that around the time being discussed (the late 1940s and early 1950s), computing devices other than the stored program kind were still in existence – and Wilkes was quite familiar with several of these. They included, e.g., the differential analyzers developed by Jay Forrester at MIT and by D. R. Hartree at Manchester and Cambridge (Wilkes 1985, chap. 2), the Automatic Sequence Controller Calculator developed by Howard Aiken, Grace Hopper, and their colleagues at Harvard (Wilkes 1985, chap. 12), and of course, the ENIAC, built at the Moore School in Philadelphia (Wilkes 1985, chap. 12). This is why rule R3 explicitly associates "functional flexibility" with *stored program* computing devices.

6

The evolution of an idea: from initial sketch to mature form

Relating the microprogram and diode matrix ideas

Consider, first, the connection between goals G2 and G5. The former stipulates that the control unit be implemented in a diode matrix. According to the latter, it is desired that this *same* control unit be realized by a microprogram.[1] Thus, it is demanded that the two entities – a diode matrix and a microprogram – *both* realize a common target entity, namely, the control unit. The question is, How can these two goals both be met in a consistent way?

Wilkes will obviously have been aware that programs (and, by implication, microprograms) are *symbolic* in nature, whereas a diode matrix is a *physical* entity. These may be stated as facts:

F13: A microprogram is an encoded structure of symbols.[2]

F14: A diode matrix is a physical structure.

Let us now postulate the following rule:

R6: *If* entity *A* is a symbolic structure
       and
       entity *B* is a physical structure,
   Then *A* is more abstract than *B*
       and
       (conversely) *B* is more concrete than *A*.

R6 exhibits several characteristics that demand notice. First, it is a *conceptual* rule in that it is concerned entirely with conceptual predicates such as "symbolic," "physical," "more abstract than," and "more concrete than." In this sense, it resembles R0 but is unlike any of the other rules introduced so far. We shall encounter several other rules of this ilk in the future.

125

Second, R6 is a rule that is applicable to entities in general – not merely to physical artifacts or organisms, but also to entities of any sort – physical or symbolic, natural or artificial – one may encounter. To this extent, its scope is broader than those of rules R0, . . . , R5. To this extent also, its scope is of the same order as those of the inference rules (e.g., R-Inst1, R-Gen1, R-Abd). In fact, the domain of R6 is, literally, the "world," and we shall encounter many such "world-specific" rules and facts in this chapter. These are to be contrasted with knowledge tokens that are "artifact-specific" or still more modest in scope, for example, "computer-specific" or even "control-unit-specific."

Third, it is not merely that the domain of applicability is broad; in addition, as a statement about entities in the world, R6 is a very *general* rule – for it claims that *any* symbolic entity is more abstract than *any* physical entity.

What grounds do I have for suggesting that someone of Wilkes's background may possess such a rule? The question is obviously important, for the plausibility of a computational or knowledge-level explanation of Wilkes's creative thinking is critically dependent on the justification or the evidence provided in support of the facts and rules that participate in the explanatory process. And the very nature of R6, especially its universal quality, may appear to make it somewhat controversial.

The nature of my justification for the claim that Wilkes's knowledge body may indeed have contained such a rule as this is one that I shall also use on other occasions. I shall claim that conceptual rules of the scope and generality of R6 (and others like it) are constructed or assimilated (consciously or otherwise – this is not important) as *generalizations that are grounded in particular or singular empirical instances* – that is, as a result of prior applications of generalization inference rules (such as R-Gen1), the premises of which are singular events or states of affairs that the agent, given his or her background, can hardly avoid knowing or observing. In the case of R6, many particular (and quite similar) instances drawn directly from the domain of computers and electronics can be identified as premises for a generalization of which the rule itself is the consequence. Consider the following, for example:

(1) A circuit diagram drawn on paper is a symbolic structure – a set of markings on paper representing other entities – and the circuit itself as a piece of electrical hardware is a physical artifact. The circuit diagram is more abstract than the circuit itself in the sense that (1) the former is not tangible whereas the latter is and (2) the former does not obey causal (i.e., physical) laws whereas the latter does.

(2) A computer program (whether written on a coding sheet or punched onto a paper tape or stored as acoustic pulses in an ultrasonic storage tank) is a

symbolic entity – a pattern of commands or a procedure that obeys no physical laws. The paper or the paper tape or the ultrasonic mercury tank encoding the program is a physical structure. The program is more abstract than its encoding or storage medium for precisely the same reasons that a circuit diagram is more abstract than the circuit.

(3) The architecture (or, as it was then referred to, the logical design) of a computer is a symbolic structure since it is a description of some properties of a computer; the computer itself is a physical entity. A computer's architecture is more abstract than the computer in the sense that (1) the former is not tangible whereas the latter is, (2) an architecture does not obey causal laws whereas the computer does, and (3) the former highlights only certain properties or features of the latter.

Rule R6 is useful, for, in conjunction with facts F13 and F14, it enables, by modus ponens, the inference

$$\frac{\text{F13, F14, R6}}{\text{I16:} \quad \text{F15}}$$

which has, as the consequence, the fact

F15: A microprogram is more abstract than a diode matrix.

Consider next the relation between goals G2 and G6. The former stipulates that the control unit is to be implemented in terms of a diode matrix. G6 requires that the selection of the micro-order "to be next executed" – and this represents a *function* to be performed by the control unit – be determined by a specification of the address of the "next" micro-order; the latter is the means or *mechanism* to achieve the function.

Thus, it is required that two entities – a diode matrix and a next micro-order address mechanism – are to realize a common function, namely, the selection of the next micro-order in the control unit. This latter function we may simply refer to as the *sequencing function*. How do these two entities relate to one another so that both goals can be achieved?

We have already noted, by way of F14, that a diode matrix is a *physical* structure. In fact, it is more than that: The diode matrix is a circuit *form* that can be used to implement many different kinds of logic functions within a computer. That a diode matrix is a physical entity is to be contrasted with the next micro-order address mechanism, which, as stated, is a *functional* entity – that is, an entity designating a particular function (in this case, the sequencing function) that can, possibly, be realized or implemented by different physical forms or structures. Suppose, then, we postulate this as a fact.

F16:   A next micro-order address mechanism is a functional
         entity.

It seems hardly plausible to claim that F16 was a token in Wilkes's knowledge body before he began to think seriously about the microprogramming problem – since there were no *direct* precursors of this notion in either the EDSAC's control unit or in any of the other control units then being designed and known to him. We may suppose, rather, that this fact was inferred. Let us postulate as the source of this inference, the rule

R7:   *If*   an artifact is a stored program computer,
        Then its next order (instruction) address mechanism is
                 a functional entity,

which, like R4 and R5, may be justifiably viewed as being a token in Wilkes's knowledge body as a result of his EDSAC experience and knowledge of stored program computer principles in general. This rule embodies the idea that every stored program computer contains, as a component, a mechanism the function of which is to select the next order or instruction for execution. Thus, the next order address mechanism is a necessary *functional component* of stored programmed computers in general.

By appealing to the rule R-Inst1 and fact F1, an *instantiation* of the form

$$\frac{\text{F1, R7}}{\text{I17:   R7.1}}$$

will yield the rule

R7.1:   *If*   a control unit is a stored program computer,
           Then (the control unit is such that) its next micro-
                    order address mechanism is a functional entity.

Finally, by invoking the goal G4 (identified earlier) and R-ModusP, the rule of modus ponens, the inference

$$\frac{\text{G4, R7.1}}{\text{I18:   F16}}$$

would allow one to generate the fact F16. Figure 6.1 shows the details of this action sequence.

Input	G6:	A goal about a control unit having a next micro-order address mechanism.
		*
Retrieve	F1:	A kind-of rule about control units and artifacts.
Retrieve	R7:	A rule about stored program computers containing next order address mechanisms as functional entities.
Retrieve	R-Inst1:	A rule about kind-of facts, entities, and rules about entities.
Apply	R-Inst1:	With R7 and F1 as substitutions.
		*
Output	R7.1:	A rule about control units that are in stored program computer form containing next order address mechanisms as functional entities.

- -

Input	R7.1:	
		*
Retrieve	G4:	A goal about control units being in stored program computer form.
Retrieve	R-ModusP:	A rule about a goal and a rule about the same goal.
Apply	R-ModusP:	With G4 and R7.1 as substitutions.
		*
Output	F16:	A fact about next micro-order addresses being functional entities.

Figure 6.1. Action sequence producing goal F16.

Consider, now, the following rule:

R8: *If* entity *A* is a functional entity
   and
   entity *B* is a physical entity,
 Then *A* is more abstract than *B*
   and
   (conversely) *B* is more concrete than *A*.

In both form and characteristics, this is rather similar to R6: It is a conceptual rule, being concerned with such abstract notions as functionality or relative abstractness; the domain of the rule is the class *entity* – it is thus a world-

specific rule; and it asserts something very general – the idea that *any* functional entity is more abstract than *any* physical entity.

As in the case of R6, the question arises as to one's justification for claiming
that R8 may have been a token in Maurice Wilkes's knowledge body. As
before, my rationale is that R8 is a *generalization* of particular instances many
of which will have been known to Wilkes either through direct experience from
the EDSAC project or as the consequence of his education, training, and
wartime activities as an applied physicist and electronics engineer.[3] Consider,
as specific instances, the following – taken from the computer domain.

(1) A "word" in the late 1940s designated an entity, means, or capacity to store
    and represent a number (Burks, Goldstine, and von Neumann 1946). A
    word thus constitutes a functional entity – that is, its meaning lies in the
    function itself. Similarly, a "memory organ" comprising a collection of
    (say) 1,024 words is an entity the meaning or significance of which lies in
    its function – that of being capable of storing or representing a set of
    numbers. In contrast, an ultrasonic storage tank of the kind used in the
    EDSAC or the Williams electronic storage tube used in the first Manches-
    ter machine (Williams and Kilburn 1948) are, indubitably, physical entities
    that can be used to *implement* words and memories. The latter are, quite
    evidently, more abstract than the former.

(2) Consider a pair of Boolean equations:[4]

$$S = X'.Y'.C_i + X'.Y.C_i' + X.Y'.C_i' + X.Y.C_i \qquad \text{(FA)}$$
$$C_o = X.Y + X.C_i + Y.C_i$$

Equations (FA) collectively define the function of what in the field of
switching theory and logic design is called a "full adder." The symbols X,
Y, and C_i (or "carry-in") are the truth-valued inputs to the function and S
("sum") and C_o ("carry-out") are the truth-valued outputs.

The equations together constitute a functional entity; they are, in fact,
equivalent to a "truth table" that shows, for all possible combination of
truth values of the inputs, what the corresponding output values will be
(Figure 6.2).[5]

In contrast, an electrical circuit that *performs* the function of the full
adder is, by virtue of its causal properties, a physical entity. Both the
functional entities – the Boolean equations and the truth table – are more
abstract than the electrical circuit itself.

We may conclude, then, that there are plausible grounds for claiming that
R8, as a generalization, may have existed in Wilkes's knowledge body circa

Inputs			Outputs	
X	Y	Ci	S	Co
0	0	0	0	0
0	0	1	1	0
0	1	0	1	0
0	1	1	0	1
1	0	0	1	0
1	0	1	0	1
1	1	0	0	1
1	1	1	1	1

Figure 6.2. Truth table for a full adder.

1950. Furthermore, given that a diode matrix and a next micro-order address mechanism are both entities, R8 can be *instantiated,* by appealing twice in succession to R-Inst1, to the following rule:

R8.1: *If*   a diode matrix is a physical entity
        and
        a next micro-order address mechanism is a functional entity,
    Then   a next micro-order address mechanism is more abstract than a diode matrix
        and
        (conversely) a diode matrix is more concrete than a next micro-order address mechanism.

Finally, R8.1, in conjunction with facts F14 and F16, allows the inference by modus ponens,

$$\frac{\text{F14, F16, R8.1}}{\text{I19:}\qquad \text{F17}}$$

where the consequence is

F17:   A next micro-order address mechanism is more abstract than a diode matrix.

The significance of the two inferred facts F15 and F17 is that they establish a relationship (of sorts) between the diode matrix idea on the one hand (goal G2) and the (micro)programming idea on the other (goals G5 and G6). Consider, further, the connection between the following:

G2:   Design a control unit to be implemented in terms of a diode matrix.

G5:   The (task to be performed by the) control unit is to be specified by a (micro)program consisting of a set of (micro)orders each held at a specified address in a memory.

F15:   A microprogram is more abstract than a diode matrix.

Suppose that there exists the following rule in Wilkes's knowledge body:

R9:   *If*   there is a goal that an entity E is to be implemented in terms of some entity E_1
            and
            there is a goal that the task or function to be achieved by E is to be specified by (or in terms of) some entity E_2
            and
            E_2 is more abstract than E_1,
      Then   establish a goal to realize E_2 in terms of E_1.

R9 is applicable to goals about entities in general but is especially pertinent to artifacts. Although it appears somewhat ad hoc and intuitively unappealing, the rule represents a simple generalization of the type that engineering practitioners (in particular) may be reasonably expected to have assimilated into their knowledge body as a result of their experiences with specific, singular instances. For someone of Wilkes's particular background, the following singular cases can be easily identified:

(1) An arithmetic "organ" (E) – the word was used by Burks, Goldstine, and von Neumann (1946) – has been (or is to be) implemented by means of an electrical circuit (E_1); the function to be performed by the arithmetic organ can be (or is to be) specified by means of an algorithm or systematic routine (E_2); an algorithm is more abstract than an electrical circuit. Thus, the arithmetic algorithm can be (or is) implemented in terms of (or by) an electrical circuit.

(2) A memory "organ" (E) has been (or is to be) implemented by means of a
set of ultrasonic tanks and the associated circuits (E_1); the task to be
performed by the memory organ (i.e., the storage and retrieval of information) has been (or is to be) specified by read/write commands, the location
of the information, and the information itself (E_2); the commands, locations, and the information (being symbol structures that signify concepts)
are, collectively, more abstract than the ultrasonic tanks and associated
circuits. The commands, locations, and information can then be (or are)
implemented in terms of the ultrasonic tanks and circuits.

By appealing to the instantiation rule

R-Inst4: *If* R is a rule about arbitrary entities $E_1, E_2, \ldots$,
possessing properties $P_1, P_2, \ldots$, respectively
and
particular entities $e_1, e_2, \ldots$, possessing (or
postulated to be possessing) $P_1, P_2, \ldots$, respectively,
Then R is a rule about $e_1, e_2, \ldots$ (after substitution),

R9 can be *instantiated* according to the inference

$$\frac{\text{R9, G2, G5, F15}}{\text{I20:} \qquad \text{R9.1}}$$

leading to the consequence

R9.1: *If* there is a goal that the control unit is to be implemented in terms of a diode matrix
and
there is a goal that the task to be achieved by
the control unit is to be specified by a microprogram (consisting of a set of micro-orders each at
a specified address in a memory)
and
a microprogram is more abstract than a diode
matrix,
Then establish a goal to implement a microprogram in
terms of a diode matrix.

Finally, using modus ponens, the inference

$$\frac{\text{G2, G5, F15, R9.1}}{\text{I21:}\qquad \text{G7}}$$

yields the goal

G7:   The microprogram (consisting of a set of micro-orders
       each at a specified address in a memory) is to be imple-
       mented in terms of (or by) a diode matrix.

The sequence of actions just described is summarized in Figure 6.3.
Similarly, consider the triplet

G2:   Design a control unit to be implemented in terms of a
       diode matrix.

G6:   (Design) a control unit in which, on completion of a
       micro-order's execution, the task of identifying the next
       micro-order normally to execute is specified by a next
       micro-order address mechanism.

F17:   A next micro-order address mechanism is more abstract
       than a diode matrix.

An *instantiation,* by virtue of rule R-Inst4,

$$\frac{\text{G2, G6, F17, R9}}{\text{I22:}\qquad \text{R9.2}}$$

yields

R9.2:   *If*   there is a goal that the control unit is to be im-
                 plemented in a diode matrix
                 and
                 there is a goal that the task of identifying the
                 next micro-order normally to execute is spec-
                 ified by a next micro-order address mechanism
                 and
                 a next micro-order address mechanism is more
                 abstract than a diode matrix,
        Then   establish as a goal the implementation of a next
                 micro-order address mechanism in terms of a
                 diode matrix.

Input	G2:	A goal about control units being implemented by diode matrices.
	G5:	A goal about control units to be specified by means of microprograms.
	F15:	A fact about microprograms being more abstract than diode matrices.
		*
Retrieve	R9:	A rule about any entity E satisfying P: a goal that E is to be implemented by some entity E_1; a goal that E is to be specified in terms of some entity E_2; and a fact that E_2 is more abstract than E_1.
Retrieve	R-Inst4:	A rule about a rule about any entity possessing a property P and about goals and/or facts about a specific entity E_1 satisfying P.
Apply	R-Inst4:	With R9, G2, G5, and F15 as substitutions.
		*
Output	R9.1:	A rule about a control unit satisfying P.
		- -
Input	G2, G5, F15, and R9.1:	
		*
Retrieve	R-ModusP:	
Apply	R-ModusP:	With G2, G5, F15, and R9.1 as substitutions.
		*
Output	G7:	A goal about microprograms being implemented in terms of diode matrices.

Figure 6.3. Action sequence producing goal G7.

The use of modus ponens

$$\frac{\text{G2, G6, F17, R9.2}}{\text{I23:} \qquad \text{G8}}$$

produces the goal

G8: The next micro-order address mechanism (for the sequencing of micro-orders) is to be implemented in terms of a diode matrix.

Figure 6.4 shows the state of the goal graph at this stage.

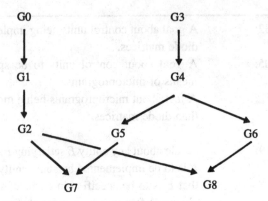

Figure 6.4. Second snapshot of the goal graph.

A diode matrix representation of the microprogram

As noted earlier (see Chapter 3, section "The Whirlwind and its control matrix" and Chapter 5, section "The idea of a diode matrix"), Wilkes was aware that

> F5:   In the MIT Whirlwind, each arithmetic operation (barring multiplication) involves exactly eight pulses issued from a control unit implemented in the form of a diode matrix.

F5 was, in fact, used in Chapter 5 to explain the formation of the diode matrix idea. Wilkes also knew, from observing the Whirlwind, the following characteristics of its control unit:

> F18:   The Whirlwind control unit is a diode matrix that consists of intersecting sets of R rows and C columns such that (1) each row i represents the set of control steps required to be activated in order to execute some distinct opcode i; (2) each column j represents a distinct control step such that a signal along column j causes the activation of the corresponding control step; and (3) the presence of a diode d_{ij} at the intersection of row i and column j causes the transmission along column j of a signal on row i (and, therefore, causes the activation of the control step in column j).[6]

Now, though F18 is an assertion about a *single* control matrix, one may plausibly *generalize* it to an assertion about *any* control matrix:

F19: A control matrix is a diode matrix that consists of inter-secting sets of rows and columns such that (1) each row *i* represents a set of control steps required to be acti-vated in order to execute some distinct opcode *i;* (2) each column *j* represents (or encodes) a distinct control step such that a signal along column *j* causes the activa-tion of the corresponding control step; and (3) the presence of a diode d_{ij} at the intersection of row *i* and column *j* causes the transmission along column *j* of a signal in row *i* (and, therefore, causes the activation of the control step in column *j*).

The legitimacy of generalizing from one or a few singular cases was discussed in Chapter 5 (section, "The idea of a diode matrix"), where two, slightly differing generalization rules, R-Gen1 and R-Gen2, were introduced. Along those same arguments, a generalization of F18 to F19 can be legitimized on the grounds that the Whirlwind control matrix, being the first and (at the time) the only one of its kind, established a schema or paradigm for "future" control matrices. Thus, while F18 is an *empirical* assertion, F19 is a *prescrip-tive* statement to the effect that anything that is a control matrix will (be expected to) be a diode matrix having the properties enunciated in F19.[7]

The generalization of F18 to F19 uses a variation of R-Gen1 and R-Gen2 that can be expressed as

R-Gen3: *If*   an entity *e* is a kind-of (or an instance-of) entity
E
and
there is a predicate *A* such that *A(e)* is the case
and
there is no known entity *e'* that is a kind-of (or an instance-of) entity *E* such that $\neg A(e')$
and
the number of instances of *E* is low,
Then   assume the fact *A(E)*.

The generalization also appeals to the fact

F20: The Whirlwind control matrix is an instance-of a con-trol matrix.

Input	G7:	A goal about microprograms implemented in terms of diode matrices.
		*
Retrieve	F18:	A fact about the Whirlwind control matrix being a diode matrix.
Retrieve	F20:	A fact about the Whirlwind control matrix being an instance-of a control matrix.
Retrieve	R-Gen3:	A rule about an entity being a kind-of some other entity and satisfying some property.
Apply	R-Gen3:	With F18 and F20 as substitutions.
		*
Output	F19:	A fact about control matrices being diode matrices.

Figure 6.5. An action generating fact F19.

and is expressible in terms of the inference

$$\frac{\text{F18, F20}}{\text{I24:}\quad\text{F19}}$$

Figure 6.5 summarizes the action leading to F19.

Contrasting goal G7 with F19, it will be noticed that, in the former, each address of the microprogram is stipulated to consist of a *single* micro-order, whereas, in the latter, each row in a control-diode matrix represents a *set* of control steps. This discrepancy between the contents of a microprogram address and those of a control-diode matrix row can be eliminated by transforming G7 to the goal

> G9: The microprogram, consisting of a set of micro-orders (each of which in turn consists of a set of micro-operations held at a specified address) is to be implemented in terms of (or by) a diode matrix.

But how could such a goal transformation take place? We may explain this by first postulating the rule

> R10: *If*   there is a goal that an entity e_1 is to be implemented in terms of an entity E
> > *and*
> > an entity e_2 is known to be implemented in terms of E,

> *Then*   establish as a goal the identification of sim-
> ilarities or mappings or equivalences between e_1
> and e_2.

By appealing to R-Inst4, R10 can be *instantiated* according to the inference

$$\frac{\text{G7, F19, R10}}{\text{I25:} \qquad \text{R10.1}}$$

producing the rule

> R10.1:   *If*   there is a goal that the microprogram (consisting
> of a set of micro-orders each at a specified ad-
> dress in a memory) is to be implemented in
> terms of (or by) a diode matrix
> *and*
> a control matrix is (implemented in terms of) a
> diode matrix that consists of . . . ,
>
>   *Then*   establish as a goal the identification of (one or
> more) similarities or mappings or equivalences
> between the microprogram and the control-diode
> matrix.

Further, by modus ponens (rule R-ModusP) we have

$$\frac{\text{G7, F19, R10.1}}{\text{I26:} \qquad \text{G10}}$$

where

> G10:   Identify one or more similarities or mappings or equiva-
> lences between a microprogram (consisting of a set of
> micro-orders each at a specified address in a memory)
> and a control-diode matrix in which each row i consists
> of . . .

Consider next the rule

R11:   *If*   there is a goal to establish a similarity or map-
                ping or equivalence between two entities e_1 and
                e_2
                and
                a component c_1 in e_1 and c_2 in e_2 are struc-
                turally similar,
       Then c_1 in e_1 and c_2 in e_2 are possibly equivalent or
                there is a possible mapping between c_1 in e_1 and
                c_2 in e_2,

and let us further assume that Wilkes *observes* that

F21:   Addresses in a microprogram and rows in a control-
       diode matrix are structurally similar

as a result of comparing the (desired) conceptual form of a microprogram (goal
G7) and the actual form of a control-diode matrix (F19). Figure 6.6 shows the
two forms. In that case, by virtue of R-Inst5, the *instantiation*

$$\frac{\text{G10, F21, R11}}{\text{I27:} \qquad \text{R11.1}}$$

yields the rule

R11.1:   *If*   there is a goal to establish a similarity or map-
                  ping or equivalence between a microprogram
                  and a control-diode matrix
                  and
                  addresses in a microprogram and rows in a
                  control-diode matrix are structurally similar,
         Then   addresses in a microprogram and rows in a
                  control-diode matrix are possibly equivalent or
                  there is a possible mapping between addresses in
                  a microprogram and rows in a control-diode
                  matrix.

Thus, by the inference by modus ponens,

$$\frac{\text{G10, F21, R11.1}}{\text{I28:} \qquad \text{F22}}$$

we obtain the hypothesis

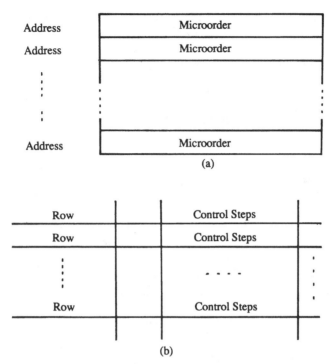

Address	Microorder
Address	Microorder
⋮	⋮
Address	Microorder

(a)

Row			Control Steps	
Row			Control Steps	
⋮			⋯	⋮
Row			Control Steps	

(b)

Figure 6.6. Structural similarity between a microprogram and a control-diode matrix.

F22: Addresses in a microprogram and rows in a control-diode matrix are possibly equivalent, or there is a possible mapping between addresses in a microprogram and rows in a control-diode matrix.

Suppose now that the following rule is invoked by association with F22,

R12: *If*   there are two entities E_1, E_2 such that e_1 in E_1, e_2 in E_2 are possibly equivalent
   and
   elements e'_1 in E_1, e'_2 in E_2 are functionally similar
   and
   e_1, e'_1 in E_1 satisfy some predicate $P(e_1, e'_1)$,
   Then assume that e_2, e'_2 in E_2 will also satisfy $P(e_2, e'_2)$,

and that the following fact (in a manner to be explained later) has been inferred:

F23:   Micro-orders in a microprogram and control steps in a
       control-diode matrix are functionally similar.

In that case, by modus ponens, the inference[8]

$$\frac{\text{F22, F23, F19, R12}}{\text{I29:} \qquad \text{G7a}}$$

will yield the goal

G7a: Each address in a microprogram will represent a set of
       micro-orders.

As the word "micro-order" has hitherto been used to denote the overall content
of an address, we will continue to employ it in that sense. The word micro-
operation will, instead, be used henceforth to designate the equivalents of the
control step – that is, the individual constituents of a micro-order.[9] Thus, G7a
can be restated as

G7b: Each address in a microprogram will represent (or con-
       sist of) a micro-order, which in turn will represent (or
       consist of) a set of micro-operations.

Goal G7b when conjoined with G7 yields G9.
     A participant in the inference I29 is the fact F23. This itself can be viewed as
an inference according to the following argument: It is quite reasonable to
assume that Wilkes's knowledge of computer architecture and programming
circa 1950 included the fact

F24:   In a stored program computer, an instruction (order)
       when executed (or activated) causes a state change in
       the relevant registers or memory words in the computer,

which may be retrieved by a spread of activation (see section, "Spreading
activation," Chapter 4) beginning with G7 as shown in Figure 6.7.[10] As the
latter shows, instrumental to this retrieval is a previously inferred goal

G4:   Specify the control unit in a stored program form.

This can, in fact, be restated as

G4′:   The control unit is to be a kind-of stored program
       computer.

In that case, by invoking R-Inst3 (see Appendix), the instantiation

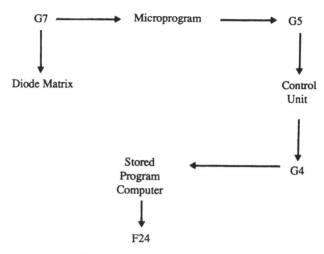

Figure 6.7. Activation network leading to fact F24.

$$\frac{\text{G4}', \text{F24}}{\text{I30}: \quad \text{F25}}$$

produces the "potential" fact

F25: In a (microprogrammed) control unit, a micro-order
when executed will cause a state change in the relevant
registers or memory words in the computer.

Furthermore, Wilkes's knowledge of the Whirlwind will include the fact

F26: Each distinct control step issued from the Whirlwind
control-diode matrix causes a state change in the relevant registers or memory words.

Keeping in mind that the Whirlwind control matrix is an instance of a
control matrix (fact F19), F26 can be *generalized* (by appealing to R-Gen4)
according to the inference

$$\frac{\text{F26}, \text{F20}}{\text{I31}: \quad \text{F27}}$$

thus generating the fact

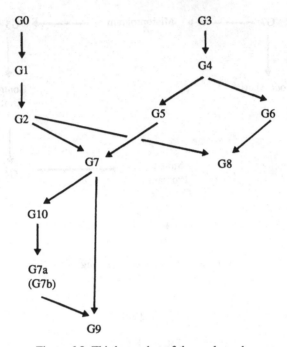

Figure 6.8. Third snapshot of the goal graph.

F27:   Each distinct control step in a control-diode matrix
       when activated or issued causes a state change in the
       relevant registers or memory words in the relevant
       computer.

Notice that F25 and F27 describe an identical behavioral effect, "state
change in the relevant registers or memory words," brought about by two
(apparently) distinct entities – micro-orders and control steps.

These two facts, in conjunction with the rule

R13:   *If*   entities $E_1, E_2, \ldots$, have the same behavioral
               effect,
       Then $E_1, E_2, \ldots$, are (postulated to be) functionally
               similar,

produces, by modus ponens, the inference

$$\frac{\text{F25, F27, R13}}{\text{I32:}\qquad \text{F23}}$$

Figure 6.8 shows the state of the goal graph at the point at which G9 has been generated. Figure 6.9 summarizes the actions leading to goal G7a/G7b, while Figure 6.10 depicts the actions whereby fact F23 is inferred.

There remains the question as to how one may plausibly justify rules R10, R11, R12, and R13. As in the case of other rules previously postulated, it is suggested that these are generalizations of singular empirical instances that a physical scientist, an engineer, or a mathematician – and Wilkes, in the course of his formal education and subsequent research career, was all of these – is quite likely to have assimilated.

Consider, for instance, R10. This is clearly a rule to help draw analogies between a given problem situation and a prior solution. Two examples that can be taken from the EDSAC experience itself are the use of a paper tape reader to implement the input function on the EDSAC and that of a teletype printer to implement the output function. Both of these are applications of previously established entities (the paper tape reader on the one hand, the teletype printer on the other) that had been used to implement somewhat different functions (i.e., sending and receiving telegraphic messages) to the domain of computer input and output. As Wilkes and Renwick noted:

> Ordinary 5-hole punched tape of the kind used in telegraphy is used for input. Each row of holes represents a 5-digit binary number and the basic input operation is to transfer this number to the store. Similarly, the output mechanism is the teleprinter and the basic output operation is to transform a 5-digit binary number to the printer and to print the corresponding character. The teleprinter code is chosen so that binary numbers up to nine are printed as the corresponding figures and a similar code is used for input. (Wilkes and Renwick 1949, p. 10)

In order to adopt the paper tape reader and teletype printer to the input and output functions, respectively, a mapping or equivalence was established between the sending/receiving of telegraphic messages and the input/output of numbers to/from the EDSAC.

R11 is a rule that may be plausibly based on the observation or previously acquired knowledge that wherever there is a structural similarity between two entities (each of which may possibly be a component of some larger entity), there is an equivalence of sorts between them. And thus, in order to seek an equivalence or mapping between entities, one may profitably inquire whether these entities (or their components) possess structural similarities.

This is a relatively subtle rule; and yet, even confining oneself to Wilkes's domain, one may find singular instances on which R11 will be founded. Consider, for example, the memory device described by Burks, Goldstine, and von Neumann (1946). This was based on the electrostatic storage (cathode-ray)

Input	G7:	A goal about microprograms being implemented in terms of diode matrices.
	F19:	A fact about control matrices being implemented in terms of diode matrices.
		*
Retrieve	R10:	A rule about two entities both being implemented in terms of another common entity.
Retrieve	R-Inst4:	A rule about a rule about entities possessing a set of properties and about facts or goals about particular entities possessing the same properties.
Apply	R-Inst4:	With G7, F19, and R10 as substitutions.
Output	R10.1:	

- -

Input	R10.1, G7, and F19:	
		*
Retrieve	R-ModusP:	
Apply	R-ModusP:	With R10.1, G7, and F19 as substitutions.
		*
Output	G10:	A goal about finding similarities or mappings between microprograms and control-diode matrices.

- -

Input	G10 and G7:	
		*
Retrieve	R11:	A rule about similarities or mappings between two entities and about components of the two entities being structurally similar.
Retrieve	F21:	A fact about microprograms and control matrices being structurally similar components.
Retrieve	R-Inst5:	A rule about a rule about entities related by a property and about a fact or a goal about particular entities related by the same property.
Apply	R-Inst5:	With G10, F21, and R11 as substitutions.
		*
Output	R11.1:	A rule about similarities or mappings between microprograms and control-diode matrices and about addresses in microprograms and rows in control-diode matrices being structurally similar.

- -

Input	G9, F21, and R11.1:	
		*
Retrieve	R-ModusP:	
Apply	R-ModusP:	With G9, F21, and R11.1 as substitutions.

		*
Output	F22:	A (potential) fact about addresses in micropro-grams and rows in control-diode matrices being equivalent.

- -

Input	F22, G7, and F19:	
		*
Retrieve	R12:	A rule about coponents of entities being equiv-alent.
Retrieve	F23:	A fact about micro-orders in microprograms and control steps in control-diode matrices being functionally similar.
Retrieve	R-ModusP:	
Apply	R-ModusP:	With F22, F23, F19, and R12 as substitutions.
		*
Output	G7a/G7b:	A goal about addresses in microprograms con-taining micro-orders consisting of micro-operations.

Figure 6.9. Action sequence producing goal G7a/G7b.

tube called the selectron. According to the design proposed by Burks et al., the memory would consist of forty such tubes each capable of storing 2^{12} bits. Structurally, the memory consisted of a regular array of forty selectrons (Figure 6.11a). Similarity, a parallel arithmetic unit (Figure 6.11b) may be described as "composed of a number of standard units each containing four flipflops (one belonging to each of four registers) together with an adder" (Wilkes 1986, p. 119).

The memory of Figure 6.11a and the arithmetic unit of Figure 6.11b are thus *structurally similar.* Their equivalence lies in the fact that (1) each element of the respective arrays holds or represents a single bit of a data item (i.e., of a word) and (2) these bits are accessible or operable in parallel.

Rule R12 is a generalization for which particular instances may be cited from both the natural and the artificial worlds. For instance, in the case of the horse-drawn carriage and the automobile, the carriage in the former and the interior of the latter are equivalent in the sense that they are both containers for passengers. In the horse-drawn carriage, the horse is responsible for providing the power that causes the vehicle to move; and in the automobile, it is the engine. The horse and the engine are thus *functionally similar.* The horse must exert sufficient power to overcome the weight of the carriage and the frictional

Input	G7:	A goal about microprograms being implemented in terms of diode matrices.
		*
Retrieve	G5:	A goal about microprograms specifying control units.
Retrieve	G4/G4′:	A goal about a control unit being a kind-of stored program computer.
Retrieve	F24:	A fact about orders in stored program computers causing state changes.
Retrieve	R-Inst3:	A rule about facts about entities and about goals or facts about other entities being kinds-of these entities.
Apply	R-Inst3:	With G4′ and F24 as substitutions.
Output	F25:	A fact about micro-orders causing state changes.
Input	F25:	
		*
Retrieve	F26:	A fact about Whirlwind control steps causing state changes.
Retrieve	F19:	A fact about the Whirlwind control matrix being a kind-of control matrix.
Retrieve	R-Gen4:	A rule about entities being kinds-of other entities and satisfying some property.
Apply	R-Gen4:	With F19 and F26 as substitutions.
		*
Output	F27:	A fact about control steps in control-diode matrices causing state changes.
Input	F25 and F27:	Two facts about identical behavioral effects.
		*
Retrieve	R13:	A rule about entities with identical behavioral effects.
Retrieve	R-ModusP:	
Apply	R-ModusP:	With F25, F27, and R13 as substitutions.
		*
Output	F23:	A fact about micro-orders and control steps being functionally similar.

Figure 6.10. Action sequence producing fact F23.

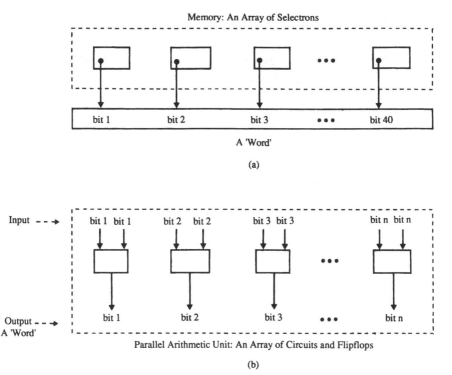

Figure 6.11. Structural similarity between a memory unit and an arithmetic unit.

resistance. The engine must correspondingly exercise sufficient power to overcome the automobile's weight and resistance due to friction.

As another example, the human heart and the mechanical pump used in a variety of machines and systems are equivalent in that they are both means of moving fluids. The corresponding sets of valves are functionally similar in that they control the entry into and exit from the organ (in one case) and the artifact (in the other) of fluids. During the operation of the pump, the inlet and outlet valves are simultaneously open (closed) and closed (open), respectively. In the operation of the heart, the tricuspid/mitral and the semilunar valves are simultaneously open (closed) and closed (open), respectively.

Finally, as a singular instance of rule R13, consider again the horse carriage–automobile example: the horse causes the carriage to move just as the engine causes the movement of the automobile. The horse and engine have the same behavioral effect; hence, they are functionally similar. As another instance, the fish gill and the human lung both behave similarly: They both take in oxygen and expel carbon dioxide. They are thus both respiratory organs – that is, they are functionally similar.

Returning now to the main line of the argument, the goal generated most recently is

G9:   The microprogram consisting of a set of micro-orders
      (each of which in turn consists of a set of micro-
      operations held at a specified address) is to be imple-
      mented in terms of (or by) a diode matrix.

Let us postulate the rule

R14:   *If*   an entity E_1 is to be implemented by (or in
                terms of) some entity E_2
                and
                an entity e_1 associated with (or an element of)
                E_1 is equivalent to an entity e_2 associated with
                (or an element of) E_2
                and
                e_1 satisfies (or is required to satisfy) some prop-
                erty P,
       Then e_2 also satisfies (or should satisfy) P.

By modus ponens, the inference[11]

$$\frac{G9, F22, R14}{I33: \quad G11}$$

leads to the goal

G11:   Each row in the diode matrix will hold (or encode) a set
       of micro-operations corresponding to a single micro-
       order.

Consider now the rule

R15:   *If*   an entity E represents (or is required to repre-
                sent) or consists of (or is required to consist of)
                a set of elements $e_1, e_2, \ldots$, of type T
                and
                the same entity E represents (or is required to
                represent) or consists of (or is required to consist
                of) a set of elements $e'_1, e'_2, \ldots$, of type T'
                and
                the types T and T' are functionally similar,

Then each element e_i of type T should correspond to (or represent or be represented by) a distinct element e'_j of type T'.

Applying R15, the inference by modus ponens

$$\frac{\text{G11, F19, F23, R15}}{\text{I34:} \qquad \text{G12}}$$

generates the goal

G12: Each control step in a row of the control-diode matrix will correspond to (or represent) a distinct micro-operation.

Figure 6.12 summarizes the actions leading to G12. Figure 6.13 shows the contents of the resulting goal graph.

Before proceeding further, it needs to be recorded that as with other previously hypothesized rules, R14 and R15 – postulated here as tokens in Wilkes's knowledge body – are taken to be generalizations founded on singular instances that are likely to have been encountered by someone of Wilkes's background. In the case of R14, for example, the following instance can be identified.

In the EDSAC, the memory that is to hold a program's orders (the entity E_1) is implemented by a bank of mercury or acoustic storage tanks (entity E_2). The address of the memory word to be accessed during the execution of an order (entity e_1) is equivalent to the contents of the location section of the order interpreter (entity e_2). The address of the memory word to be accessed enables the contents (of the desired word) to be extracted directly (e_1 satisfying property P). The contents of the location section of the order interpreter enables (or should enable) the contents (of the desired memory location) to be extracted directly (e_2 satisfying P).

As a plausible singular basis for R15, consider a memory (entity E) consisting of a set of locations $l_1, l_2, \ldots, l_n$. Consider also that the memory consists of, or is represented by, a set of positions on a set of cathode-ray tubes (Figure 6.11a), these positions being denoted by $p_1, p_2, \ldots, p_n$. The types "location" and "position" are functionally similar since they both signify where each digit or order (as the case may be) is to be stored. Thus, each location l_i corresponds to a distinct position p_j; or conversely, each position p_i represents (or should represent) a distinct location l_j.

At this stage, the significant immediate goals are G8, G9, and G12. The last of these, in conjunction with fact F19(3) and the rule

Input	G9:	A goal about microprograms (consisting of micro-orders held at specified addresses) implemented by diode matrices.
		*
Retrieve	R14:	A rule about a goal about entities implemented by other entities and about the equivalence of the entities or their components.
Retrieve	F22:	A fact about the equivalence of addresses in microprograms and rows in diode matrices.
Retrieve	R-ModusP:	
Apply	R-ModusP:	With G9, F22, and R14 as substitutions.
		*
Output	G11:	A goal about rows in diode matrices encoding the micro-operations of a micro-order.

- -

Input	G11:	
		*
Retrieve	F19(1):	A fact about rows in control-diode matrices representing control steps.
Retrieve	F23:	A fact about micro-operations and control steps in control-diode matrices being functionally similar.
Retrieve	R15:	A rule about an entity representing two distinct entities that are functionally similar.
Retrieve	R-ModusP:	
Apply	R-ModusP:	With G11, F19(1), F23, and R 15 as substitutions.
		*
Output	G12:	A goal about distinct control steps in rows in a diode matrix representing distinct micro-operations.

Figure 6.12. Action sequence leading to goal G12.

R16: *If* an entity E_1 represents (or is intended to represent) some entity E_2
and
some behavioral property $P(E_1)$ is the effect of some causal agent A,

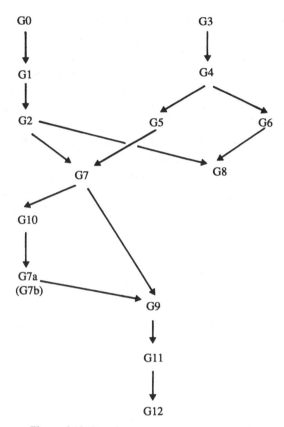

Figure 6.13. Fourth snapshot of the goal graph.

> *Then*   the causal agent A will also produce the same
> behavioral property $P(E_2)$ in E_2.

produces, by modus ponens,

$$I35: \quad \frac{F19(3), G12, R16}{G13}$$

the goal

G13:   The presence of a diode d_{ij} at the intersection of row i
and column j will cause the activation of micro-
operation j whenever there is a signal along row i.

Rule R16 describes the situation in which if an entity is represented by (or is implemented in terms of) another entity, then the behavioral properties of the latter are likely to be inherited by the former when so represented. To take a particular example, consider once more the computer design presented by Burks, Goldstine, and von Neumann (1946) and suppose that a set of cathode-ray tubes represents the main memory of a computer. More precisely, suppose that the set of identical positions i on the forty cathode-ray tubes (entity E_1) – see Figure 6.11 – represents location i of main memory (entity E_2). In this situation, issuing the contents of the address register to the control input of the bank of tubes (the causal agent A) will result in the contents of positions i of all the tubes to be accessed in parallel (the behavioral property $P(E_1)$). Clearly, then, issuing the contents of the address register will result in the contents of the computer's main memory to be accessed in parallel ($P(E_2)$).

Suppose further that goal G13 invokes, by the spread of activation, the rule

R17: *If*   there is a goal that an entity E_1 (having a certain operational characteristic $O(E_1)$) is to cause an entity E_2 to behave in a certain way,

  Then establish as a goal the representation or implementation of E_2 by E_1.

Then, by modus ponens, the inference

$$\frac{\text{G13, R17}}{\text{I36: \quad G14}}$$

generates the goal

G14: Micro-operation j (on row i) is implemented (or represented) by a diode d_{ij} at the intersection of row i and column j of the control-diode matrix.

As was the case with other postulated rules, R17 can be justified as a generalization of particular instances, such as the following: An acoustic delay line (E_1), when operated such that a signal sent to its input control results in the "contents" of the line to appear at the output ($O(E_1)$), causes the simulation of a memory word being read out. Thus a memory word can be implemented by means of an acoustic delay line. A circuit consisting of a pair of relay switches connected in series causes the circuit to simulate the logical AND function (or causes the simulation of an AND gate). Thus, an AND gate can be implemented by (or the AND function can be represented by) a pair of relays in series.

Consider now the two goals

G14: Micro-operation j on row i is implemented (or represented) by a diode d_{ij} at the intersection of row i and column j of the control-diode matrix,

G11: Each row in the diode matrix will hold (or encode) a set of micro-operations corresponding to a single micro-order.

Their conjunction, which appeals to the rule

R-And: *If*   a fact (goal) (rule) A is the case
                  and
                  a fact (goal) (rule) B is the case,
        Then   the fact (goal) (rule) A *and* B is the case

produces, by way of the inference

$$\frac{\text{G11, G14}}{\text{I37: \quad G15a}}$$

the goal

G15a: Each row i of the diode matrix will hold (or encode) a set of micro-operations corresponding to a single micro-order and each micro-operation j in row i will be implemented by a diode d_{ij} at the intersection of row i and column j.

This can be reformulated more simply as

G15: Each row i of the diode matrix will consist of a set of diodes $d_{i1}, d_{i2}, \ldots$, representing the set of distinct micro-operations corresponding to a single micro-order.

Finally, given G15 and the previously established "potential" fact F22, their conjunction, according to

$$\frac{\text{G15, F22}}{\text{I38: \quad G16}}$$

produces, as a consequence, the goal

G16:   Each row i of the control-diode matrix will consist of a
       set of diodes d_{i1}, d_{i2}, . . . , representing the set of dis-
       tinct micro-operations corresponding to a single micro-
       order where row i represents (or is equivalent to) an ad-
       dress of the microprogram.

The resulting goal graph is as shown in Figure 6.14. Furthermore, at this point,
a diode matrix realization of the microprogram – as demanded by and in
response to goal G9 – has been achieved. The form of this implementation and
its basic operating characteristics are defined by the following previously
established items:

G16:   Each row i of the control-diode matrix will consist of a
       set of diodes d_{i1}, d_{i2}, . . . , representing the set of dis-
       tinct micro-operations corresponding to a single micro-
       order, where row i represents (or is equivalent to) an
       address of the microprogram.

G13:   The presence of a diode d_{ij} at the intersection of row i
       and column j will cause the activation of micro-
       operation j whenever there is a signal along row i.

G12:   Each control step in a row of the control-diode matrix
       will correspond to (or represent) a distinct micro-
       operation.

F20(2): Each column j represents (or encodes) a distinct control
       step, such that a signal along column j causes the ac-
       tivation of the corresponding control step.

This diode matrix is depicted in Figure 6.15. We shall refer to this as diode
matrix A.

Diode matrix representation of next micro-order addresses

Referring to Figure 6.14, it can be seen that the developments leading to diode
matrix A, as described in the preceding section, are captured by the subgraph
rooted in G7. In fact, the latter was one of the two goals connecting the idea of
microprograms to diode matrices. Consider now, the second of these goals:

G8:   The next micro-order address mechanism (for the se-
       quencing of micro-orders) is to be implemented in
       terms of a diode matrix.

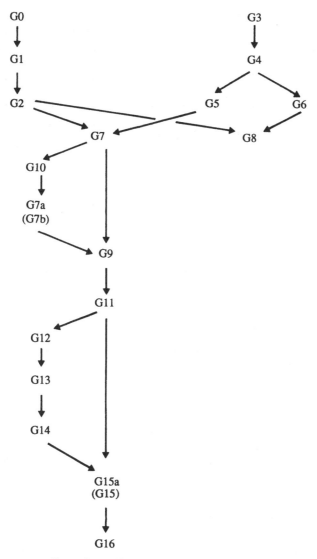

Figure 6.14. Fifth snapshot of the goal graph.

Recall that although both G7 and G8 refer to diode matrices, nothing was said (when deriving these goals – see section, "Relating the microprogramming and diode matrix ideas," this chapter) about whether they refer to the same matrix or to distinct matrices. However, diode matrix *A* (Figure 6.15) was derived by a process in which G8 was ignored.

This may imply one of two assumptions or options:

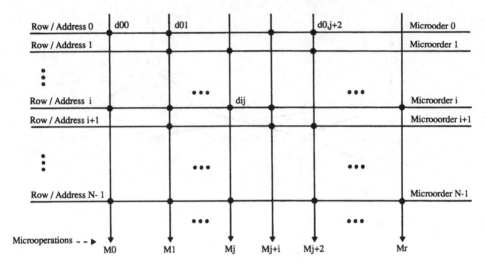

Figure 6.15. Organization of diode matrix A.

(1) That G7 and G8 will, in fact, have separate diode matrix solutions – that is, the overall solution will entail a *dual* diode matrix approach.

(2) That the diode matrix solution to G7 will be *modified* so as to accommodate or satisfy G8.

It is worth noting that there were no a priori reasons for Wilkes to have conceived of a diode matrix solution to the next micro-order addressing problem. In the case of the EDSAC, no such solution was employed for the problem of determining the address of the next order to be executed. In fact, in both the EDSAC and the design proposed by Burks, Goldstine, and von Neumann (1946) – and these were the principal sources of Wilkes's empirical knowledge concerning next address generation – a very different mechanism had been proposed. In the case of the EDSAC,

At the beginning of each operation, the sequence control tank contains the address of the order due to be executed next. *Before* the completion of the operation, unity is added to the address contained in this tank so as to *prepare* for the executing of the next order. (Wilkes 1956, p. 49; italics added)

Orders are normally placed in storage locations numbered in the sequence in which the machine is required to carry out the operations specified. The control unit is designed so that the machine having carried out the operation specified by the order in [location] *m* automatically takes (*m* + 1) [i.e., the contents of location *m* + 1] as the next order. (Wilkes, Wheeler, and Gill 1951, p. 7)

Furthermore,

> When the order which passes into the order tank . . . is a conditional order, and the condition is satisfied, a connexion is established . . . between the order tank [i.e., the instruction register] and the sequence control tank [i.e., the program counter]; the order then passes into the sequence control tank and replaces what was there before. The result . . . is that the sequence control tank now contains the address specified in the conditional order so that . . . the order to be [next] executed is taken from that address. (Wilkes 1956, p. 53)

Thus (as we have hypothesized in the section "Relating the microprogramming and diode matrix ideas," this chapter), G8 was derived in order to satisfy the *global* goal of using diode matrices (G2). There is, then, no prior *computer-specific* rationale of any kind to suggest which of the two options, (1) or (2), to pursue profitably. Nevertheless, there are, I believe, two arguments that can be advanced in support of the first option being a preference:

(1) Given that both goals G7 and G8 are progenies of an earlier goal to realize the control unit in the form of a stored program device (goal G4), Wilkes's knowledge of and experience with programming may suggest a clean separation between the mechanism for the storage of instructions in memory and the mechanism to select instructions from memory. A similar separation of functions may be suggested *analogically* in the present case.
(2) Satisfying goals G7 and G8 independently (if possible or to the extent possible) appears to be a more manageable task than deriving a common or simultaneous solution to them.

These observations, in conjunction, constitute a plausible reason for selecting the first of the two approaches.

Consider now G8. Given the earlier comment on the absence of any precedence in using diode matrices for the next address mechanism, it may be suggested that some sort of analogical reasoning was brought into play to achieve this goal. Accordingly, we postulate the presence, in Wilkes's knowledge body, of the general analogical rule

R18: *If* an entity E is used (or to be used) to implement an entity E_1
and
entity E is used (or to be used) to implement an entity E_2
and
E is used in a particular way in the case of E_1,

Then E may (perhaps) be used in a similar way for
      E_2,

which when invoked by association with G8 and G9 produces, according to the
inference by modus ponens

$$\frac{\text{G8, G9, R18}}{\text{I39: \qquad G17}}$$

the goal

> G17: Use a diode matrix to implement the next micro-order
> address mechanism in a way that is similar to the use of
> the diode matrix for implementing the microprogram
> function.

Figure 6.16 summarizes the nature of this action. As to the justification of
R18, this is the kind of generalization for which many particular instances can
be cited from both the artificial and organic worlds. Thus, for example, paper
tape readers (E) were used to implement telegraphic devices (E_1). Such a tape
device was also used in the EDSAC (E_2) and in other machines of that period,
including the Manchester Computer and the Whirlwind I (Wilkes 1956). In the
former case, each row of the tape encoded a character of the message word,
which was then sensed by the reader and transmitted electrically. In the case of
the EDSAC, each row of the tape was used to encode a character of data or the
order, which is then "read" and transmitted electrically to the computer.

As another example, a cathode-ray tube or "iconoscope" (E) was developed
by J. Rachman of the RCA Princeton Laboratories to store electrical information for television images (E_2). In their original plans for what came to be
called the Institute of Advanced Study (IAS) computer, Burks, Goldstine, and
von Neumann (1946) had decided to implement the memory organ (E_1) of their
computer using the same type of device in a similar manner, since, in the case
of the memory, it was also required to store information electrically.

A solution to G17 demands knowledge of *how* the diode matrix is used to
implement the microprogram function. This knowledge is, in fact, encoded in
the artifactual form named diode matrix A (Figure 6.15), the characteristics of
which can be summarized (from goals G9, G12, G13, and G16 and fact F19(2))
by means of the following fact:

Input	G8:	A goal about an entity E_1 to be implemented in terms of an entity E (a diode matrix).
		*
Retrieve	G9:	A goal about an entity E_2 to be implemented in terms of entity E (a diode matrix).
Retrieve	R18:	A rule about an entity E used to implement distinct entities E_1 and E_2.
Retrieve	R-ModusP:	
Apply	R-ModusP:	With G8, G9, and R18 as substitutions.
		*
Output	G17:	A goal about diode matrix usage.

Figure 6.16. An action producing goal G17.

F28: Diode matrix A

A1: The microprogram consists of a set of micro-orders $M_1, \ldots, M_m$ at addresses $1, \ldots, m$, respectively.

A2: Each micro-order consists of a set of micro-operations (which is a subset of the set of distinct micro-operations).

A3: Each column j of the diode matrix will represent a distinct micro-operation.

A4: Each row i of the diode matrix will consist of a set of diodes $d_{i1}, d_{i2}, \ldots$, representing the set of micro-operations corresponding to a single micro-order at address i.

A5: The presence of a diode d_{ij} at the intersection of row i and column j will cause the activation of micro-operation j whenever there is a signal along row i.

Consider now goal G17. This demands, explicitly, the use of some form of *analogical* reasoning to produce a diode matrix solution for the next micro-order address function. Analogical reasoning takes many different forms as discussed, for example, by Hesse (1966) and Holland et al. (1986).[12] In this particular case, the application of a rule of the following form may be suggested:

R19:   *If*   an analogical solution is sought between a
                 source situation S and a target situation T,
       Then   establish a mapping between the known entities
                 (in the *function* parts) of S and T
                 and
                 then substitute the known entities of T for the
                 corresponding known entities of S in the *method
                 of solution* part of S.

This rule refers to a particular representation of the analogical situation. *Source* denotes the known entity that is to serve as a basis for drawing the analogy. *Target* refers to the entity the solution to which is sought. The source and the target are both represented in terms of a *function* part, a *goal* part, and a *method of solution* part as depicted in Figure 6.17.[13] Here, Source and Target signify the particular source S and target T, respectively, for the given problem.

It will be noted that the information contained in the Source half of this table is merely a concise restatement of F28. The Target half, however, characterizes the next address function in terms of a property that has not hitherto been explicitly stated. This is a general empirical fact that would obviously have been known to Wilkes:

F29:   In a binary digital computer, addresses (locations) of or-
       ders (instructions) and numbers (data) can be encoded
       and represented by binary numbers (bit strings).

The upper section of Figure 6.17 shows the mapping between Source and Target when R19 is applied to the ⟨Source, Target⟩ pair of Figure 6.17. The lower section describes the result after substitution has been effected. The crucial step in this mapping is the depiction (in Source) of a micro-order M_i at address i as a *vector* $(\mu_{i1}, \mu_{i2}, \ldots, \mu_{in})$ of size n (the number of distinct micro-operations) where μ_{ij} is either mj, an element of M, or $\neg mj$ (i.e., not mj). This vector can be held in correspondence to the vector $(b_{i1}, b_{i2}, \ldots, b_{ip})$ (in Target). The substitutions under the "method of solution" part follow almost automatically.

The question may arise as to whether we can further elucidate the manner in which this crucial step – that is, the seeing of a micro-order as a vector – may have taken place. We first note that the goal to map from Source to Target is the result of applying rule R19. This produces – after the appropriate instantiation – the inference, by modus ponens,

Source	Target
(1) *Function:*	(1) *Function:*
(a) Address of a micro-order $1 \le i \le m$	(a) Address of a micro-order $1 \le i \le m$
(2) *Goal:*	(2) *Goal:*
(a) M_i: Micro-order at address i $= \{m_{i1}, m_{i2}, \ldots, m_{iji}\}$, where $m_{ik} \in M$, $M = (m_1, \ldots, m_n)$	(a) Succ(i): successor to address i = a binary integer $[b_{i1}, b_{i2}, \ldots, b_{ip}]$ where $p = [\log_2 m]$
(b) That is, M_i = micro-order at address i $= [\mu_{i1}, \mu_{i2}, \ldots, \mu_{in}]$, where $\mu_{ij} \in \begin{cases} mj \\ \neg mj \end{cases}$	(b) That is, Succ(i) $= [b_{i1}, b_{i2}, \ldots, b_{ip}]$ where $b_{ij} \in \begin{cases} 1 \\ 0 \end{cases}$
(3) *Method of solution:* Implement using a diode matrix (a) Diode matrix of m rows × n columns (b) $d_{ij} = 1$ if $\mu_{ij} = mj$ $= 0$ if $\mu_{ij} = \neg mj$	(3) *Method of solution:* Implement using a diode matrix (a) Diode matrix of m rows × p columns (b) $d_{ij} = 1$ if $b_{ij} = 1$ $= 0$ if $b_{ij} = 0$

Figure 6.17. Mapping from Source to Target (action part of rule R19).

$$\frac{G17, R19}{I40: \quad G18}$$

the consequence of which is

G18: Establish a mapping between the known entities (in the *function* parts of Source and Target), *and* then substitute the known entities of Target for the corresponding known entities of Source in the *method of solution* part of Source.

We may note that there is no obvious mapping between (2)(a) of Source (in Figure 6.17) and (2)(b) of TARGET. However, given G18, a strenuous effort to *establish* such a mapping may be made.

Suppose Wilkes had drawn on the *method of solution* of Source to gain further insight. He may have appealed to the form of the diode matrix A (Figure 6.15) for clues and used the fact that each micro-order $M_i = \{m_{i1}, m_{i2}, \ldots, m_{iji}\}$ is actually *implemented* as a vector that *does* bear a correspondence with the bit vector for Succ(i).

One way in which this kind of reasoning may have been effected is by using "means–ends analysis," a very general, domain-independent problem-solving heuristic first proposed by Allen Newell and Herbert Simon (see Newell and Simon 1972; Simon 1981). This can be stated as:

> R20:   Means–ends analysis heuristic.
> *If*   the goal state is GS and the current state is CS,
> *Then*   establish the difference between GS and CS
>   *and*
>   then apply an operator that reduces the
>   difference.

The means–ends rule is an instance of a *grand* strategy that can be summoned when no other, more specific, rules are available. In the discussion that follows, I shall not give the details of the action sequence that would be generated when applying means–ends analysis to the problem at hand. Suffice it to say that the actions can be constructed at the cost of some tedium.

For the present problem, the current state may be described, based on entries (2)(a) and (2)(b) of Figure 6.17 as

Current:
(1) M_i: micro-order at address $i = (m_{i1}, m_{i2}, \ldots, m_{iji})$ such that $m_{ik} \in M = (m_1, \ldots, m_n)$
(2) Succ(i): successor to address i $= [b_{i1}, b_{i2}, \ldots, b_{ip}]$ where $b_{ij} \in \{0,1\}, p = [\log_2 m]$,

whereas the goal state, based on the first subgoal in G18 can be stated as

Goal: Establish a mapping or equivalence or correspondence between (representations of) M_i and Succ-(i).

The difference between Current and Goal can be stated as follows:[14]

(1) Each M_i is a variable element set, *not* a fixed-size vector.
(2) Each M_i specifies only the presence of micro-operations in the micro-order, *not* both the presence and the absence of micro-operations.

An *operator* that may be suggested from the *method of solution* for Source (entry (3) in Figure 6.17) is

Make M_i a vector of size n: $[\mu_{11}, \mu_{12}, \ldots \mu_{in}]$ such that
$\mu_{ij} = m_j$ if $d_{ij} = 1$ in "method of solution" for Source
      $= \neg m_j$ if $d_{ij} = 0$ in "method of solution" for Source.

Clearly, however, this operator must have been assimilated into Wilkes's knowledge body in order for it to be available for application. This raises the question as to how such an operator may have been identified at all.

Consider the following possibility: Assume the existence of a general rule for digital systems:[15]

R21:   *If*   an entity E_1 is in the form of a binary pattern
             and
             E_1 implements an entity E_2,
     Then E_2 may itself be (represented) in the form of a
             vector of elements that are present or absent ac-
             cording to the binary pattern.

Several obvious singular cases of this rule appear in the realm of digital systems.

There also exists a goal that is engendered as a result of computing the difference between Current and Goal states:

G19:   Make each micro-order M_i a fixed-size vector, showing
        both the presence and the absence of micro-operations.

G19 may cause R21 to be retrieved by spread of activation and the latter, when *instantiated,* by virtue of rule R-Inst5, according to the inference

$$\frac{\text{R21, F28 (A4, A5)}}{\text{I41:} \qquad \text{R21.1}}$$

yields the domain specific rule

R21.1:   *If*   each row i of a $(m \times n)$ diode matrix is in the
            form of (present and absent) diodes
            and
            each row i of the diode matrix implements a
            micro-order M_i (consisting of a set of micro-
            operations such that
            $d_{ij} = 1$ (d_{ij} is present) if mj is in M_i
              $= 0$ (d_{ij} is absent) if mj is not in M_i

Then M_i can be represented as a vector $(\mu_{i1}, \mu_{i2}, \ldots, \mu_n)$

where

$$\mu_{ij} = mj \quad \text{if} \quad d_{ij} = 1$$
$$\quad = \neg mj \quad \text{if} \quad d_{ij} = 0.$$

Thus, the subsequent inference, by modus ponens,.

$$\frac{\text{F28(A4, A5), R21.1}}{\text{I42:} \qquad \text{G20}}$$

produces the goal

G20: Represent each M_i as a vector of size n:$[\mu_{i1}, \mu_{i2}, \ldots, \mu_{in}]$ such that

$$\mu_{ij} = m_j \quad \text{if} \quad d_{ij} = 1$$
$$\quad = \neg m_j \quad \text{if} \quad d_{ij} = 0.$$

G20, then, is the operator used to reduce the difference when applying the means–ends rule. Figure 6.18 shows, in summary, the action sequence producing goal G20. This goal can be directly achieved and results in the entry (2)(b) of Figure 6.17. And as was noted earlier, once this crucial mapping or equivalence between the micro-orders M_i ($i = 1, \ldots, m$) in Source and the addresses Succ(i) ($i = 1, \ldots, m$) in Target is achieved, the *method of solution* shown in entry (3) for Target follows immediately.

I shall refer to this solution as diode matrix B, and Figure 6.19 summarizes the situation obtained thus far by juxtaposing the two diode matrices. The characteristics of matrix B can also be summarized (as F28 does in the case of matrix A) in the form of a fact:

F30: Diode Matrix B

B1: The successor address, Succ(i), to an address i of a micro-order is a binary integer $[b_{i1}, b_{i2}, \ldots b_{ip}]$ where $p = [\log_2 m]$ and $1, \ldots, m$ are the addresses of micro-orders.

B2: Each column j of the diode matrix represents a distinct bit position of the binary address.

B3: Each row i of the diode matrix will contain diodes for those bit positions in Succ(i) that are 1s, while diodes are absent (in row i) for those bit positions in Succ(i) that are 0s.

B4: A signal along row i will cause the selection of Succ(i).

Input	G19:	A goal about an entity (the micro-orders in a microprogram) being in a binary pattern.
	F28:	A set of facts about diode matrix *A*.
		*
Retrieve	R21:	A rule about an entity in a binary pattern implementing another entity.
Retrieve	R-Inst5:	
Apply	R-Inst5:	With R21 and F28 (A4, A5) as substitutions.
		*
Output	R21.1	A rule about a diode matrix consisting of a binary pattern of diodes implementing micro-orders.

- -

Input	R21.1 and F28:	
		*
Retrieve	R-ModusP:	
Apply	R-ModusP:	With R21.1 and F28 (A4, A5) as antecedents.
		*
Output	G20:	A goal about micro-orders being in binary patterns.

Figure 6.18. Action sequence producing goal G20.

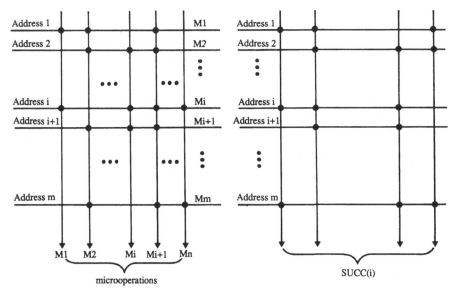

Figure 6.19. Coupled diode matrices D1.

Coupling the diode matrices

We now have the two matrix forms A and B. These may be collectively referred to as the matrix form D1. Figure 6.20 shows the state of the goal graph at this stage, with D1 appended at the appropriate location.[16]

D1 is clearly a design and is intended, as Figure 6.20 shows, to satisfy goals G7 and G8. However, as the goal graph further reminds us, G7 and G8 were both subgoals generated for the purpose of satisfying the earlier and more general goals:

G2: Design a control unit to be implemented in terms of a
     diode matrix.

G4: Specify the control unit in a stored program computer
     form.

Suppose that, at this stage, Wilkes had asked himself whether or not D1 *actually* satisfies G2 and G4. In order for such a question to arise, we postulate the following high-level general rule applicable to the realm of design.

R22: Misfit identification and elimination rule
      If   there exists a goal G specifying a requirement
               for an artifact
               and
               there exists a design D that is intended to satisfy
               G,
      Then   determine the misfit M(D, G) between D and G
               and
               then apply an action to eliminate or reduce M
               (D, G),

which might be retrieved by association with, or through spread of activation from, the design D1.[17] R22 in turn might cause G2 or G4 – which happen to be the highest-level common ancestors of G7 and G8 in the goal graph that led, respectively, to the A and B components of D1 – to be retrieved.

Suppose that G4 was the goal that was retrieved rather than G2.[18] Then, by modus ponens, the inference

$$\frac{\text{G4, D1, R22}}{\text{I43:} \quad \text{G21}}$$

would produce the goal

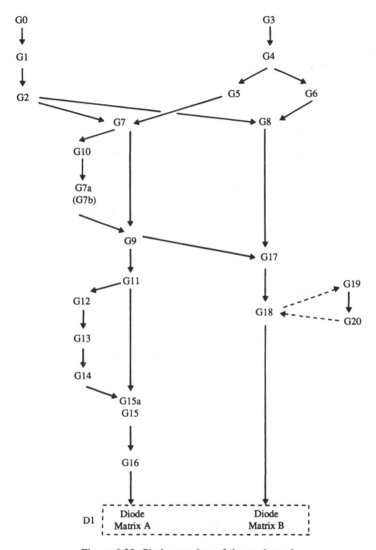

Figure 6.20. Sixth snapshot of the goal graph.

G21: Identify a misfit M(D1, G4) between design D1 and
goal G4
and
then apply an action to eliminate or reduce M(D1, G4).

In order to identify any misfit that might exist between D1 and G4, it will be
necessary to invoke *relevant* knowledge about the stored program computer

form. Clearly, such knowledge should be part of Wilkes's knowledge body and should include such facts as, for example, F9 and F24 and such rules as R3, R4, and R5. Thus, the very attempt to achieve G21 will cause diverse facts about stored program computers to be retrieved.

The various discussions of the EDSAC by Wilkes and his colleagues (Wilkes, Wheeler, and Gill 1951, p. 7; Wilkes 1956, p. 49 and 53; see also, the excerpts in the preceding section) include some EDSAC-specific facts concerning the temporal relationship between the *current instruction activation* and the *next instruction address selection* phases. It may reasonably be supposed, then, that the following empirical fact – a generalization of the EDSAC experience – was a token in Wilkes's knowledge body:

> F31: In a stored program computer form, the phases or
> events "current instruction (or order) activation" and
> "next instruction (or order) address selection" are ordered in time.

By *ordered in time* is meant that the *current instruction execution* phase begins (but does not necessarily end) before the *selection of the next instruction address* phase begins.

Given goal G4 – according to which the control unit is a kind-of stored program computer – and taking into account that the term corresponding to *order* in the case of the control unit is *micro-order,* F31 can be *instantiated* by appealing to R-Inst3, according to the inference

$$\frac{\text{G4, F31}}{\text{I44: \quad F31.1}}$$

the consequence of which is the fact

> F31.1: In a microprogrammed control unit, the phases or
> events *current micro-order activation* and *next micro-order address selection* are ordered in time.

This fact becomes relevant when testing for the presence of a misfit between the current design D1 and goal G4, for, if D1 is to satisfy G4, it must, inter alia, satisfy F31.1. And a comparison of D1 against F31.1 would reveal the following: Matrix A encodes the microprogram such that (according to F28) a signal along row i activates the micro-order at address i within the microprogram. Each row i of matrix B represents the successor address to the micro-order at address i, and a signal along row i of B causes the selection of the successor to address i (according to F30). However, the overall design D1 = {Matrix A,

Matrix B} *does not* satisfy the required temporal orderings of the events implemented by matrices A and B.

The misfit may, therefore, be stated as follows:

> There is no ordering in time between *current micro-order activation* in matrix A and *next micro-order address selection* in matrix B.

An appropriate operator or action that would eliminate this misfit can be stated in the form of the goal:[19]

> G22: Establish a relationship between matrices A and B such that a temporal ordering obtains between *current micro-order activation* in matrix A and *next micro-order address selection* in matrix B.

Now, the event *current micro-order activation from address i* is caused by a signal along row *i* of matrix A (according to F28). Likewise, the event *next micro-order address selection* – that is, the selection of Succ(i) – is caused by a signal along row *i* of matrix B (according to F30). These two cause–effect situations are depicted in Figure 6.21. Therefore, if the signal along row *i* of matrix A is *also* the signal along row *i* of matrix B, and row *i* of A precedes row *i* of B in the signal's path, then

(1) The signal will activate the current micro-order at address *i and* will select the next micro-order address, Succ(i), and
(2) The former event will be initiated before the latter event is initiated.

This situation can be characterized more precisely as follows. It uses a token of hardware-specific knowledge.

> R23: *If*   a signal activates (or is required to activate) a process/device/circuit P_1
>   *and*
>   a signal activates (or is required to activate) a process/device/circuit P_2
>   *and*
>   the activation of P_1, P_2 are to be ordered in time,
>   *Then*   pass the same signal *S* through P_1, P_2 such that P_1 precedes P_2 in *S*'s path,

which is retrieved by association with (or spread of activation from) goal G22. The deduction, by modus ponens,

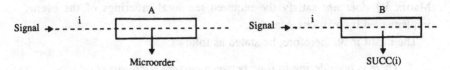

Figure 6.21. Relationship between a signal and the activations of a micro-order and a successor address.

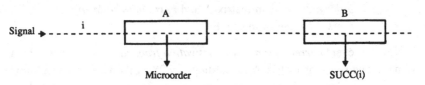

Figure 6.22. Realization of goal G24.

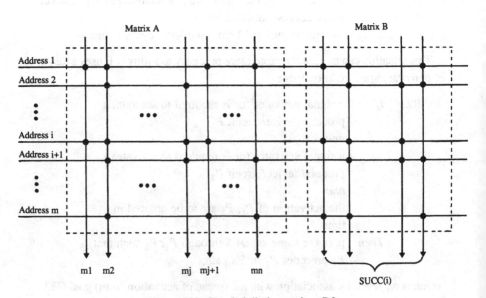

Figure 6.23. Coupled diode matrices D2.

$$\frac{\text{G22, F28(A4, A5), F30(B4), R23}}{\text{I45:} \qquad \text{G23}}$$

produces, as a consequence, the goal

G23: Pass signal along row *i* of matrix A to row *i* of matrix B such that row *i* of A precedes row *i* of B in the signal's path.

This goal, in conjunction with the hardware-specific rule

R24: *If*   a signal *S* is to pass through the processes/devices/circuits P_1, P_2
             and
             P_1 is to precede P_2 in *S*'s path,
    Then   connect P_1, P_2 in series

leads, by modus ponens,

$$\frac{\text{G23, R24}}{\text{I46:} \quad \text{G24}}$$

to the goal

G24: Row *i* of diode matrix A is (to be) connected in series to row *i* of diode matrix B.

This goal, when realized, is shown schematically by Figure 6.22. The resulting structure of the *coupled diode matrices* is depicted in Figure 6.23. This matrix complex will constitute and be referred to as design D2. Figure 6.24 shows the revised state of the goal graph after the appropriate insertion of D2.

The problem of alternative successor addresses

A revised design D2 having been obtained, we may postulate a second invocation of the misfit identification and elimination rule R22, applied to the goal G4 and design D2. The inference, by modus ponens,

$$\frac{\text{G4, D2, R22}}{\text{I47:} \quad \text{G25}}$$

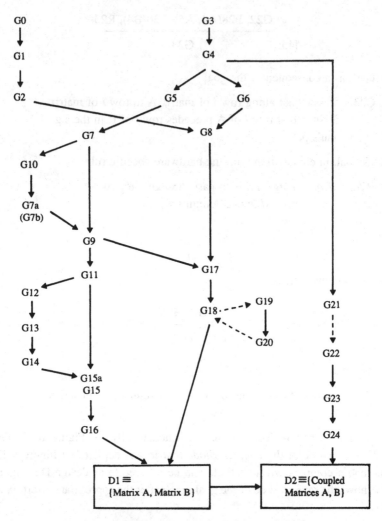

Figure 6.24. Seventh snapshot of the goal graph.

yields, as a consequence

G25: Identify a misfit M(D2, G4) between design D2 and
goal G4
and
then apply an action or operator to eliminate or reduce
M(D2, G4).

As in the earlier case of misfit identification (see goal G21), it may be necessary to invoke many kinds of knowledge associated with G4 – that is, tokens relevant to the stored program computer form. One such token is the following fact, which, it is quite reasonable to believe, will have been assimilated into Wilkes's knowledge body as a generalization extracted from both the EDSAC experience and other contemporary projects on computer design:

> F32: In an entity that is in the stored program computer form, it is possible to select between (at least) two alternative successor orders, Succ-1(i), Succ-2(i), to an order at address i, as a function of the state of some condition flag.

In fact, F32 is simply another way of characterizing the functional flexibility of the stored program computer form and was, tacitly, a basis for one of the original goals, G3 (see Chapter 5, section "Identifying a stored program computer-like form").

Given that a control unit is (intended to be) a kind-of stored program computer form (goal G4), the inference, by instantiation (invoking R-Inst3),

$$\frac{\text{F32, G4}}{\text{I48:} \quad \text{F32.1}}$$

produces the fact

> F32.1: In a control unit that is (intended to be) in stored program computer form, it is (or should be) possible to select between (at least) two alternative successor micro-orders, Succ-1(i), Succ-2(i), to a micro-order at address i, as a function of the state of some condition flag.

This fact is pertinent when testing for the presence of a misfit between D2 and G4; for, if the former is to satisfy the latter, it must, inter alia, satisfy F32.1. However, a comparison of D2 against G4 would reveal the following: Matrix A encodes the microprogram such that (according to F28) a signal propagated along row i activates the micro-order specified in row (i.e., address) i; and since row i of matrix A is connected to row i of matrix B (as per design D2), the same signal that passes along row i of A also selects the *single* address Succ(i) of the micro-order in address i (by F30).

Thus, the misfit, as identified, can be stated as follows:

In design D2, it is not possible to select between (at least) two successor micro-orders, Succ-1(i), Succ-2(i), to a micro-order at address i as a function of the state of some condition flag.

The operator or action most obviously suggested for eliminating this misfit can be stated in the form of a goal:

G26: Modify the design D2 such that one of (at least) two alternative successor micro-orders, Succ-1(i), Succ-2(i), to a micro-order at address i can be selected as a function of the state of some condition flag.

Consider now, the processsby which D2 may plausibly be modified so as to meet G26.

The design D2 engenders the following fact:

F33: In D2, matrix B is responsible for the representation and selection of the successor address, Succ(i), to a micro-order in row (address) i of matrix A.

This fact may be invoked by activation spreading from G26. We further postulate the presence and retrieval, by association with G26 and F33, of the rule

R25: *If*   there is a goal "An entity E is to satisfy some property P"
and
a component or subentity E_1 of E is known to be functionally responsible for a *related* property P_1,
Then modify the goal to "The subentity E_1 is to satisfy property P."

This rule is arguably somewhat more subtle than most of the general rules postulated thus far. Yet it merely captures the engineering notion that if a structure with a certain functional capability is already in place, then additions to such functions may be profitably effected by *modifying the existing structure* (rather than, say, by proposing a new structure). One can certainly identify singular instances of this rule. In the case of a particular computer, for example, suppose that the arithmetic unit (consisting of the pertinent combinational circuits and associated registers) performs the "add" and "subtract" operations. If the computer design is to be extended or modified so as to include the "multiply" operation, then the designer would first seek or attempt to modify the existing arithmetic unit rather than propose a new unit or attempt to augment some other part of the system.

R25, when instantiated (by appealing to R-Inst4) according to the inference

$$\frac{\text{G26, F33, R25}}{\text{I49:} \quad \text{R25.1}}$$

results in the rule

R25.1: *If*   the goal is "Modify D2 such that one of (at least) two alternative successor micro-orders, Succ-1(i), Succ-2(i), to a micro-order at address i (in matrix A) can be selected as a function of the state of some condition flag"
and
in D2, matrix B is responsible for the representation and selection of the successor address Succ(i), to a micro-order in row (address) i of matrix A,
Then   modify the goal to "Matrix B is to satisfy the property that one of (at least) two alternative successor micro-orders, Succ-1(i), Succ-2(i), to a micro-order at address i (in matrix A) can be selected as a function of the state of some condition flag."

Application of R-ModusP yields, according to the deduction

$$\frac{\text{G26, F33, R25.1}}{\text{I50:} \quad \text{G27}}$$

the goal

G27:   Modify matrix B so that one of (at least) two alternative successor micro-orders, Succ-1(i), Succ-2(i), to a micro-order at address i (of matrix A) can be selected as a function of the state of some condition flag.

Figure 6.25 summarizes the actions leading from G26 to G27.

Assuming the availability of the following rule pertaining to electrical circuits,

Input	G26:	A goal about modifying design D2 so as to satisfy a property (involving two or more successor addresses).
	D2:	A design involving two diode matrices.
		*
Retrieve	F33:	A fact about a component of D2 satisfying a related property (involving one successor address).
Retrieve	R25:	A rule (1) about a goal about an entity satisfying a property and (2) about a fact about a subentity of the entity satisfying a related property.
Retrieve	R-Inst4:	
Apply	R-Inst4:	With G26, F33, and R25 as substitutions.
		*
Output	R25.1	A rule (1) about a goal about D2 satisfying a property (involving successor addresses) and (2) about a fact about matrix *B* in D2 satisfying a related property (involving successor addresses).

- -

Input	R25.1, G26, and F33:	
		*
Retrieve	R-ModusP:	
Apply	R-ModusP:	With R25.1, G26, and F3 as substitutions.
		*
Output	G27:	A goal about matrix B in D2 satisfying a property.

Figure 6.25. Action sequence leading to goal G27.

R26: *If*   a signal along an electrical path *P* is to be transmitted along one of two alternative electrical paths *Q, R* based on the state of a device *D*,

    Then insert a switch in the circuit with input *P* and outputs *Q, R* and let the output of D be connected to the control input of the switch,

the instantiation, by appealing to R-Inst5,[20]

$$\frac{G27, R26}{I51: \quad R26.1}$$

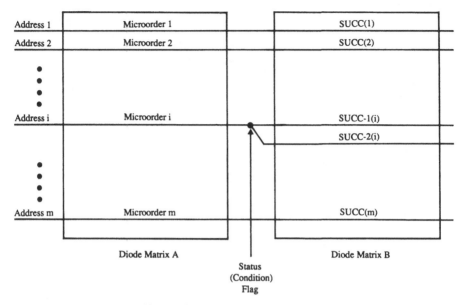

Figure 6.26. Coupled diode matrix D3.

yields

    R26.1:　*If*　　a signal along row *i* of matrix A is to be trans-
               mitted along (or selects) one of two alternative
               successor rows, Succ-1(i), Succ-2(i,) in matrix B
               based on the state of a condition flag,
        Then　insert a switch with input row *i* of matrix A and
               outputs Succ-1(i), Succ-2(i) of matrix B and let
               the outputs of the condition flag be connected to
               the control input of the switch.

By modus ponens, the inference

$$\frac{G27, R26.1}{I52: \quad G28}$$

produces the goal

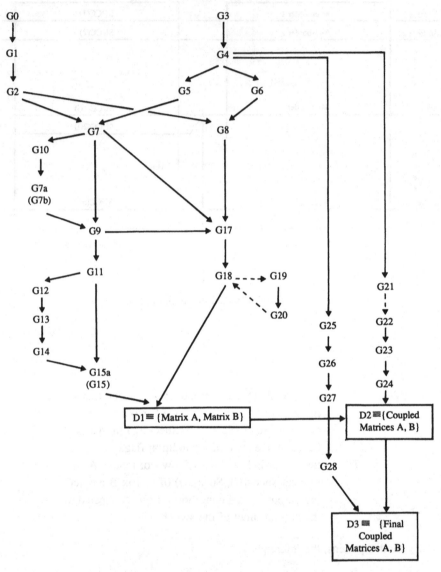

Figure 6.27. Final state of the goal graph.

G28:   Insert a switch with input row *i* of matrix A and outputs
       rows/addresses Succ-1(*i*), Succ-2(*i*) of matrix B and let
       the outputs of the condition flag be connected to the
       control input of the switch.

This goal, then, is the means whereby the design D2 can be modified in order to achieve G27. Its enaction leads to the final diode matrix complex D3, shown in Figure 6.26. This, of course, is the essence of Wilkes's model of the micro-programmed control unit (see Figure 3.11). Figure 6.27 shows the final state of the goal graph.

Notes

1. Henceforth, I shall use the words *microprogram, micro-order,* and *microinstruction* without parenthesizing the prefix *micro.*
2. It may seem odd to assert that F13 was part of Wilkes's knowledge body at a time when not a single instance of a microprogram was known to exist. However, the general nature of what such an entity would "look like" had already emerged by virtue of the inferred rule R4.1 (see chapter 5, section "Deriving the broad principle of microprogramming"; also, Table C in the Appendix). According to R4.1, a microprogram is a program – i.e., composed of a set of instructions or orders. Thus, there is nothing untoward in supposing that a fact about microprograms exists as a knowledge token even though microprograms have yet to come into being. One might think of F13 as (part of) a *specification* of what a microprogram has to be.
3. In 1931, Wilkes went up to Cambridge, where he took the Mathematical Tripos, graduating in 1934. As he records in his *Memoirs,* in pursuit of his long-standing interest in radio (acquired during his school days), he both read books and attended lectures on electronics and electrical engineering during his tenure as an undergraduate (Wilkes 1985, pp. 14–15). His postgraduate research, conducted at the Cavendish Laboratory – at that time, still headed by Lord Rutherford – was on radio physics and culminated in the completion of his Ph.D. in 1938 (Wilkes 1985, chap. 3). During the Second World War, Wilkes was a member of the British group responsible for the development and implementation of what later came to be known as radar (Wilkes 1985, chaps. 4 and 5). It was, perhaps, his wartime activities that led to his emergence as a practical-minded engineer and scientist with a strong pragmatic and empirical approach to research – traits very much in evidence in the subsequent developments of the EDSAC, programming techniques, microprogramming, and slightly later, the EDSAC-2.
4. A Boolean equation (named after George Boole, the nineteenth-century English mathematician and originator of this algebra) differs from other types of algebraic equations in that (1) its variables can only have "truth values," i.e., the values "true" or "false." More conveniently, these are represented by "1" and "0"; and (2) the basic operations that appear in it are the logical operations "AND" (denoted by "." here), "OR" (denoted by "+") and the negation or NOT (denoted here by "'"). Thus x' is 0 when the value of x is 1 and 1 when x is 0. $x.y$ has the value 1 when the values of x *and* y are 1; it is 0 otherwise. $x + y$ has the value 1 when either x *or* y has the value 1 or when *both* have values 1; it is 0 otherwise.
5. This particular truth table indicates, e.g., that $S = 1$ whenever $X = 0$ AND $Y = 0$ AND $C_i = 1$ OR when $X = 0$ AND $Y = 1$ AND $C_i = 0$ OR when $X = 1$ AND Y

$= 0$ AND $C_i = 0$ OR when $X = 1$ AND $Y = 1$ AND $C_i = 1$. Since $X = 0$ means that $X' = 1$ and so on, the above conditions, collectively, represent the equation for S in (FA).

6. The reader may recall the principal characteristics of the Whirlwind control unit by referring to Chapter 3, section "The Whirlwind and its control matrix" and, esp., Figure 3.10.

7. In the artificial sciences, such generalizations are not uncommon, particularly in the earliest stages of the evolution of a class of artifacts. A new design or concept for a particular artifact may become, in terms of some of its significant structural, behavioral, or functional features, a model, schema, or paradigm for a new class of artifacts, i.e., such significant features establish the defining characteristics of an artifact class. For example, the architecture of the stored program computer as enunciated by von Neumann (1945) and Burks, Goldstine, and von Neumann (1946) established the defining characteristics of the stored program computer in general. For that matter, the significant features underlying Wilkes's concept of the microprogrammed control unit defined, for at least some years, the architecture of microprogrammed control units in general (Husson 1970, chap. 2). Of course, such a state of affairs lasts only as long as new designs or concepts are not advanced as alternative competitive instances of the artifact category itself.

8. Strictly speaking, R12 will first be instantiated and it is the resulting instantiated version of R12 that will appear as an antecedent in the deductive inference leading to G7a. Thus far, all instantiations have been explicitly stated. Henceforth, unless a new instantiation rule of inference (of the type R-Inst1, R-Inst2, etc.) is to be demonstrated or the instantiation is nonobvious, the instantiation steps will be omitted from the explanation. That is, they will, henceforth, be mostly implicit.

9. It is fascinating to note the vacillation in the terminology of microprogramming. For, in his early writings, Wilkes is somewhat inconsistent in his use of such terms as "micro-order" and "micro-operation." In his 1951 paper, he first says:

Each operation called for by an order in the order code of the machine involves a sequence of steps which may include transfers from the store to control or arithmetic registers or *vice versa* and transfers from one register to another. Each of the steps . . . I will refer to . . . as a "micro-operation." Each true machine operation is thus made up of a sequence or "micro-programme" of micro-operations. (Wilkes 1986, p. 120)

Thus, here, Wilkes used "micro-operation" to mean what I have been referring to as *micro-order* and which later came to be called "microinstruction" – the modern standard term (see the section "The emergence of the microprogramming principle" in Chapter 3). Later in the same paper, however, Wilkes actually substitutes "micro-order" for "micro-operation":

The system as described would enable a fixed cycle of operations only to be performed. Its utility can be greatly extended by making some of the micro-orders conditional in the sense that they are followed by one of two alternative micro-orders according to the state of the machine. (Wilkes 1986, p. 120)

And, again:

The matrix A [see Figure 3.11, Chapter 3] contains sequences of micro-orders for performing all the basic operations in the order code of the machine. (Wilkes 1986, p. 120)

These uses of "micro-order" are clearly along the lines of the usage in the present text. In the next paper on the topic (Wilkes and Stringer 1953), we find, however:

The operation called for by a single machine order can be broken down into a sequence of more elementary operations. . . . These elementary operations will be referred to as *micro-operations*. Basic machine operations such as addition, subtraction, multiplication, etc., are thought of as being a *micro-programme* of micro-operations, each micro-operation being called for by a *micro-order*. (Wilkes 1986, pp. 121–2; italics in the original)

Thus, here, it seems that a "micro-order" is the specification of a command that causes an event, a micro-operation, to take place!
In the next paper from the Cambridge group (Wilkes, Renwick, and Wheeler 1958) – which discusses the design of the control unit of the EDSAC-2 – the terms "micro-programming" and "micro-programme" (*sic*) are basically abandoned (for reasons explained by the authors). Correspondingly, the terms "individual step" or "individual operation" are used instead of "micro-operation" or "micro-order." However, in a well-known paper published slightly earlier, Mercer (1957) makes a clear distinction between a micro-order (i.e., each horizontal line of Wilkes's original "matrix A"; see Figure 3.11, chapter 3) and micro-operations (the vertical lines in matrix A – i.e., the encoded constituents of a micro-order).
Finally, in a brief but important literature review of the topic published a decade later, Wilkes (1969) uses the standard term "microinstruction" to mean the earlier "micro-order." And yet, even in this relatively late paper there remains ambiguity in his use of "micro-operation" since this word is used here to denote the event or the effect of a microinstruction! For a complete discussion of the terminology of microprogramming, the interested reader may refer to Dasgupta (1979, 1989a, chap. 5).

10. The EDSAC was an "accumulator"-based computer, which also included an additional multiplier register. The EDSAC arithmetic instructions changed the states of the accumulator and/or the multiplier register. The STORE instruction changed the state of memory words (Wilkes, Wheeler, and Gill 1951; Wilkes 1956).
11. The goal G9, shown as one of the antecedents in this inference, actually serves two functions in the (implied instantiation and the subsequent) deduction by modus ponens: It provides the subgoal that "the microprogram . . . is to be implemented in terms of (or by) a diode matrix" – which matches the first *If* part of R14; it also provides the (rephrased) subgoal that "an address (in a microprogram) will hold (or encode) a set of micro-operations corresponding to a single micro-order" – which matches the third *If* part of R14.
12. Holland et al. (1986), esp. chap. 10, is a detailed discussion of the general nature of analogical reasoning. Hesse (1966) discusses the role of analogy in scientific reasoning. Langley et al. (1987) describe how analogy was embedded in their BACON.5 program and used in "discovering" Joule's law for the conservation of energy. Thagard (1988) discusses the place of analogical reasoning in his PI system.
13. This representation is an adaptation of the slightly more elaborate representation suggested by Holland et al. (1986).
14. This, of course, is not the only difference between Current and Goal states. An alternative is defined by the pair of assertions:

(1) Succ(i) is a fixed-size vector, *not* a variable element set.

(2) Succ(i) specifies both $b_{ij} = 1$ and $b_{ij} = 0$, *not* merely $b_{ij} = 1$.

However, if this difference had been identified first and an attempt was made to reduce it by changing the representations of Succ(i) to conform to that of M_i, it is reasonable to believe that this would have led to a failure. Eventually, the more fruitful difference already identified would have been pursued. My account of the invention process does not discuss failures or blind alleys.

15. This obviously is not the only general rule of digital systems. There are others, corresponding to the different ways in which binary patterns are used to represent and implement different states of affairs, e.g., sequences of high and low voltages, "yes" and "no" responses, magnetized and nonmagnetized states.

16. The goals G19 and G20 are shown here as placed outside the main graph since, as will be recalled, they were generated in the course of applying means–ends analysis. Computationally speaking, these goals may be viewed as having been generated during a subroutine (or, more appropriate to this discussion, subprocess) call!

17. Karl Popper's (1968, 1972) theory of the scientific method can be schematically summarized as

$$P1 \to TT \to EE \to P2,$$

where P_1 is a given problem situation, TT is a tentative theory advanced as an explanation for P1, EE is the process of error elimination applied to TT, and P2 is the resulting new problem situation (Popper 1972, p. 145). In Dasgupta (1989c, 1991), it is suggested that design problem solving in general follows an evolutionary pattern along the lines of Popper's model. The schematic for design is

$$R1/D1 \to CT \to MI \to ME \to R2/D2$$

where R1/D1 is a complex consisting of a set of *requirements* R1 and a *design* D1 that has been proposed in response, CT is a *critical test* (to determine whether D1 meets R1), MI is the *identification of a misfit*, and ME signifies the *elimination* (or reduction) *of the misfit* – which may entail modifying the design, modifying the requirements, or both – thereby producing R2/D2, a new requirements/design complex. In the present context, R1/D1 consists of the goal G4 together with the matrix form D1 = {matrix A, matrix B}.

If this evolutionary model is indeed a universal characterization of design problem solving – and there is considerable empirical evidence to believe this to be the case (Dasgupta 1991) – then the misfit rule R22 is very likely to be a part of most engineers' knowledge body. In fact, it can be seen that the misfit rule is a special case of the means–ends rule, R20.

The claim of universality of evolution as an intrinsic property of design processes has been further asserted by Dasgupta (1992) in the form of a law of design called the *hypothesis law*, according to which a design process that reaches completion does so through one or more cycles of hypothesis creation, testing, and (if necessary) modification.

18. G2 would, of course, be trivially satisfied by D1. Thus, had G2 been selected rather than G4, the application of the critical test rule would have yielded a null misfit.

19. Keeping in mind that the misfit identification and elimination rule R22 is a special case of means–ends rule R20, the identification of the misfit and that of the

operator or action for its elimination can be conducted along the lines described earlier for applying the means–ends rule.

20. This instantiation is shown here in a slightly simplified form. It relies on the fact that (1) every row of matrix A is an electrical path, (2) every row i of matrix B is an electrical path, (3) a row i of matrix B is referred to as Succ(i) because it encodes the successor address of the micro-order in row/address i of matrix A, and (4) a signal along row i of matrix A propagates along row i of matrix B.

Finally, given that R26 is a rule about general entities "electrical paths P, Q, R" and "device D" satisfying the property "signal P to Q or R as a function of D," the instantiation relies on the goal G27, which stipulates that the particular entities "row i of matrix A, rows Succ-1(i), Succ-2(i) of matrix B" and "condition flag" satisfy the property "signal from row i of matrix A to Succ-1(i) or Succ-2(i) of matrix B as a function of the condition flag."

Part III

Reflections on the nature of inventing

7

Eight hypotheses about the nature of inventing

There we have it: an account – an explanation – of how a particular act of inventive design in the domain of one particular science of the artificial might have taken place. The explanation takes the form of a computation at the level of cognitive description known as the knowledge level. Just as the proof of a theorem stated as an organized, stepwise set of arguments is an explanation of why the theorem is (believed or should be believed by an individual or community to be) true, so also our explanation takes the form of a symbolic process – that is, a structured set of symbol-transforming actions. Extending this parallel further, just as a mathematical argument draws on a body of assertions (axioms, lemmas, and theorems) that are assumed or known to be true prior to the onset of the argument or are produced along the way, so also the process described in these pages appeals to a corpus of knowledge the tokens of which are in part postulated to have existed at the time Maurice Wilkes began to think about the problem and in part generated by the process itself.

Let us, at this stage, recall a point already emphasized in Chapters 1 and 4. Historical episodes of a certain type bear the stamp of contingency. Past episodes of cognitive acts such as the invention of a theory or the design of a new type of artifact belong to this category. Thus, any explanation of such an episode will inherit the burden of contingency. We can hardly ever claim that the episode *must* have happened in one particular way rather than some other. One can only seek to construct, with the benefit of hindsight, a causal account that is, in some sense "better" than its competitors, consistent with what we know of the circumstances, and founded on assumptions that are plausible under the circumstances.

Thus, if we ask the question, How can one *test* the knowledge-level process I have advanced as an account of Wilkes's thought processes? we have to answer that insofar as theories about contingent events do not lead to prediction, the "standard" approach – in which one deduces observable or measurable consequences of the theory – cannot be applied. In the case of this particular case study, this means that we cannot apply the usual methodological criteria of the experimental sciences to make any claims about the validity of the explanation. We *can*, however, advance the following two claims:

(1) The computation-based explanation of the invention of microprogramming suggested here is founded on facts, rules, and actions that, to a large degree, are both individually *plausible* and collectively *consistent* (i.e., noncontradictory), given the documented circumstances surrounding the state of computer design circa 1950 and given what is known of Wilkes's academic and professional background. It is precisely by these criteria, namely, the extent of the plausibility and the consistency of the supporting evidence, that one tests the validity of historical explanations.

(2) A knowledge-level, computation-based explanation of the kind presented in the preceding two chapters offers an account of a particular act of scientific creativity that is considerably more detailed and specific (and, therefore, more testable in the sense just mentioned) than any other presently known modes of explanation for creative phenomena.

Both claims – in particular, the issue of the plausibility of the knowledge ascribed to Maurice Wilkes and the advantages of the detailed computational account relative to other accounts of creative acts – will be discussed further. However, if these two claims *are* valid and have evidential support, then they constitute, I think, sufficiently compelling reasons for us to take the computational theory of creativity seriously – in which case, the question of immediate interest is *What have we learned (or can we learn) about the process of inventing in the artificial sciences and about the nature of creativity in general from this single case study?* This chapter is comprised of some reflections pertinent to this question.

Invention as a goal-directed endeavor

In essence, the entire process, beginning with goal G0 to develop a control unit that would be easy to design, maintain and repair, and ending with the coupled diode matrix form D3, is captured by the goal graph, the final state of which is shown in Figure 6.27. I shall refer to this final graph as GG.

A goal graph, it will be recalled, reveals the dependencies or the causal structure between goals in the sense that a directed edge from a goal (node) Gi to goal (node) Gj implies that the achievement of Gi depends on, or is effected by, the attainment of Gj. Gj may be referred to as a subgoal for Gi, or alternatively, we may call Gi a *parent* goal and Gj a *daughter* goal.

The suggestion that we can explain how Wilkes may have invented the microprogramming principle in terms of an organized network of goals and the achievement of such goals lends support to the thesis that creative processes are *purposive, goal-directed,* or *teleological* in nature. By *teleological* I do not, of course, refer to some unseen or hidden *final* cause; quite the contrary, in fact! By *teleological* I simply mean that such processes are governed by the identification of ends and the determination of means to achieve such ends.

The goal-directedness of creative thinking is an idea that constitutes what I believe is one of the core elements in D. N. Perkins's (1981) highly eclectic study of creativity; Gruber's (1981) investigation of Darwin's development of the theory of evolution concludes with the similar notion of "creative thought" as "the work of purposeful beings." The picture I have painted of Wilkes in the foregoing pages is one in which Wilkes, beginning with a given objective, goal, or problem, determines what requires to be done to satisfy the goal, sets up the latter as a subgoal or new problem, identifies what needs to be done to achieve the subgoal, and so the process continues. At every stage, *the inventive process is driven, controlled or directed by the immediate goal on hand.* Like Gruber's Darwin, the portrait is one of Wilkes as a highly purposeful being. In this particular sense, the process of invention or that of highly creative design is no different from any other process of problem solving – an observation that is in accordance with the hypothesis, framed three decades ago by Newell, Shaw, and Simon (1962), that creative thinking is only a special kind of problem-solving behavior.

Goals as working hypotheses in inventive design

A further characteristic of the goal graph GG worth noting is that, for the most part, each goal spawned (and, in consequence, was dependent on) only a very small number of daughter goals. Referring to Figure 6.27, we see that G7 generated three daughters, and G2, G4, and G9 each generated two subgoals; the other goals in GG produced one daughter each. Conversely, each goal was the daughter of a small number of parents. In particular, G17 had three parents, G7, G8, and G15 each had two, and the others had only one each.[1]

If we accept GG as a plausible expression of the way in which microprogramming came into being, the graph suggests not only the goal-directedness of the inventive act, but also that the pursuit of the original goal (G0) was conducted in a narrow, focused manner. That is, success was attained by pursuing a rather small number of trails. At several points, the trail was linear, as, for example, when G0 produced G1 and G1 produced G2 or as in the sequences (G12, G13, G14), (G25, G26, G27, G28), and (G21, G22, G23, G24). Thus, to add to the emerging portrait of Wilkes, this would suggest that in addition to being purposeful and goal-oriented, he was *highly focused* in his endeavor. Whether this has any general significance for our understanding of the creative act is not entirely clear. The matter, however, is worth exploring, even if only briefly, for reasons I shall shortly make clear.

Consider, with reference to GG, the goal sequence (G0, G1, G2), in which, it will be recalled, the goals are as follows:

G0: To develop a control unit that is easy to design, maintain, and repair.

G1: Design a control unit that has a simple, repetitive, and regular structure.

G2: Design a control unit to be implemented in terms of a diode matrix.

We see here a train of ideas that is entirely linear. Superficially, this seems to suggest a highly confident and knowledgeable agent who did not *need* to refine G0 into more than one goal (i.e., G1) or to produce more than one daughter (i.e., G2) from G1. However, this was unlikely to have been the case. We know that Wilkes was working on a problem that, as far as was known to him, had not been previously recognized, let alone been solved. Thus, Wilkes could hardly have *known* that G1 was the "right" subgoal of G0 or that G2 was the "right" subgoal of G1.

An alternative interpretation is that, given G0, Wilkes invoked (through either rational/conscious or nonrational/unconscious means)[2] tokens from his knowledge body that enabled him to identify, *as a working hypothesis,* goal G1 as a subgoal of G0. Likewise, given the need to achieve G1, he established, as a working hypothesis, G2 as a subgoal.

Working hypotheses are᾽ *highly provisional* in form; by their very nature, they serve as *means to making progress* in solving problems. Clearly, progress can be best made by postulating and working with one or, at most, a very small number of hypotheses at one time. This was precisely the role that the generation of G1 and G2 played in this sequence.

The gradualistic nature of an insight

The literature on creativity is replete with anecdotal evidence of the place of sudden insight, mental leaps, or "Eureka" moments in creative thinking.

Among the most celebrated of these – in addition, that is, to the original Eureka experience attributed to Archimedes – are the poet Samuel Taylor Coleridge's account of how a fragmented poem "Kubla Khan" came to be written in 1797[3] and Henri Poincaré's (1913/1946) recollections of the circumstances attending his discovery of a particular class of mathematical functions (see the section "Metaphors as explanatory models," Chapter 1). Indeed, in his still widely quoted lecture "Mathematical Creation," Poincaré gives several examples of the suddenness with which mathematical ideas came to him.

The extent to which thinkers on creativity have, in the past, ascribed a central role to moments of sudden insight is best exemplified by the four-stage Helmoltz–Poincaré–Wallas–Hadamard model (discussed in the section "Metaphors as explanations of creativity," Chapter 1) in which the *illumination* step occupies the central place in the act of creation.

In recent years, largely as a result of detailed historical and psychological research into particular creative episodes, some writers have rejected, at least in the cases of the episodes they have studied, the validity of the very idea of sudden insights or great mental leaps as being the sine qua non of the creative act.

Consider, for example, the case of Darwin's theory of evolution. According to Darwin's own account in his *Autobiography,* the key moment in the development of his theory was when he read Malthus's *An Essay on the Principles of Population* (6th edition, 1826) in September 1838. It was this that apparently provided him immediately with the idea of natural selection.[4] However, Gruber (1981, pp. 168–74), in discussing this "great Malthusian moment," has pointed out that contrary to Darwin's later recollections, his notebook for that period (specifically, the entry for September 28, 1838, the day of the Malthusian moment) gives no indication that this was a moment of Eureka-like illumination that immediately transformed his thinking. In a more recent article in which this episode is again discussed, Gruber (1989) concluded that the Malthusian moment was significant insofar as it allowed Darwin to *recognize* an idea that had almost been within his grasp for some time.

As another example, Holmes's (1985) study of Lavoisier's work on respiration and other aspects of biochemistry – to which I alluded at some length in Chapter 1 – concludes with his observation that what might at one level of abstraction appear to be a great leap of conceptual insight can be shown, on more detailed inspection, to consist of a protracted series of small steps.

In the case of microprogramming, as I have already described in Chapter 3, the development of Wilkes's ideas seemed to have begun during or after the summer of 1949; and the solution was at hand by the winter of 1950. There is no documentary evidence to indicate the occurrence of a Eureka-like moment except, possibly, his remark in the *Memoirs* that "sometime during the winter [of 1950] the ideas fell into shape" (Wilkes 1985, p. 128). Yet if one were to "step back" (as it were) and read the conventional historical account of the matter – as I have presented, for instance, in Chapter 3 – one is tempted to think of the falling "into shape" of the ideas as *the* moment of illumination; for, given the problem at hand, it would appear that the two principal ingredients, namely, the use of a diode matrix and the need for the flexibility of a stored program computer, *combined* in some fashion to produce the solution.

What the computational mode of description reveals is that *it is possible to explain episodes of great insight or Eureka-like events in gradualistic terms*. In fact, the goal graph GG is a record of how one particular "moment" of illumination might have occurred. The transition from the goals

G2:   Design a control unit to be implemented in terms of a
         diode matrix,

G3:   The control unit must be functionally flexible,

to the design D3 (Figure 6.26) seems indeed a large leap. The transition to D3 from G3 and the other original goal

G0:   To develop a control unit form that is easy to design,
         maintain, and repair,

seems a still greater leap. The goal graph shows that this "leap" is composed of an organized and interdependent set of considerably smaller changes.

On the mechanics of "bisociation" or the combining of ideas

While discussing computation as a metaphorical model of the creative process in Chapter 1, I remarked on the widely held view that an essential ingredient of the creative act is the effective combination of possibly disparate or uncon-nected ideas (see, e.g., Livingstone Lowes 1927; Hadamard 1945; Gruber 1981; Perkins 1981; Johnson-Laird 1988a). This particular attribute was made the central element by Koestler (1964) in his theory of creativity under the name of "bisociation."

Koestler's *Act of Creation* is arguably one of the most monumental studies of the creative process. Its dense, rich complex of ideas and examples from such diverse domains as humor, technical invention, artistic endeavor, and science remains, I think, unmatched in the literature on creativity; in spite of Medawar's (1964) severe criticism of this work, no student of creativity can afford to ignore it.

Following the Helmoltz–Poincaré–Wallas–Hadamard line of thinking, Koestler associates creativity with the unconscious combining of ideas drawn from different domains: "The creative act . . . does not create something out of nothing; it uncovers, selects, reshuffles, combines, synthesizes already existing facts, ideas, faculties, skills" (p.120). "Bisociation" is the name he gives to the mechanism or process whereby such combination or synthesis comes about. As a preliminary to this notion, Koestler introduces the idea of "frames of reference" or "planes" or, as he later called them, "conceptual *matrices.*" By "matrix," Koestler meant "any ability, habit or skill, any pattern of ordered behavior governed by a *code* of fixed rules" (p. 38; italics in the original). The perception of an idea or a situation in the creative act entails the linkage of that idea not just to a single matrix – as it is, according to Koestler, in the case of routine skills – but to (at least) two normally incompatible or disparate matrices. The idea or situation is then said to be *bisociated* with the two matrices:

I have coined the term "bisociation" in order to make a distinction between the routine skills of thinking on a "plane," as it were, and the creative act which, as I shall try to show, always operates on more than one plane. (p. 135)

Furthermore, "The bisociative act connects previously unconnected matrices of experience" (p. 45).

Koestler's overall analysis of the act of creation is not unlike the Helmoltz–Poincaré–Wallas–Hadamard scheme. His main point of departure lies in his notion of conceptual matrices (or frames of reference, schemata, mental structures, etc.) and the place of bisociation in the creative act. He gives several examples of (his interpretation of) bisociation.

(1) Gutenberg's invention of the printing press involving, as matrices, printing from wooden blocks by rubbing and the winepress.
(2) Kepler's discovery of the laws of planetary motion: Here, the relevant matrices were the descriptive geometry of astronomy and the (then) known principles of physics.
(3) Darwin's theory of evolution. In this case, according to Koestler, there were three relevant matrices: first, the "evolutionists' credo" that the various species in the animal/vegetable kingdom had not been independently created but had descended as varieties from other species; second, the principle of artificial selection; and last, Malthus's theory of population.

There is unfortunately, a distinctly archaic air to Koestler's language – sufficiently so to make the scientist uneasy. Metaphors of the more airy sort abound. This raises the question as to the testability of his ideas. One way of testing his theory would be to examine in detail the very examples Koestler cites in much the same way historians of science and technology examine such events and determine whether the historical data is consistent with Koestler's interpretation.

However, independent of such investigations, there remains the serious problem that Koestler leaves unexplained the *mechanics* of bisociation. I suggest that computational explanations offer considerable insight into how ideas may combine (or, equivalently, matrices may bisociate).

Considering once more the case of Wilkes's invention, it was noted (see, e.g., the preceding section) that the idea of microprogramming emerged as a result of combining two essential and very unrelated ideas, namely, the use of the diode matrix for effecting regularity, order, and structure in electronic artifacts and the employment of the stored program computer form for realizing flexibility or variability in control signal sequences. In Koestlerian terms, the bisociation of these two conceptual matrices resulted in the microprogrammed control unit. The mechanics of this bisociation happens to have been described in detail by the knowledge-level process discussed in Chapters 5 and 6. We see, in fact, that the combination of these two "grand" ideas can be explained in terms of a series of more elementary knowledge-level actions in which an action entails, first, the *retrieval of tokens* (by association and activation spreading) and then *inferences,* resulting in new goals, rules, or facts as output. The latter then enters as input to further actions, and so on.

The role of logic and reasoning in acts of creation

This brings us to what is perhaps the most surprising and, to some, the most controversial implication of the computational theory of creativity: the idea that reasoning and logic may play a key and ubiquitous role in the creative process – at least in the domain of invention, discovery, and design.

To many, logic or reasoning is the very antithesis of creativity. I have already referred, in Chapter 1, to Karl Popper's (1934/1968) dismissal of the process of discovery from his "logic of scientific discovery." Medawar (1964), in his critical review of *The Act of Creation,* protested against Koestler's description of the creative act as involving the selection or combining of existing ideas by remarking that the act of creation so conceived is not creative at all.

Among recent writers on this topic, the educational psychologist D.N. Perkins (1981) is certainly one who has sought, through his protocol-based empirical studies, to refute the belief that reasoning is anathema to creativity.

As he put it, following an analysis of one of his experimental subjects who wrote a poem and others who solved a mathematical puzzle, "Far from being contrary to insight, reasoning is an important means to insight, and often a neglected one" (1981, p. 71).

However, it is only when we enter the realm of computation that we can see quite explicitly *how it is possible for logic and reasoning to serve as means to creative ends.* Consider the situation, for example, in which an agent, posed with a series of observed values for a set of variables, is seeking to determine whether there is a mathematical relationship among the variables and, in the event there is, the form of this relationship. Herbert Simon, Pat Langley, and their co-workers have referred to this as "data-driven" discovery (Langley et al. 1987; Qin and Simon 1990), and it reminds us of a philosophy of science – according to which one begins with a body of singular instances and seeks a theory, a generalization, that explains the instances – often referred to as "inductivism."[5] While inductivism as *the* theory of the scientific method has fallen entirely into disrepute, the underlying strategy – namely, generalizations from observed instances – remains one of the common approaches for reasoning, not only in everyday affairs but also in science.

In their important book *Scientific Discovery,* Langley et al. (1987) explored in great detail the nature of the reasoning that might serve to effect data-driven discovery in the natural sciences. Their principle vehicle was a collection of rule-based computer programs (called BACON GLAUBER, STAHL, and DALTON), which successfully uncovered, inductively, several quantitative and qualitative laws in the physical sciences.

Since our present concern is the question of how logic and reasoning can participate in creative acts, it is sufficient to consider BACON.1 and its derivation of Kepler's third law of planetary motion.[6] This law, it may be recalled, is of the form

$$T^2 = KR^3,$$

where T is the period of any given planet, R is the mean orbital radius of that planet, and K is a constant, having the same value for *all* planets.

BACON.1 is given a series of pairs of (T, R) values, and it applies a sequence of heuristics or rules to derive the law. Of particular interest are the program's rules for inferring regularities:

(1) Constant:

    If   the goal is to find laws

and

the variable *V* has the same value *u* in all cases,

Then   infer that *V* always has the value *u*.

(2) Linear:

If   the goal is to find laws

and

there exists a set of values for the variable *X*

and

there exists a set of values for the variable *Y*

and

the values of *X*, *Y* are linearly related with slope *M* and intercept *B*,

Then   infer a linear relationship between *X*, *Y* with slope *M* and intercept *B*.

(3) Increasing:

If   the goal is to find laws

and

there exists a set of values for the variable *X*

and

there exists a set of values for the variable *Y*

and

the absolute value of *X* increases as the value of *Y* increases

and

these values are not linearly related,

Then   consider the ratio of *X* and *Y*.

(4) Decreasing:

If: the goal is to find laws

and

there exists a set of values for the variable *X*

and

there exists a set of values for the variable *Y*

and

the absolute value of *X* increases as the absolute value of *Y* decreases

and

these values are not linearly related,

Then   consider the product of *X* and *Y*.

Using both idealized data and the actual data used by Sir Isaac Newton as a basis for his verification of Kepler's third law, Langley et al. (1987) describe how, using these (and other) rules, BACON.1 succeeds in discovering the law.

The hypothesis we are tempted to form is that such rules become, through both conscious and unconscious means, assimilated into the scientist's (or the scientifically trained person's) knowledge body in the course of his or her education and training. The scientific problem solver then draws on and applies these rules whenever posed with a problem of the kind presented to BACON.1[17] This hypothesis is supported by Qin and Simon's (1990) protocol studies of human subjects, who, given the same kind of data for *T* and *R*, were required to determine a mathematical relationship between the variables. Of the nine subjects, five were undergraduates in science or engineering, one was a graduate student in physics, one an engineer, and the remaining two graduate students in art history and education, respectively. The subjects had no knowledge of the source of the data or of their physical significance. Only two of them, a freshman and the physics graduate student were able to discover Kepler's third law, while the electrical engineering student came close. The others failed.

Qin and Simon found, from the protocol analysis, that all nine subjects applied rules resembling BACON.1's Constant and Linear heuristics. Procedures similar to Increasing and Decreasing were also used frequently, though not to the same extent by all subjects: The successful subjects used these rules more, and more successfully, than the others. In general, Increasing was used more frequently than Decreasing.

From the perspective of this book, the significant point about these studies of scientific law discoveries – and others conducted by Lenat (1976, 1977) in mathematics, Kulkarni and Simon (1988) in biochemistry, and Thagard (1988) in physics – is not that scientific discovery can be automated but that they allow us to uncover and identify explicit rules of reasoning that may be fundamentally instrumental in the creative discovery process. This is a far cry from Popper's (1934/1968) flat denial of there being a logic in the discovery process.

This brings us back to Maurice Wilkes and microprogramming. If we admit the plausibility of the knowledge-level account given in Chapters 5 and 6, then, if asked whether there is a discernible logic or evidence of reasoning in this particular act of invention, the answer must be an emphatic *yes.* Furthermore, the foundations for this act of invention lie in the set of *inference rules,* which are the most general and domain-independent of all the tokens in the knowledge body postulated for Wilkes (see Appendix, Table A) and which facilitate the inference of new rules or (less often) new facts.

Let us recapitulate the general nature of these rules. They consist of four classes:

(1) *Instantiation rules,* which allow the instantiation or particularization of a general rule or fact in the context of a particular situation. An example is the rule

R-Inst1:   *If*   R is a rule-about a class of entities C_1
                   and
                   entity class C_2 is (postulated to be) a kind-of C_1,
           Then R is (postulated to be) a rule-about C_2 (after
                   substitution of terms/concepts from C_2 in C_1).

(2) *Rules of deduction,* which are the rules of classical (deductive) logic. In this particular case study, the one most frequently used is modus ponens:

R-ModusP: *If*   a fact or goal or rule A is the case
                   and
                   there is a rule "*If* A is the case, *Then* the fact
                   or rule or goal B is the case,"
           Then establish B as a fact or goal or rule.

(3) *The rule of abduction,* which is of the form

R-Abd: *If*   P is a problem to be solved/goal to be achieved,
                   and
                   there exists a rule "*If* the proposition H is the
                   case/subgoal H is achieved, *Then* P is
                   solved/achieved,"
           Then (Assume) H is the case/subgoal,

and which allows hypotheses or subgoals to be established "retroductively."

(4) *Generalization rules,* which are the main means by which general rules or facts can be induced from particular instances. An example is

R-Gen4:   *If*   for all known entities e that are a kind-of entity
                   E there are predicates A, B such that $A(e)$ and
                   $B(e)$ are known to be the case
                   and
                   the number of co-occurrences of $A(e)$ *and* $B(e)$
                   is significantly large,
           Then assume the rule *If* $A(E,)$ *Then* $B(E)$."

In contrast to the other less general or more domain-specific rules used by the process, no justification has been provided to support the presence of these rules of inference in Wilkes's postulated knowledge body. Simply stated, no justification seems necessary. The implicit claim is that rules such as these are acquired, certainly by those with a scientific background, but also by most humans in the course of everyday problem solving.

In addition to the inference rules, other general, domain-independent heuristics that are appealed to include R20 (means–ends analysis) and R22 (the misfit identification and elimination rule (see Appendix, Table C).

One rather surprising aspect of the computational process described here is the fact that abduction appears only twice in the fifty-two inferences shown; it was used to generate goals G1 and G4. (See Chapter 5, section "Identifying a stored program computer-like form.") This was surprising in the sense that this writer had expected, having been influenced strongly by Norwood Russell Hanson's (1958) suggestion that abduction is the fundamental mode of inference in discovery (see Chapter 1, section "The significance of philosophy of science"), a prominent role for this inference rule in the inventive process under study. This belief had been further strengthened by March's (1976) view that in the domain of the artificial sciences, the "logic of design" was fundamentally abductive. This case study clearly indicates otherwise. Each of the other forms of inference was used more frequently than was abduction.

To conclude, as in the case of discovery in the physical sciences as described by Langley et al. (1987) and others, we see that invention or highly creative design in the artificial sciences can be explained in terms of a *logic of invention and design*. Such a logic is not strictly deductive, though deduction is one of its elements. It is comprised of many different kinds of very general rules that allow inferences to be made. But unlike strictly deductive inferences, these inferences are not formally or provably correct. Rather, they are tentative and subject to empirical tests; they are potentially falsifiable. The logic of invention, like that of discovery in the natural sciences, is not inexorable in nature. However, it allows progress to be made in a reasoned manner. Perhaps most significantly, the rules of inference cited in the preceding chapters, along with the means–ends and misfit identification rules, appear to be no different from or at variance with the kinds of rules that are applied to more mundane or less creative types of problem solving, even those of everyday life.

On the richness and quality of the knowledge body

However, whereas the logical basis of the inventive process consists of a small number of quite commonplace inference rules, the amount and the variety of the total knowledge body is seen to be considerable (see Appendix, Tables A, B, and C). Furthermore, when one follows the process described in Chapters 5 and 6, one notices that most of the tokens (excluding the inference rules) are used only once in the course of the process. There is certainly no parsimony in the use of knowledge.

In Tables B and C of the Appendix, some indication as to the general nature of the tokens are given. Broadly speaking, the knowledge tokens are either *assumed* (labeled "A") to have existed in Wilkes's knowledge body at the start of the process or are generated or *inferred* (labeled "I") in the course of the process. In a few cases, namely, F28, F30, and F33, the facts are true "by construction" – that is, by virtue of having been designed, (labeled "D").

In addition, the facts can be organized into the following types:

(1) Facts that are *known empirically* to be true. That is, there exist certain entities in the world with certain objectively determinable properties. Examples include:

> F5: In the MIT Whirlwind, each arithmetic operation (bar-
> ring multiplication) involves exactly eight pulses issued
> from a control unit implemented in the form of a diode
> matrix.

> F9: An order interpreter is a kind-of computer component.

These are facts pertaining to (the then) extant computers or known hardware principles.

(2) Facts that pertain to *concepts* and may be thought to be true. Such facts signify that there exist certain entities in the physical world that exhibit certain abstract, conceptual, or value-related (and, therefore, subjectively perceived) properties. Examples are:

> F2: Difficulty of design, maintenance, and repair constitutes
> a negative property of an artifact.

> F6: EDSAC's order interpreter is simple, repetitive, and
> regular.

These facts, though pertaining to conceptual properties (e.g., "negative property of," "simple in structure") also relate to (the then) extant computers or hardware principles.

(3) Facts that are *hypothesized* to be empirically true. That is, certain entities are postulated to exist though they actually do not (at least at the time being considered) – these may be referred to also as *theoretical* entities – and to which certain properties are attributed such that if the theoretical entities

were to exist, these properties could be tested for their presence or absence. Examples include:

F13:   A microprogram is an encoded structure of symbols.

F25:   In a (microprogrammed) control unit, a micro-order
       when executed will cause a state change in the relevant
       registers or memory words in the computer.

Both facts refer to such entities as microprogram, micro-order, micro-programmed control unit, of which (at the time) there were no instances in the physical world. They are, thus, theoretical entities until such time as a microprogrammed control unit is in existence or (at the very least) has been designed.

(4) Facts that are hypothesized and pertain to *concepts.* That is, certain entities are postulated to which certain conceptual properties are attributed. Examples include:

F15:   A microprogram is more abstract than a diode matrix.

F21:   Addresses in a microprogram and rows in a control-
       diode matrix are structurally similar.

Both facts refer to the (then) hypothetical or theoretical entity micropro-gram and to such conceptual properties as "more abstract than," and "structurally similar."

It may be remarked here that the distinction between empirical and conceptual facts is not always clear. For example, the fact

F0:   Extant control units are difficult to design, maintain,
      and repair because of their complexity

is described in Table B of Appendix as being empirical. One could argue that a property such as "difficult to . . . " is vague and subjective, and hence, F0 is really a conceptual fact. Nevertheless, the categories just identified, even though fuzzy to some extent, provide a useful framework for understanding the kinds of knowledge employed.

Along a very different dimension, each of the tokens in the knowledge body can be assigned to one of a number of distinct conceptual *domains,* which, by and large, form a hierarchy of abstraction levels. These domains and their relationships are shown in Figure 7.1; roughly speaking, they become more abstract upward. The single-bordered rectangles signify concepts that were already in place at the time Wilkes began to think about microprogramming (see also Figures 3.3, 3.4, and Chapter 5), while the double-bordered box at the

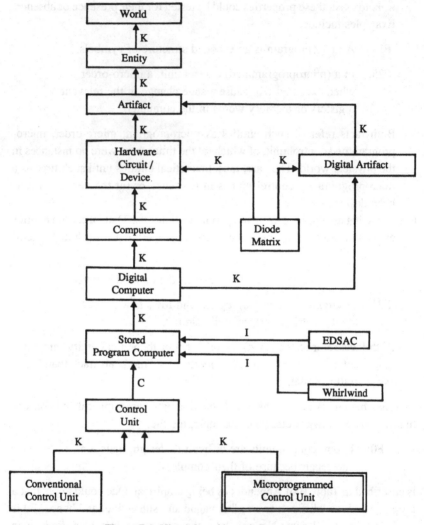

Figure 7.1. Hierarchy of knowledge domains.

bottom signifies the addition to the network resulting from the invention of the microprogramming concept.

Figure 7.2 lists all the knowledge tokens according to the relevant domain. Note that since some of the tokens are relevant to more than a single domain, they accordingly appear in more than one row of the table.

Two other characteristics of this knowledge body also deserve attention:

Domain/level	Assumed	Inferred
World	R-Inst1, R-Inst2, R-Inst3, R-Inst4, R-Inst5, R-ModusP, R-And, R-Abd, R-Gen1, R-Gen2, R-Gen3, R-Gen4, R19, R20, R22	
Entity	F3; R6, R8, R9, R10, R11, R12, R13, R14, R15, R16, R17, R18, R25	
Artifact	F1, F2, F3, F12; R0, R1, R4, R5, R7	R3.1
Hardware circuit	R23, R24, R26	
Diode matrix	F14, F18, F19, F21, F26	F15, F17, F20, F22, F23, F27; R2, R8.1, R9.1, R9.2, R10.1, R11.1, R21.1
Digital artifact		
Computer	F9; R3	R2.1
Stored program computer	F24, F31, F32; R3, R4, R5, R7	R2, R3.1
EDSAC	F4, F6, F8	
Whirlwind	F5, F7, F8, F10, F18, F19, F26	
Control unit	F0, F1, F10, F11	F32.1; R0.1, R0.1.1, R1.1, R2.1.1, R3.1.1, R4.1, R5.1, R7.1, R9.1, R9.2
Microprogrammed control unit	F13, F21	F15, F16, F17, F22, F23, F28, F30, F31.1, F33; R10.1, R11.1, R21.1, R25.1, R26.1

Figure 7.2. Knowledge tokens – by domain.

(1) It includes a sizeable chunk of facts and rules that have nothing to do with computers, digital circuits, or hardware per se. Rather, it refers to properties or characteristics of artifacts in general and, even more sweepingly, of "entities" in general. Thus, if we desire to seek a larger insight into the

nature of invention and design from this particular case study, one such insight is that *engineering knowledge* – the knowledge that is brought to bear in design problem solving, especially of the more innovative kind – encompasses far more than the design knowledge pertaining only to the relevant class of artifacts. It also includes, in particular, rules or facts pertaining to abstract relationships between properties of things in general (e.g., F2, F15, R6, R8, R9, and R10), to the causal connection between function, structure, and behavior (e.g., R13, R15, and R18), and to the taxonomic relationship between entities and artifacts (e.g., F1, F3, and F12).

(2) Every token used in the process described was *qualitative* in nature. According to conventional wisdom, modern engineering is grounded securely on the bedrock of mathematics. The practice of design is *calculational* and *mensurative* in nature – and parts of it have been so since the Middle Ages (Pacey 1992). Yet if we are to believe that Wilkes's invention of the microprogramming concept was along the lines of the process described in the preceding two chapters, not a single token of knowledge pertaining to calculation or measurement was necessary in arriving at the form of the microprogrammed control unit. We may surmise that at least in the realm of *inventive* design, where new artifactual concepts and forms are at stake, *qualitative* reasoning and knowledge may be of more significance than their quantitative or calculational counterparts. The latter obviously becomes more important in the case of *detailed* design or in the realm of less innovative or more routine design.

To conclude then, the broad picture that emerges is of a Maurice Wilkes who freely draws on *a wide variety of knowledge tokens spanning across many different domains and levels of abstraction* as and when required to advance the solution to his particular problem.

On an assumption concerning the retrieval of knowledge

It will be recalled that the computational process described here is founded on a knowledge-level theory of creativity. At the knowledge level, the means by which tokens are accessed or retrieved are transparent. All that is admitted about the knowledge body is that "it is there" and that its tokens are accessible, as well as that, at the knowledge level, an action – which, as we have seen, involves the retrieval of facts and rules from the knowledge body and the application of the rules – is performed according to the principle of rationality and constrained by bounded rationality.

The one assumption made about the general nature of the retrieval of knowledge is that it is *associative* and entails the *spread of activation* (see section "Spreading activation," Chapter 4). This assumption has at least one important implication for our understanding of the nature of the creative process. Consider, for example, the very first action described in Chapter 5 (Figure 5.1). Here, given an input fact

F0:   Extant control units are difficult to design, maintain, and repair,

several tokens are retrieved by association and activation spreading:

F1:   A control unit is a kind-of artifact.

F2:   Difficulty of design, maintenance, and repair constitutes a negative property of an artifact.

F3:   An artifact is a kind-of entity.

R0:   *If*   an artifact demonstrates some negative or disad-vantageous character,

    Then   establish as a goal/problem the elimination of that character.

R-Inst1:   *If*   R is a rule-about a class of entities C_1

    and

    entity class C_2 is (postulated to be) a kind-of C_1,

    Then   R is (postulated to be) a rule about C_2 (after substitution of terms/concepts from C_1 in C_2).

As Figure 5.2 indicates, several distinct activation sequences can be discerned in the retrieval process:

(1) F0 activates the concept "control unit" which in turn activates F1; F1 activates the concept "artifact."

(2) F0 activates the concept "difficulty of design, maintenance, and repair," which, in turn, activates F2; F2 activates the concept "negative properties of artifact."

(3) The concept "artifact" and "negative properties of artifact" together activate R0; R0 activates the concept "rule about entities."

(4) F1 activates the concept "kind-of fact."

(5) The concepts "artifact" and "kind-of fact" together activate F3, which in turn activates the concepts "entity" and "kind-of fact."

(6) The concepts "kind-of fact," "entity," and "rule about entities" together activate R-Inst1.

The point is, of course, that from any given concept (including facts or rules), many other very different concepts could have been activated. These other, possibly false trails are not part of the process shown here for the reason that the documentary records give no clues as to whether any such false trails were at all pursued.[8] The activations described are exactly those that allow us to explain how a particular inference (to rule R0.1) took place. Our computational account or model of Wilkes's act of invention remains silent about why these particular activation sequences took place and not others.

However, this account does provide what I think is one quite crucial insight about this particular act of creation and, possibly, about creativity in general: Not only does the proposed model presuppose a rich and varied knowledge body (as discussed in the preceding section), but also it suggests *an ability (and a willingness) on the part of our "postulated" Wilkes to roam freely across the span of knowledge* using the mechanisms of association-by-activation spreading – to have "an open mind" as it were – so that no knowledge token, however seemingly remote from the immediate goal or fact on hand, is discounted or rejected out of hand.

The eight hypotheses

Suppose we allow ourselves the luxury of extrapolating from this one case study. Then, in response to the question, What have we learnt about the nature of invention and discovery and about creativity in general? we may sum up the situation by formulating the following hypotheses:

(H1) *Inventing – that is, creating an original artifactual form – is a goal-directed, purposive, or teleological endeavor.* In this regard, the process whereby a new form is brought into being appears no different from more mundane design activities – or, for that matter, from problem-solving processes of any kind.

(H2) *Acts of creation, at least in the realm of the (artificial and natural) sciences are opportunistic in nature.* Thus, although the overall process may be goal directed, the goals (or subgoals) are provisional or tentative: Goals are working hypotheses, and because of bounded rationality, there are no guarantees that either (1) a goal will, in fact, be satisfied in the future or (2) a goal, even if satisfied, is in fact the appropriate or "correct" descendent of an earlier goal.

(H3) *Large insights are composed of a possibly intricate but describable network of small steps.* Acts of creation by humans, like those of nature, are incremental or gradualistic.

(H4) Creative acts or processes certainly seem to entail the combination or the bisociation of apparently unrelated ideas – and this seems a criterion whereby creative acts can be distinguished from acts that are noncreative. However, *such combinations or bisociations are explicable in terms of quite commonplace rules of inference* – of the kind that participate in more mundane problem solving and even everyday reasoning.

(H5) *Creative processes are reasoning processes* in the sense that they involve the use of rules of inference and other general rules such as means–ends analysis and the misfit identification and elimination heuristic to make progress, to bring into existence new rules and facts, and to generate goals.

(H6) *Acts of creation, at least in the domain of the sciences, are knowledge intensive.* They entail access to and retrieval from a broad, rich spectrum of knowledge ranging from tokens highly specific to the domain or task at hand to the most abstract, even philosophical, propositions. We surmise that this knowledge intensiveness is one of the critical ways in which creative processes may differ from processes considered as noncreative.

(H7) The creative agent is not only knowledge rich; *he or she also has the capability to freely and associatively wander about the knowledge space and retrieve whatever tokens seem related to the goal at hand.* As in (H6), it is conjectured that this is also one of the central ways in which creative acts (and agents) are distinguishable from their more humdrum counterparts.

These hypotheses are by no means the only ones that characterize acts of creation. Nor is it claimed that they apply to domains outside the natural and the artificial sciences. These hypotheses are, however, the ones that emerge most significantly from this particular case study. Furthermore, they have the considerable merit of being translatable into computational terms (since it is from the computational model that they arose in the first place), which means that as general hypotheses they can be tested and possibly refuted by conducting further cognitive-computational studies of actual episodes of invention and discovery.

In fact, we already have other prior experiments the results of which are entirely consistent with these hypotheses. The BACON series of programs developed by Langley et al. (1987), which discovered several of the fundamental laws in the physical sciences; Kulkarni and Simon's (1988) KEKADA system, which reconstructed Hans Krebs's discovery of the biochemical mechanism for urea synthesis; and Thagard's (1988) PI system, which was able to invent the wave theory of sound, all provide powerful corroboration of each of the hypotheses (H1)–(H7).

The suggestion that (H1)–(H7) apply to both the discovery of natural laws and the inventive design of artifactual forms implies the presence of a strong connection between science and design. Such a connection had been recognized before in a slightly different context by Dasgupta (1991), who, in a recent work on the theory of design, advanced the proposition named the *design-as-scientific-discovery (DSD) hypothesis,* according to which

> Design problem solving is a special instance of (and is indistinguishable from) the process of scientific discovery.

The argument for the DSD hypothesis rested on the observation that although it is mostly true that the *aims* of the natural and the artificial sciences differ, one should not confuse the differences in aims for differences in *methodology.* Thus, the DSD hypothesis, if accepted as valid, would signify that science (i.e., the natural sciences) and engineering (i.e., the artificial sciences) share a methodological basis; they are methodologically indistinguishable.

The reasoning advanced in support of the DSD hypothesis involved, first, presenting a "reference" model of science that was itself a synthesis of the theories of Kuhn (1962, 1970a, 1970b), Popper (1934/1968), Hanson (1958), Lakatos (1978), and Laudan (1977) and then constructing a model of the design process that (1) was consistent with what we know about design and (2) was strongly isomorphic to the reference model of science.

However, neither the reference model of science nor the model of design addressed the issue of how, given a scientific problem, a theory is initially born or how, given a design problem, a design is initially formulated. The DSD hypothesis is essentially concerned with the factors that influence the *subsequent* fate of theories and designs – in fact, with Reichenbach's celebrated context of justification. (See Chapter 1, section "The significance of philosophy of science".)

Our concern in the present study has been the context of discovery, or, rather, the context of discovery and invention. Thus, if the seven hypotheses (H1)–(H7), which are generalizations founded on a particular instance of invention in the *artificial* sciences, are indeed supported by studies of the discovery process in the *natural* sciences, then this suggests yet a further general principle about the nature of creativity, namely:

> The process of inventing artifactual forms (or creating original designs) in the artificial sciences is cognitively indistinguishable at

the knowledge level from the process of inventing theories or discovering laws in the natural sciences.

By "is cognitively indistinguishable at the knowledge level" is meant that exactly the same cognitive features attend the knowledge-level processes of creativity in both the natural and the artificial sciences. These features are, at the very least, the ones described as hypotheses (H1)–(H7).

Let us call this the *central hypothesis of scientific creativity.* To those who have investigated creativity from a computational perspective, this hypothesis is hardly surprising. It is an obvious corollary to CTSC, the computational theory of scientific creativity. (See Chapter 2, section "A computational theory of scientific creativity: the hypothesis".) Nevertheless, the central hypothesis is worth stating explicitly if only for its directness and because it abstracts away from computational influence. The central hypothesis can be tested by appealing to (H1)–(H7): If it can be shown that a given act of invention or discovery satisfies each of (H1)–(H7), the central hypothesis is (further) corroborated. If, on the other hand, a particular instance fails to satisfy one or more of (H1)–(H7), it will be held up to doubt (if not peremptorily abandoned, as the "pure" Popperian would have it). Like the lesser hypotheses on which it rests, the central hypothesis is falsifiable.

Notes

1. In the formal language of the mathematical theory of directed graphs, this means that the "outdegrees" and "indegrees" of goal nodes were one, two, or three.
2. See the section "Problem recognition and formulation" in Chapter 5 for a discussion of nonrational actions and their relationship to unconscious thinking.
3. According to the "Kubla Khan" story, Coleridge had apparently been ill and was living at the time in the country. One afternoon, he took an "anodyne" and fell asleep while reading a book describing Kubla Khan's capital city. He slept deeply for about three hours in the course of which he dreamt of images and associated expressions. Upon waking, he recalled distinctly the whole dream and was able, instantly, to write down the poem.
   Coleridge's account of this episode (reprinted in Ghiselin's [1952] anthology) and, in particular, the suddenness with which the poem came about has since been challenged by John Livingston Lowes (1927). For a brief discussion of the "Kubla Khan" episode, the reader may consult Perkins (1981).
4. The original manuscript of Darwin's autobiography (which he called "Recollections") was dated May 31, 1876. Its most recent version, *The Autobiography of Charles Darwin, 1804–1882,* was edited and published in 1958 by Nora Barlow, Darwin's granddaughter (Clark 1984).
5. Inductivism, also called the "inductive model of science," is usually associated with the name of the late sixteenth/early-seventeenth-century thinker and man of affairs Francis Bacon – to the extent that inductivism is also referred to as the

Baconian method. In actual fact, inductivism can be traced back to such medieval scholars as Roger Bacon, John Duns Scotus, and William of Occam and even further back to Aristotle (Losee 1980). Its more modern exponents were the Victorians John Herschel, William Whewell, and in particular, John Stuart Mill (Losee 1980; Harré 1985)

6. BACON is the collective name given to a series of six programs or program versions. To give some idea about their capabilities, the first of the BACON programs, BACON.1 discovered Boyle's law, Kepler's third law, Galileo's law and Ohm's law. BACON.3 discovered, in addition, the ideal gas law and Coulomb's law. BACON.4 discovered Ohm's law, Archimedes' principle, Snell's law of refraction, Black's specific heat law, the conservation of momentum principle, and Newton's law of gravitation.

7. Thomas Kuhn (1970a, 1970b) in later clarifications of *The Structure of Scientific Revolutions* (1962) noted that one of the essential components of what he called "paradigms" was "exemplars or shared examples." These are the actual problem–solution complexes that the students of a particular scientific discipline encounter in the course of their apprenticeship and that serve to sharpen the students' abilities to solve problems in the relevant disciplines. Kuhn insists, however, that exemplars play yet a deeper role in the "upbringing" of a scientist. He suggests that in the course of dealing with exemplars relevant to a particular topic, the student learns to traverse among several alternative "symbolic generalizations" (e.g., different forms of the same law) attending the discipline.

   Kuhn's own example is taken from Newton's second law of motion which, in addition to its standard form, $F = ma$, is represented as $mg = m(d^2s/dt^2)$ in the case of free fall and by $mg \sin\theta = ml(d^2\theta/dt^2)$ in the case of the simple pendulum.

   In solving a problem in that discipline, the student learns to recognize which symbolic generalizations are relevant in given situations. Exemplars are, thus, means of acquiring *ways of seeing* and *intimately knowing* a discipline. BACON.1's rules are, similarly, ways of inferring based on assimilation of intimately known rules of inference.

8. Apropos this point, in answer to my question to Wilkes about the extent to which he considered or explored or searched alternative approaches to the problem, his response was that he did not consider any alternatives to the one he did adopt (i.e., the one involving the use of diode matrices). Thus, there was no significant search in the course of his thinking about the problem. This would seem to imply that, at least at the more general level, there were no false trails (meeting with M. V. Wilkes, Olivetti Research Laboratory, Cambridge, December 19, 1991).

8

Epilogue

This brings us to the end of this particular inquiry. We began with a central concern: the nature of creativity as it is manifested in the development or design of artifacts. Not all acts of design count as creative acts. Like ideas and theories about nature or works of literature and art, the creation of artifacts is deemed *creative* when the outcome is *original* in some sense. Drawing on a distinction made by Johnson-Laird (1988a), Boden (1991), and others, we saw that it is possible to establish criteria of originality either from the perspective of the individual agent or from that of the society or community to which the agent belongs. When the outcome of an act of design is an artifactual form that satisfies one or more of the criteria of originality, the design act is called *inventive* or *creative* design. More simply, we call it *invention*. Inventing artifactual forms corresponds to discovering laws or inventing theories about natural phenomena. Thus, it seemed reasonable to suppose that studies of creativity in the natural sciences might provide insight into the nature of creativity in the sciences of the artificial.

We saw that philosophy of science, having been primarily preoccupied with the logic of justification, had little to contribute to our inquiry. Fortunately, there has emerged in relatively recent times a new kind of inquiry into scientific activity that draws on the ideas of cognitive psychology, history of science, and artificial intelligence; it was to these sources we turned.

There next arose the issue of methodology. How should or can one investigate creativity? The history of the subject tells us that one might resort to introspection as such luminaries as Poincaré, Helmoltz, Kekulé, and Hadamard have done. A second approach is to conduct studies of human subjects under laboratory conditions, in vitro, as it were. This was what Perkins (1981) did, at least in part, as also Qin and Simon (1990). Yet another strategy is the case study approach in which particular acts of creation or significantly creative periods in the lives of particular persons are studied in detail.

Richard Ellman's (1982) biography of James Joyce and his analysis of the development of T. S. Eliot's *The Waste Land* (1988), Rudolph Arnheim's (1962) study of the birth and growth of Picasso's "Guernica," John Livingston Lowes's (1927) dissection of Coleridge's "Kubla Khan" and *The Rime of the Ancient Mariner,* and Linda Jeffrey's (1989) study of Wordsworth's writing (and rewriting) of *The Prelude* are all instances of this approach from the literary and painterly worlds. Howard Gruber's (1981) examination of Darwin, Holmes's (1985, 1989, 1991) investigations of Lavoisier and Hans Krebs, and Arthur Miller's (1986) work on the role of imagery in the thinking of Poincaré, Einstein, Neils Bohr, Ludwig Boltzmann, and Heisenberg are important examples of the case study approach in the realm of the sciences. Finally, although Root-Bernstein's (1989) remarkable recent book is somewhat more encyclopedic in scope then those just cited, much of its general thesis on scientific creativity is based on detailed studies of particular scientists such as the chemists Svante Arrenius, Claude Berthollet, Wilhelm Ostwald, and Van't Hoff and such figures from the biological field as Pasteur, Darwin, and Claude Bernard.

The merit of this approach is that it is firmly rooted in the history of the person or of the particular episode of interest. The historical data provides an empirical anchor from which the investigation can never stray too far. This was the approach chosen here. A particular achievement that took place in the relatively early days of computer design, the invention of microprogramming by Maurice Wilkes, became the vehicle of this investigation.

The circumstances surrounding the genesis of microprogramming is unusual among episodes in the history of computing in that it has been rather well documented by the originator himself, not only through the usual channels of scientific communication, that is, papers in scientific journals and conference proceedings, but also by virtue of several retrospective accounts including – what is quite a distinctive element in the history of computing to date – a personal memoir. Unfortunately, computer design as a research field is not a laboratory science in the classical sense that physics, chemistry, and biology are: Thus, Wilkes did not maintain anything in the nature of a laboratory notebook for the relevant period. He did keep diaries, however, during his travels in Europe and North America. Since his deliberations on the problem that eventually led to the concept of microprogramming partially coincided in time with his (second) visit to the United States in the summer of 1950, one might be justified in hoping that Wilkes's diary of the U.S. trip would reveal some of his thoughts on the matter. My examination of this diary proved disappointing in this regard. Thus, the documentary roots of this study are located entirely in the published papers and articles, the *Memoirs,* a videotaped lecture on the topic, as well as several personal conversations and correspondence between this writer and Wilkes.

Science is conducted within certain "worldviews." Kuhn (1962, 1970a, 1970b) called such worldviews "paradigms," and this term and the complex of concepts associated with it have prevailed. Others, in critical response to Kuhn's original concept, have referred to the slightly different notions of "research programs" (Lakatos 1978) and "research traditions" (Laudan 1977). Investigating creativity within a setting that we claim to be "scientific" is no exception in this regard. We need a paradigm to which we subscribe and within which we can systematically study our subject matter. In the case of this work, the paradigm is provided by the computational metaphor and takes the shape of a knowledge-level computational framework. To be sure, the adoption of a paradigm may smack of scientific relativism (Laudan 1990) in the sense that there is the danger that one's analysis and comprehension, the choice of evidence and the mode of interpretation, are all a function of, and relative to, the paradigm. But paradigms or research traditions survive only as long as they are useful and there are no other competing and more effective alternatives. Science is a problem-solving activity; theories and hypotheses and their containing paradigms prevail only if they offer solutions to problems that are better (in some sense) than their rivals. Paradigms are, thus, heuristic devices. The computational paradigm – and CTSC, the theory of scientific creativity that derives from it – is no exception. It provides a powerful language and a set of formal symbol manipulation tools for the investigation of cognitive phenomena.

This raises the specter of the old debate: When it comes to theorizing about the human mind, even the mention of computation is – and has been ever since Turing's (1950) celebrated article – controversy-prone (see, e.g., Dreyfus 1979; Searle 1984); the primary objection, of course, is to the very idea that computers can "think," "exhibit intelligence," "be creative," and so on. However, that particular debate is not germane *at all* to the issues covered in this book. We can only reiterate what was stated in Chapter 1: The computational metaphor is precisely that – a metaphor that can serve as an aid, a scaffolding, for thinking about creativity as other metaphors are employed in thinking about problems in chemistry, physics, evolution, and other disciplines. (See Chapter 1, section "Metaphors as explanatory models" et seq.) In this sense, the explanatory model constructed in these pages of Wilkes's invention of microprogramming is entirely in keeping with – indeed, is framed within – the computational or (as some prefer to call it) information-processing paradigm that guides and informs cognitive psychology and cognitive science (Lachman, Lachman, and Butterfield 1979; Anderson 1983; Simon and Kaplan 1989; Newell 1991).

What has emerged from this approach insofar as this particular case study is concerned is, first, a plausible description of a cognitive process whereby Maurice Wilkes, given his specific circumstances, his weltanschauung, might have arrived at the idea of microprogramming. Second, it led to a set of generalizations stated in the form of the seven hypotheses, (H1)–(H7) in Chapter 7, which, we assert, characterize creativity in the artificial sciences. These in turn, being entirely consistent with what others have discovered in the natural sciences, led, finally, to an eighth and somewhat broader proposition – the *central hypothesis* of scientific creativity – which simply claims that the processes whereby discoveries are made about the natural world and those by which we invent new artifactual forms are of a kind.

It hardly needs to be said that the systematic study of creativity in the sciences has only just begun. Having said that, it must also be noted that albeit "only just," it has *indeed* begun. We now have descriptions of processes whereby laws such as Boyle's and Kepler's can be discovered (Langley et al. 1987), the wave theory of sound can be invented (Thagard 1988), paradigm shifts such as the ones brought about in chemistry in the eighteenth century and geology in this century, can be explained (Thagard 1990; Thagard and Nowak 1990), biochemical pathways can be elucidated (Kulkarni and Simon 1989), and, now, a principle of computer design can be invented. Collectively, they constitute what we believe is the embryo of a testable theory of scientific creativity and, by consequence, a new philosophy of the natural *and* the artificial sciences.

Appendix

Table A. *Inference rules*

I. Instantiation rules

R-Inst1

If   R is a rule about a class of entities C_1
and
entity class C_2 is (postulated to be) a kind-of C_1,

Then   R is (postulated to be) a rule-about C_2 (after substitution of terms/concepts from C_2 in C_1).

R-Inst2

If   R is a rule about an entity class C possessing a type-of property P_1
and
type-of property P_2 is a kind-of P_1,

Then   R is a rule about C possessing type-of property P_2 (after substitution).

R-Inst3

If   F is a fact about a class of entities C_1
and
entity class C_2 is (postulated to be) a kind-of C_1,

Then   F is a rule about C_2 (after substitution).

R-Inst4

If   R is a rule about arbitrary entities $E_1, E_2, \ldots$, possessing properties $P_1, P_2, \ldots$, respectively
and
particular entities $e_1, e_2, \ldots$, possessing (or postulated to be possessing) $P_1, P_2, \ldots$, respectively,

Then   R is a rule about $e_1, e_2, \ldots$ (after substitution).

R-Inst5:

If   R is a rule about arbitrary entities $E_1, E_2, \ldots$, related by one or more predicates $P_1, P_2, \ldots$
and
particular entities $e_1, e_2, \ldots$, are (postulated to be) related by $P_1, P_2, \ldots$,

Then   R is a rule about $e_1, e_2, \ldots$ (after substitution).

II. Deduction

R-ModusP:

If   a fact or goal or rule A is the case
and
there is a rule "*If* A is the case, *Then* the fact or goal or rule B is the case,"

Then   establish B as a fact or goal or rule.

217

R-And:	*If*	a fact (goal) (rule) A is the case
		and
		a fact (goal) (rule) B is the case
	Then	the fact (goal) (rule) A *and* B is the case.

III. Abduction

R-Abd	*If*	P is a problem to be solved/goal to be achieved
		and
		there exists a rule "*If* the proposition H is the case/subgoal H is achieved, *Then* P is solved/achieved,"
	Then	(Assume) H is the case/subgoal.

IV. Generalization

R-Gen1:	*If*	an entity e is an instance-of or a kind-of entity E
		and
		there are predicates A, B such that A(e) and B(e) are known to be the case
		and
		there is no known entity e' that is an instance-of or a kind-of E such that A(e') and ¬B(e') is known to be the case
		and
		the variability of B with respect to A is known to be low,
	Then	assume the rule "*If* A(E), *Then* B(E)."

R-Gen2:	*If*	an entity e is an instance-of or a kind-of entity E
		and
		there are predicates A, B such that a rule of the form "*If* A(e), *Then* B(e)" is known to be the case
		and
		there is no known entity e' that is an instance-of or a kind-of E such that a rule of the form "*If* A(e'), *Then* ¬B(e')" is known to be the case
		and
		the variability of B with respect of A is known to be low,
	Then	assume the rule "*If* A(E), *Then* B(E)."

R-Gen3	*If*	an entity e is a kind-of (or an instance-of) entity E
		and
		there is a predicate A such that A(e) is the case
		and
		there is no known entity e' that is a kind-of (or an instance-of) E such that ¬A(e')
		and
		the number of instances of E is low,
	Then	assume the fact A(E).

R-Gen4:	*If*	for all known entities e that are a kind-of entity E there are predicates A, B such that A(e) and B(e) are known to be the case
		and
		the number of co-occurrences of A(e) and B(e) is significantly large,
	Then	assume the rule "*If* A(E), *Then* B(E)."

Table B. *Facts*

Id.	Description	Type and origin	Reference chapter
F0	Extant control units are difficult to design, maintain, and repair because of their complexity.	E; A	5
F1	A control unit is a kind-of artifact.	E; A	5
F2	Difficulty of design, maintenance, and repair constitutes a negative property of an artifact.	C; A	5
F3	An artifact is a kind-of entity.	E; A	5
F4	The EDSAC order interpreter (which issues control signals to arithmetic, input/output, memory units) is (partially) implemented in the form of a diode matrix.	E; A	5
F5	In the MIT Whirlwind, each arithmetic operation (barring multiplication) involves exactly eight pulses issued from a control unit implemented in the form of a diode matrix.	E; A	5 6
F6	EDSAC's order interpreter is simple, repetitive, and regular	C; A	5
F7	Whirlwind's control unit is simple, repetitive and regular.	C; A	5
F8	The EDSAC order interpreter is an instance-of an order interpreter.	E; A	5
F9	An order interpreter is a kind-of computer component.	E; A	5
F10	A control unit is a kind-of computer component.	E; A	5
F11	The Whirlwind control unit is an instance-of a control unit.	E; A	5
F12	A computing device is a kind-of device or artifact.	E; A	5
F13	A microprogram is an encoded structure of symbols.	E; A	6
F14	A diode matrix is a physical structure.	E; A	6
F15	A microprogram is more abstract than a diode matrix.	C; I	6
F16	A next micro-order address mechanism is a functional entity.	C; I	6
F17	A next micro-order address mechanism is more abstract than a diode matrix.	C; I	6

Id.	Description	Type and origin	Reference chapter
F18	The Whirlwind control matrix is a diode matrix that consists of intersecting sets of R rows and C columns such that (1) each row i represents the set of control steps required to be activated in order to execute some distinct opcode i; (2) each column j represents a distinct control step such that a signal along column j causes the activation of the corresponding control step; and (3) the presence of a diode d_{ij} at the intersection of row i and column j causes the transmission along column j of a signal on row i (and, therefore, causes the activation of the control step in column j).	E; A	6
F19	A control matrix is a diode matrix that consists of intersecting sets of rows and columns such that (1) each row i represents a set of control steps required to be activated in order to execute some distinct opcode i; (2) each column j represents (or encodes) a distinct control step such that a signal along column j causes the activation of the corresponding control step; and (3) the presence of a diode d_{ij} at the intersection of row i and column j causes the transmission along column j of a signal in row i (and, therefore, causes the activation of the control step in column j).	E; I	6
F20	The Whirlwind control matrix is an instance-of a control matrix	E; A.	6
F21	Addresses in a microprogram and rows in a control-diode matrix are structurally similar.	C; A	6
F22	Addresses in a microprogram and rows in a control-diode matrix are possibly equivalent, or there is a possible mapping between addresses in a microprogram and rows in a control-diode matrix.	C; I	6
F23	Micro-orders in a microprogram and control steps in a control-diode matrix are functionally similar.	C; I	6
F24	In a stored program computer, an instruction (order) when executed (or activated) causes a state change in the relevant registers or memory words in the computer.	E; A	6
F25	In a (microprogrammed) control unit, a micro-order when executed will cause a state change in the relevant registers or memory words in the computer.	E; I	6
F26	Each distinct control step issued from the Whirlwind control-diode matrix causes a state change in the relevant registers or memory words.	E; A	6

Id.	Description	Type and origin	Reference chapter
F27	Each distinct control step in a control-diode matrix when activated or issued causes a state change in the relevant registers or memory words in the relevant computer.	E; I	6
F28	Diode matrix A: A1: The microprogram consisting of a set of micro-orders $M_1, \ldots, M_m$ at addresses $1, \ldots, m$, respectively. A2: Each micro-order consists of a set of micro-operations (which is a subset of the set of distinct micro-operations). A3: Each column j of the diode matrix will represent a distinct micro-operation. A4: Each row i of the diode matrix will consist of a set of diodes $d_{i1}, d_{i2}, \ldots$, representing the set of micro-operations corresponding to a single micro-order at address i. A5: The presence of a diode d_{ij} at the intersection of row i and column j will cause the activation of micro-operation j whenever there is a signal along row i.	E; D	6
F29	In a binary digital computer, addresses (locations) of orders (instructions) and numbers (data) can be encoded and represented by binary numbers (bit strings).	E; A	6
F30	Diode Matrix B: B1: The successor address, Succ(i), to an address i of a micro-order is a binary integer $[b_{j1}, b_{i2}, \ldots, b_{ip}]$ where p = $[\log_2 m]$ and $1, \ldots, m$ are the addresses of micro-orders. B2: Each column j of the diode matrix represents a distinct bit position of the binary address. B3: Each row i of the diode matrix will contain diodes for those bit positions in Succ(i) that are 1s, while diodes are absent (in row i) for those bit positions in Succ(i) that are 0s. B4: A signal along row i will cause the selection of Succ(i).	E; D	6
F31	In stored program computer form, the phases or events *current instruction (or order) activation* and *next instruction (or order) address selection* are ordered in time.	E; A	6
F31.1	In a microprogrammed control unit, the phases or events *current micro-order activation* and *next micro-order address selection* are ordered in time.	E; I	6

Id.	Description	Type and origin	Reference chapter
F32	In an entity that is in the stored program computer form, it is possible to select between (at least) two alternative successor orders, Succ-1(i), Succ-2(i), to an order at address i, as a function of the state of some condition flag.	E; A	6
F32.1	In a control unit that is (intended to be) in stored program computer form, it is (or should be) possible to select between (at least) two alternative successor micro-orders, Succ-1(i), Succ-2(i), to a micro-order at address i, as a function of the state of some condition flag.	E; I	6
F33	In D2, matrix B is responsible for the representation and selection of the successor address, Succ(i), to a micro-order in row (address) i of matrix A.	E; D	6

Legend
E: Empirical
I: Inferred
D: Design-based
A: Assumed
C: Conceptual

Table C. *Noninference rules*

Id.		Description	Origin	Reference chapter
R0	*If*	an artifact demonstrates some negative or disadvantageous character,	A	5
	Then	establish as a goal/problem the elimination of that character.		
R0.1	*If*	a control unit demonstrates some negative or disadvantageous character,	I	5
	Then	establish as a goal/problem the design of a control unit in which the negative character is eliminated.		
R0.1.1	*If*	a control unit is difficult to design, maintain, and repair,	I	5
	Then	establish as a goal/problem the design (or development) of a control unit (form) that is easy to design, maintain, and repair.		
R1	*If*	an artifact has a simple, repetitive, and regular structure,	A	5
	Then	the artifact is easy to design, maintain, and repair.		

Id.		Description	Origin	Reference chapter
R1.1	*If*	a control unit has a simple, repetitive, and regular structure,	I	5
	Then	the control unit is easy to design, maintain, and repair.		
R2	*If*	an order interpreter is (partially) implemented using a diode matrix,	I	5
	Then	(that part of) the order interpreter is simple, repetitive, and regular.		
R.2.1	*If*	a computer component is implemented using a diode matrix,	I	5
	Then	the component is simple, repetitive, and regular.		
R2.1.1	*If*	a control unit is implemented using a diode matrix,	I	5
	Then	the control unit is simple, repetitive, and regular.		
R3	*If*	a computing device is in the stored program computer form,	A	5
	Then	the computing device is functionally flexible.		
R3.1	*If*	a device or artifact is in the stored program computer form,	I	5
	Then	the artifact is functionally flexible.		
R3.1.1	*If*	a control unit is in the stored program computer form,	I	5
	Then	the control unit is functionally flexible.		
R4	*If*	an artifact is a stored program computer,	A	5
	Then	the task to be performed by the artifact will be specified by a program *and* the program is composed of a set of instructions (orders) *and* the program will be stored in a memory with each instruction (order) having a distinct memory address.		
R4.1	*If*	a control unit is (to be specified as) a stored program computer,	I	5
	Then	the task to be performed by the control unit will be specified by a (micro)program *and* the (micro)program is composed of a set of (micro)instructions (orders) *and* the (micro)program will be stored in a memory with each (micro)instruction (order) having a distinct memory address.		

Appendix

Id.		Description	Origin	Reference chapter
R5	*If*	an artifact is a stored program computer,	A	5
	Then	on completion of an instruction (order's) execution, the task of identifying the next instruction (order) normally to execute is specified by a *next instruction address* mechanism.		
R5.1	*If*	a control unit is (to be specified as) a stored program computer,	I	5
	Then	(the control unit is such that) on completion of a (micro)order's execution, the task of identifying the next (micro)order normally to execute is specified by a *next (micro)order address* mechanism.		
R6	*If*	entity A is a symbolic structure *and* entity B is a physical structure,	A	6
	Then	A is more abstract than B *and* (conversely) B is more concrete than A.		
R7	*If*	an artifact is a stored program computer,	A	6
	Then	its next order (instruction) address mechanism is a functional entity.		
R7.1	*If*	a control unit is a stored program computer,	I	6
	Then	(the control unit is such that) its next micro-order address mechanism is a functional entity.		
R8	*If*	entity A is a functional entity *and* entity B is a physical entity,	A	6
	Then	A is more abstract than B *and* (conversely) B is more concrete than A.		
R8.1	*If*	a diode matrix is a physical entity *and* a next micro-order address mechanism is a functional entity,	I	6
	Then	a next micro-order address mechanism is more abstract than a diode matrix.		
R9	*If*	there is a goal that an entity E is to be implemented in terms of some entity E_1 *and* there is a goal that the task or function to be achieved by E is to be specified by (or in terms of) some entity E_2 *and* E_2 is more abstract than E_1,	A	6

Id.		Description	Origin	Reference chapter
	Then	establish a goal to realize E_2 in terms of E_1.		
R9.1	*If*	there is a goal that the control unit is to be implemented in terms of a diode matrix *and* there is a goal that the task to be achieved by the control unit is to be specified by a microprogram (consisting of a set of micro-orders each at a specified address in a memory) *and* a microprogram is more abstract than a diode matrix,	I	6
	Then	establish a goal to implement a microprogram in terms of a diode matrix.		
R9.2	*If*	there is a goal that the control unit is to be implemented in a diode matrix *and* there is a goal that the task of identifying the next micro-order to normally execute is specified by a next micro-order address mechanism *and* a next micro-order address mechanism is more abstract than a diode matrix,	I	6
	Then	establish as a goal the implementation of a next micro-order address mechanism in terms of a diode matrix.		
R10	*If*	there is a goal that an entity e_1 is to be implemented in terms of an entity E *and* an entity e_2 is known to be implemented in terms of E,	A	6
	Then	establish as a goal, the identification of similarities or mappings or equivalences between e_1 and e_1.		
R10.1	*If*	there is a goal that the microprogram (consisting of a set of micro-orders each at a specified address in a memory) is to be implemented in terms of (or by) a diode matrix *and* a control matrix is (implemented in terms of) a diode matrix that consists of . . .,	I	6
	Then	establish as a goal the identification of (one or more) similarities or mappings or equivalences between the microprogram and the control-diode matrix.		

Id.		Description	Origin	Reference chapter
R11	*If*	there is a goal to establish a similarity or mapping or equivalence between two entities e_1 and e_2 *and* components c_1 in e_1 and c_2 in e_2 are structurally similar,	A	6
	Then	c_1 in e_1 and c_2 in e_2 are possibly equivalent or there is a possible mapping between c_1 in e_1 and c_2 in e_2.		
R11.1	*If*	there is a goal to establish a similarity or mapping or equivalence between a microprogram and a control-diode matrix *and* addresses in a microprogram and rows in a control-diode matrix are structurally similar,	I	6
	Then	addresses in a microprogram and rows in a control-diode matrix are possibly equivalent or there is a possible mapping between addresses in a microprogram and rows in a control-diode matrix.		
R12	*If*	there are two entities E_1, E_2 such that e_1 in E_1, e_2 in E_2 are possibly equivalent *and* elements e'_1 in E_1, e'_2 in E_2 are functionally similar *and* e_1, e'_1 in E_1 satisfy some predicate $P(e_1, e'_1)$,	A	6
	Then	assume that e_2, e'_2 in E_2 will also satisfy $P(e_2, e'_2)$.		
R13	*If*	entities $E_1, E_2, \ldots$, have the same behavioral effect,	A	6
	Then	$E_1, E_2, \ldots$, are (postulated to be) functionally similar.		
R14	*If*	an entity E_1 is to be implemented by (or in terms of) some entity E_2 *and* an entity e_1 associated with (or is an element of) E_1 is equivalent to an entity e_2 associated with (or is an element of) E_2 *and* e_1 satisfies (or is required to satisfy) some property P,	A	6
	Then	e_2 also satisfies (or should satisfy) P.		
R15	*If*	an entity E represents (or is required to represent) or consists of (or is required to consist of) a set of elements $e_1, e_2, \ldots$, of type T *and*	A	6

Id.		Description	Origin	Reference chapter
		the same entity E represents (or is required to represent) or consists of (or is required to consist of) a set of elements $e'_1, e'_2 \ldots$, of type T' *and* the types T and T' are functionally similar,		
	Then	each element e_i of type T should correspond to (or represent or be represented by) a distinct element e'_j of type T'.		
R16	*If*	an entity E_1 represents (or is intended to represent) some entity E_2 *and* some behavioral property $P(E_1)$ is the effect of some causal agent A,	A	6
	Then	the causal agent A will also produce the same behavioral property $P(E_2)$ in E_2.		
R17	*If*	there is a goal that an entity E_1 (having a certain operational characteristic $O(E_1)$) is to cause an entity E_2 to behave in a certain way,	A	6
	Then	establish as a goal the representation or implementation of E_2 by E_1.		
R18	*If*	an entity E is used (or to be used) to implement an entity E_1 *and* entity E is used (or to be used) to implement an entity E_2 *and* E is used in a particular way in the case of E_1,	A	6
	Then	E may (perhaps) be used in a similar way for E_2.		
R19	*If*	an analogical solution is sought between a source situation S and a target situation T,	A	6
	Then	establish a mapping between the known entities (in the *function* parts) of S and T *and* then substitute the known entities of T for the corresponding known entities in the *method of solution* part of S.		
R20		Means–ends analysis heuristic	A	6
	If	the goal state is GS and the current state is CS,		
	Then	establish the difference betwen GS and CS *and* then apply an operator that reduces the difference.		

Id.		Description	Origin	Reference chapter
R21	*If*	an entity E_1 is in the form of a binary pattern *and* E_1 implements an entity E_2,	A	6
	Then	E_2 may itself be (represented) in the form of a vector of elements that are present or absent according to the binary pattern.		
R21.1	*If*	each row i of (a $m \times n$) diode matrix is in the form of (present and absent) diodes *and* each row i of the diode matrix implements a micro-order M_i (consisting of a set of micro-operation) such that $d_{ij} = 1$ (d_{ij} is present) if m_j is in M_i $= 0$ (d_{ij} is absent) if m_j is not in M_i,	I	6
	Then	M_i can be represented as a vector $\mu_{i1}, \mu_{i2}, \ldots, \mu_{in}]$ where $\mu_{ij} = m_j$ if $d_{ij} = 1$ $\qquad\quad\; = \neg m_j$ if $d_{ij} = 0.$		
R22		Misfit identification and elimination rule	A	6
	If	there exists a goal G specifying a requirement for an artifact *and* there exists a design D that is intended to satisfy G,		
	Then	determine the misfit M(D, G) between D and G *and* then apply an action to eliminate or reduce M(D, G).		
R23	*If*	a signal activates (or is required to activate) a process/device/circuit P_1 *and* a signal activates (or is required to activate) a process/device/circuit P_2 *and* the activation of P_1, P_2 are to be ordered in time,	A	6
	Then	pass the same signal S through P_1, P_2 such that P_1 precedes P_2 in S's path.		
R24	*If*	a signal S is to pass through the processes/devices/circuits P_1, P_2 *and* P_1 is to precede P_2 in S's path,	A	6
	Then	connect P_1, P_2 in series.		
R25	*If*	there is a goal "An entity E is to satisfy some property P" *and*	A	6

Id.		Description	Origin	Reference chapter
		a component or subentity E_1 of E is known to be functionally responsible for a *related* property P_1,		
	Then	modify the goal to "The subentity E_1 is to satisfy property P."		
R25.1	*If*	the goal is "Modify D2 such that one of (at least) two alternative successor micro-orders, Succ-1(i), Succ-2(i), to a micro-order at address i (in matrix A) can be selected as a function of the state of some condition flag" *and* in D2, matrix B is responsible for the representation and selection of the successor address Succ(i) to a micro-order in row (address) i of matrix A,	I	6
	Then	modify the goal to "Matrix B is to satisfy the property that one of (at least) two alternative successor micro-orders, Succ-1(i), Succ-2(i), to a micro-order at address i (of matrix A) can be selected as a function of the state of some condition flag."		
R26	*If*	a signal along an electrical path P is to be transmitted along one of two alternative electrical paths Q, R based on the state of a device D,	A	6
	Then	insert a switch in the circuit with input P and outputs Q, R and let the output of D be connected to the control input of the switch.		
R26.1	*If*	a signal along row i of matrix A is to be transmitted along (or select) one of two alternative successor rows, Succ-1(i), Succ-2(i), in matrix B based on the state of a condition flag,	I	6
	Then	insert a switch with input row i of matrix A and outputs Succ-1(i), Succ-2(i) of matrix B and let the outputs of the condition flag be connected to the control input of the switch.		

Legend
I: Inferred
A: Assumed

Table D. *Goals*

Id.	Description	Reference chapter
G0	To develop a control unit that is easy to design, maintain, and repair.	5
G1	Design a control unit that has a simple, repetitive, and regular structure.	5
G2	Design a control unit to be implemented in terms of a diode matrix.	5, 6
G3	The control unit must be functionally flexible.	5
G4	Specify the control unit in a stored program computer form.	5,6
G4′	The control unit is to be a kind-of stored program computer.	6
G5	The (task to be performed by the) control unit will be specified by a (micro)program consisting of a set of (micro)orders each held at a specified address in a memory.	5,6
G6	(Design) a control unit in which, on completion of a (micro)order's execution, the task of identifying the next (micro)order normally to execute is specified by a *next (micro)order address* mechanism.	5,6
G7	The microprogram (consisting of a set o micro-orders each at a specified address in a memory) is to be implemented in terms of (or by) a diode matrix.	6
G7a	Each address in a microprogram will represent a set of micro-orders.	6
G7b	Each address in a microprogram will represent (or consist of) a micro-order, which in turn will represent (or consist of) a set of micro-operations.	6
G8	The next micro-order address mechanism (for the sequencing of micro-orders) is to be implemented in terms of a diode matrix.	6
G9	The microprogram, consisting of a set of micro-orders (each of which in turn consists of a set of micro-operations held at a specified address) is to be implemented in terms of (or by) a diode matrix.	6
G10	Identify one or more similarities or mappings or equivalences between a microprogram (consisting of a set of micro-orders each at a specified address in a memory) and a control-diode matrix in which each row i consists. . . .	6
G11	Each row in the diode matrix will hold (or encode) a set of micro-operations corresponding to a single micro-order.	6
G12	Each control step in a row of the control-diode matrix will correspond to (or represent) a distinct micro-operation.	6
G13	The presence of a diode d_{ij} at the intersection of row i and column j will cause the activation of micro-operation j whenever there is a signal along row i.	6

Id.	Description	Reference chapter
G14	Micro-operation j (on row i) is implemented (or represented) by a diode d_{ij} at the intersection of row i and column j of the control-diode matrix.	6
G15	Each row i of the diode matrix will hold (or encode) a set of micro-operations corresponding to a single micro-order, and each micro-operation j in row i will be implemented by a diode d_{ij} at the intersection of row i and column j.	6
G15a	Each row i of the diode matrix will consist of a set of diodes $d_{i1}, d_{i2}, \ldots$, representing the set of distinct micro-operations corresponding to a single micro-order.	6
G16	Each row i of the control-diode matrix will consist of a set of diodes $d_{i1}, d_{i2}, \ldots$, representing the set of distinct micro-operations corresponding to a single micro-order, where row i represents (or is equivalent to) an address of the microprogram.	6
G17	Use a diode matrix to implement the next micro-order address mechanism in a way that is similar to the use of the diode matrix for implementing the microprogram function.	6
G18	Establish a mapping between the known entities (in the *function* parts of Source and Target) *and* then substitute the known entities of Target for the corresponding known entities of Source in the *method of solution* part of Source.	6
G19	Make each micro-order M_i a fixed-size vector, showing both the presence and the absence of micro-operations.	6
G20	Represent each M_i as a vector of size n: $[\mu_{i1}, \mu_{i2}, \ldots, \mu_{in}]$ such that $\mu_{ij} = mj$ if $d_{ij} = 1$ $= \neg mj$ if $d_{ij} = 0$.	6
G21	Identify a misfit $M(D1, G4)$ between design D1 and goal G4 *and* then apply an action to eliminate or reduce $M(D1, G4)$.	6
G22	Establish a relationship between matrices A and B such that a temporal ordering obtains between *current micro-order activation* in matrix A and *next micro-order address selection* in matrix B.	6
G23	Pass signal along row i of matrix A to row i of matrix B such that row i of A precedes row i of B in the signal's path.	6
G24	Row i of diode matrix A is (to be) connected in series to row i of diode matrix B.	6

Id.	Description	Reference chapter
G25	Identify a misfit M(D2, G4) between design D2 and goal G4 *and* then apply an action or operator to eliminate or reduce M(D2, G4).	6
G26	Modify the design D2 such that one of (at least) two alternative successor micro-orders, Succ-1(i), Succ-2(i), to a micro-order at address i can be selected as a function of the state of some condition flag.	6
G27	Modify matrix B so that one of (at least) two alternative successor micro-orders Succ-1(i), Succ-2(i) to a micro-order at address i (of matrix A) can be selected as a function of the state of some condition flag.	6
G28	Insert a switch with input row i of matrix A and outputs rows/ addresses Succ-1(i), Succ-2(i) of matrix B and let the outputs of the condition flag be connected to the control input of the switch.	6

References

Addis, W. (1990), *Structural Engineering: The Nature of Theory and Design,* Horwood, New York.

Alexander, C. (1964), *Notes on the Synthesis of Form,* Harvard University Press, Cambridge, MA.

Alexander, C., Neis, H., Anninou, A., and King, I. (1987), *A New Theory of Urban Design,* Oxford University Press, New York.

Anderson, J. R. (1983), *The Architecture of Cognition,* Harvard University Press, Cambridge, MA.

Arnheim, R. (1962), *Picasso's Guernica: The Genesis of a Painting,* University of California Press, Berkeley.

Ashenhurst, R. L., and Graham, S. (Eds.) (1987), *ACM Turing Award Lectures: The First Twenty Years, 1966–1985,* ACM Press, New York/Addison-Wesley, Reading, MA.

Aspray, W. (1991), *John von Neumann and the Origins of Modern Computing,* MIT Press, Cambridge, MA.

Atanasoff, J. V. (1984), "Advent of Electronic Digital Computing," *Annals of the History of Computing,* 6, 6, 279–82.

Barr, A., and Feigenbaum, E. (1981), *Handbook of Artificial Intelligence, Vol. 1.,* Morgan Kaufman, San Mateo, CA.

Basalla, G. (1988), *The Evolution of Technology,* Cambridge University Press.

Bell, C. G., and Newell, A. (1971), *Computer Structures: Readings and Examples,* McGraw-Hill, New York.

Berry, J. R. (1986), "Clifford Edward Berry, 1918–1963: His Role in Early Computers," *Annals of the History of Computing,* 8, 4, Oct., 361–9.

Billington, D. P. (1979), *Robert Maillart's Bridges: The Art of Engineering,* Princeton University Press, Princeton, N. J.

Billington, D. P. (1983), *The Tower and the Bridge,* Basic, New York.

Black, M. (1962), *Models and Metaphors,* Cornell University Press, Ithaca, NY.

Blockley, D. I., and Henderson, J. R. (1980), "Structural Failures and the Growth of Engineering Knowledge," *Proceedings of the Institution of Civil Engineers, Part 1,* 68, Nov., 719–28.

Boden, M. A. (1977), *Artificial Intelligence and Natural Man,* Harvester, Hassocks.

Boden, M. A. (1989), *Artificial Intelligence in Psychology,* MIT Press, Cambridge, MA.

Boden, M. A. (1991), *The Creative Mind,* Basic, New York.

Brachman, R., and Levesque, H. (Eds.) (1985), *Readings in Knowledge Representation*, Morgan Kaufman, San Mateo, CA.

Brown, D. C., and Chandrasekaran, B. (1989), *Design Problem Solving*, Pitman, London/Morgan Kaufman, San Mateo, CA.

Bruner, J. S. (1962), "The Conditions of Creativity," in Gruber, Terrell, and Wertheimer (Eds.) (1962), 1–30.

Bugliarello, G., and Doner, D. B. (Eds.) (1979), *The History and Philosophy of Technology*, University of Illinois Press, Urbana.

Burks, A. W. (1980), "From ENIAC to the Stored-Program Computer: Two Revolutions in Computers," in Metropolis, Howlett, and Rota (Eds.), (1980), 311–44.

Burks, A. W., and Burks, A. R. (1981), "The ENIAC: First General Purpose Electronic Computer," *Annals of the History of Computing*, 3, 4, Oct., 310–89.

Burks, A. W., Goldstine, H. H., and von Neumann, J. (1946), "Preliminary Discussions of the Logical Design of an Electronic Computer Instrument," Institute of Advanced Studies, Princeton University. Reprinted in Randell (1975), 371–86.

Butterfield, H. (1968), *The Origin of Modern Science, 1300–1800*, Clarke, Irwin, Toronto.

Carnap, R. (1966), *Philosophical Foundations of Physics*, Basic, New York.

Carr, E. H. (1961), *What is History?* Macmillan, London.

Chandrasekhar, S. (1987), *Truth and Beauty*, University of Chicago Press, Chicago.

Chomsky, N. (1957), *Syntactic Structures*, Mouton, The Hague (Eight Printing, 1969).

Clark, R. W. (1984), *The Survival of Charles Darwin: A Biography of a Man and an Idea*, Random House, New York.

Cohen, I. B. (1985), *Revolution in Science*, Harvard University Press, Cambridge, MA.

Collins, A. M., and Loftus, E. F. (1975), "A Spreading-Activation Theory of Semantic Processing," *Psychological Review*, 82, 407–28.

Conant, J. B. (Ed.) (1950a), *The Overthrow of the Phlogiston Theory: The Chemical Revolution of 1755–1789* (Harvard Case Histories in Experimental Science), Harvard University Press, Cambridge, MA.

Conant, J. B. (Ed.) (1950b), *Robert Boyle's Experiments in Pneumatics* (Harvard Case Histories in Experimental Sciences), Harvard University Press, Cambridge, MA.

Coyne, R. D., Rosenman, M. A., Radford, A. D., Balachandran, M., and Gero, J. S. (1989), *Knowledge Based Design Systems*, Addison-Wesley, Reading, MA.

Cross, N. (Ed.) (1984), *Developments in Design Methodology*, Wiley, New York.

Csikszentmihalyi, M. (1988), "Society, Culture and Person: A Systems View of Creativity," in Sternberg (1988a), 325–39.

Dasgupta, S. (1979), "The Organization of Microprogram Stores," *ACM Computing Surveys*, 11, 1, Mar., 39–65.

Dasgupta, S. (1984), *The Design and Description of Computer Architectures*, Wiley (Wiley-Interscience), New York.

Dasgupta, S. (1989a), *Computer Architecture: A Modern Synthesis, Vol. 1: Foundations*, Wiley, New York.

Dasgupta, S. (1989b), *Computer Architecture: A Modern Synthesis, Vol. 2: Advanced Topics*, Wiley, New York.

Dasgupta, S. (1989c), "The Structure of Design Processes," *Advances in Computers*, Vol. 28 (M. C. Yovits, Ed.), Academic Press, New York, 1–68.

Dasgupta, S. (1991), *Design Theory and Computer Science*, Cambridge University Press.

Dasgupta, S. (1992), "Two Laws of Design," *Intelligent Systems Engineering*, 1, 2, Winter, 146–56.

Dasgupta, S., and Shriver, B. D. (1985), "Developments in Firmware Engineering," *Advances in Computers*, Vol. 24 (M. C. Yovits, Ed.), Academic Press, New York.

Dennett, D. C. (1978), *Brainstorms*, MIT Press, Cambridge, MA.

Dennett, D. C. (1988), *The Intentional Stance*, MIT Press, Cambridge, MA.

Dreyfus, H. L. (1979), *What Computers Can't Do* (Revised Edition), Harper & Row, New York.

Duheim P. (1914/1954), *The Aim and Structure of Physical Theory*, Princeton University Press, Princeton, N. J.

Ellmann, R. (1982), *James Joyce*, Oxford University Press.

Ellmann, R. (1988), " 'He Do the Police in Difference Voices,' " in *A Long the Riverrun: Selected Essays*, Hamish Hamilton, London.

Fetzer, J. H. (1991), *Philosophy and Cognitive Science*, Paragon, New York.

Fetzer, J. H. (1992), *Philosophy of Science*, Paragon, New York.

Feyerabend, P. (1978), *Against Method*, Verso, London.

Findlay, A. (1948), *A Hundred Years of Chemistry*, Gerald Duckworth, London.

Findler, N. V. (Ed.) (1979), *Associative Networks: Representation and Use of Knowledge by Computers*, Academic Press, New York.

Foder, J. A., and Pylyshyn, Z. A. (1988), "Connectionism and Cognitive Architecture: A Critical Analysis," in S. Pinker and J. Mehler (Eds.), *Connections and Symbols*, MIT Press, Cambridge, MA, 30–72.

Gardiner, P. (1961), *The Nature of Historical Explanation*, Oxford University Press.

Ghiselin, B. (Ed.) (1952), *The Creative Process*, University of California Press, Berkeley.

Goldstine, H. H. (1972), *The Computer from Pascal to von Neumann*, Princeton University Press, Princeton, N. J.

Gould, S. J. (1981), *The Mismeasure of Man*, Norton, New York.

Gould, S. J. (1990), *The Individual in Darwin's World* (2d Edinburgh Medal lecture), Edinburgh University Press, Edinburgh.

Gries, D. G. (1981), *The Science of Programming*, Springer-Verlag, New York.

Gruber, H. E. (1981), *Darwin on Man: A Psychological Study of Scientific Creativity* (2d Edition), University of Chicago Press, Chicago.

Gruber, H. E. (1989), "The Evolving Systems Approach to Creative Work," in Wallace and Gruber (Eds.), (1989) 3–24.

Gruber, H. E., Terrell, G., and Wertheimer, M. (Eds.) (1962), *Contemporary Approaches to Creative Thinking*, Atherton, New York.

Habib, S. (Ed.) (1988a), *Microprogramming and Firmware Engineering Methods*, Van Nostrand Reinhold, New York.

Habib, S. (1988b), "A Brief Chronology of Microprogramming Activity," in Habib (1988a), 1–32.

Hadamard, J. (1945), *Psychology of Invention in the Mathematical Field*, Princeton University Press, Princeton, N. J. (Dover reprint, 1954).

Hanson, N. R. (1958), *Patterns of Discovery*, Cambridge University Press.

Hardy, G. H. (1940), *Ramanujan*, Cambridge University Press.

Hardy, G.H. (1969), *A Mathematician's Apology*, Cambridge University Press. (1st Edition, 1941).

Harré, R. (1985), *The Philosophies of Science: An Introductory Survey*, Oxford University Press.

Hayes, J. P. (1984), *Digital System Design and Microprocessors*, McGraw-Hill, New York.

Hempel, C. G. (1965), *Aspects of Scientific Explanation*, Free Press, New York.

Hesse, M. (1966), *Models and Analogies in Science*, Sheed & Ward, London.

Hoare, C. A. R. (1985), *Communicating Sequential Processes*, Prentice-Hall, Englewood Cliffs, N. J.

Hoare, C. A. R. (1986), "The Mathematics of Programming," Inaugural lecture, University of Oxford, Oxford University Press.

Hodges, A. (1983), *Alan Turing: The Enigma*, Simon & Schuster, New York.

Hofstadter, D. R. (1979), *Godel, Escher, Bach: An Eternal Golden Braid*, Basic, New York.

Holland, J. H., Holyak, K. J., Nisbett, R. E., and Thagard, P. R. (1986), *Induction*, MIT Press, Cambridge, MA.

Holmes, F. L. (1980), "Hans Krebs and the Discovery of the Ornithine Cycle," *Federation Proceedings*, 39, 215–25.

Holmes, F. L. (1985), *Lavoisier and the Chemistry of Life*, University of Wisconsin Press, Madison.

Holmes, F. L. (1989), "Lavoisier and Krebs: Two Styles of Scientific Creativity," in Wallace and Gruber (Eds.) (1989), 44–68.

Holmes, F. L. (1991), *Hans Krebs: The Formation of a Scientific Life, 1900–1937*, Oxford University Press, New York.

Holton, G. (1952), *Introduction to Concepts and Theories in Physical Science*, Addison-Wesley, Reading, MA.

Holton, G. (1973), *Thematic Origins of Scientific Thought*, Harvard University Press, Cambridge, MA.

Hume, D. (1748/1977), *An Enquiry Concerning Human Understanding*, Edited by E. Steinberg, Hackett, Indianapolis, IN.

Husson, S. S. (1970), *Microprogramming: Principles and Practices*, Prentice-Hall, New York.

Hwang, K., and Briggs, F. A. (1984), *Computer Architecture and Parallel Processing*, McGraw-Hill, New York.

Ihde, D. (1991), *Instrumental Realism*, Indiana University Press, Bloomington.

Jaynes, J. (1976), *The Origin of Consciousness in the Breakdown of the Bicameral Mind*, University of Toronto Press, Toronto.

Jeffrey, L. R. (1989), "Writing and Rewriting Poetry: William Wordsworth," in Wallace and Gruber (Eds.) (1989), 69–90.

Johnson-Laird, P. M. (1988a), *The Computer and the Mind*, Harvard University Press, Cambridge, MA.

Johnson-Laird, P. M. (1988b), "Freedom and Constraint in Creativity," in Sternberg (1988a), 202–19.

Jones, J. C. (1980), *Design Methods: Seeds of Human Futures*, 2d Edition, Wiley, New York.

Kilburn, T. (1949), "The Manchester University Digital Computing Machine," *Report of the Conference on High Speed Automatic Calculating Machines*, University Mathematical Laboratory, Cambridge, June, 119–21.

Koestler, A. (1964), *The Act of Creation*, Hutchinson, London.

Kuhn, T. S. (1962), *The Structure of Scientific Revolutions*, University of Chicago Press, Chicago.

Kuhn, T. S. (1970a), "Postscript – 1969," *The Structure of Scientific Revolutions*, 2d Edition Enlarged, University of Chicago Press, Chicago.

Kuhn T. S. (1970b), "Reflections on My Critics," in Lakatos and Musgrave (Eds.) (1970), 231–78.

Kuhn, T. S. (1977), "Second Thoughts on Paradigms," in Suppe (1977a), 459–82.

Reprinted in T. S. Kuhn, *The Essential Tension,* University of Chicago Press, Chicago.

Kulkarni, D., and Simon, H. A. (1988), "The Processes of Scientific Discovery: The Strategy of Experimentation," *Cognitive Science,* 12, 139–76.

Lachman, R., Lachman, J. L., and Butterfield, E. C. (1979), *Cognitive Psychology and Information Processing: An Introduction,* Erlbaum, Hillsdale, NJ.

Laird, J. E., Newell, A., and Rosenbloom, P. S. (1987), "SOAR: An Architecture for General Intelligence," *Artificial Intelligence,* 33, 1–64.

Lakatos, I. (1976), *Proofs and Refutations,* Cambridge University Press.

Lakatos, I. (1978), *The Methodology of Scientific Research Programmes,* Cambridge University Press.

Lakatos, I., and Musgrave, A. (Eds.) (1970), *Criticism and the Growth of Knowledge,* Cambridge University Press.

Langley, P., Simon, H. A., Bradshaw, G. L., and Zytkow, J. M. (1987), *Scientific Discovery,* MIT Press, Cambridge, MA.

Laudan, L. (1977), *Progress and Its Problems,* University of California Press, Los Angeles.

Laudan, L. (1984), *Science and Values,* University of California Press, Berkeley.

Laudan, L. (1990), *Science and Relativism: Some Key Controversies in the Philosophy of Science,* University of Chicago Press, Chicago.

Lawson, B. (1980), *How Designers Think: The Design Process Demystified,* Architectural Press, London.

Lenat, D. B. (1976), "AM: An Artificial Intelligence Approach to Discovery in Mathematics as Heuristic Search," Ph.D. Diss., Stanford University, Stanford, CA.

Losee, J. (1980), *Historical Introduction to the Philosophy of Science,* Oxford University Press.

Lowes, J. L. (1927), *The Road to Xanadu,* Houghton-Mifflin, Boston.

McCluskey, E. J. (1986), *Logic Design Principles with Emphasis on Testable Semicustom Circuits,* Prentice-Hall, Englewood Cliffs, NJ.

Mallach, E., and Sondak, N. (Eds.) (1983), *Advances in Microprogramming,* Artech House, Dedham, MA.

March, L. (1976), "The Logic of Design and the Question of Value," in L. March (Ed.) *The Architecture of Form,* Cambridge University Press, 1–40.

Masterman, M. (1970), "The Nature of a Paradigm," in Lakatos and Musgrave (Eds.), (1970), 59–90.

Mayr, E. (1988), *Towards a New Philosophy of Biology,* Harvard University Press, Cambridge, MA.

Medawar, P. B. (1964), *"The Act of Creation:* Koestler's Theory of the Creative Act," *New Statesman,* June 19, reprinted in P. B. Medawar (1982), *Pluto's Republic,* Oxford University Press, New York, 252–62.

Medawar, P. B. (1990), "Creativity – Especially in Science," in P. B. Medawar, *The Threat and the Glory,* Oxford University Press, 83–90.

Mercer, R. J. (1957), "Micro-programming," *Journal of the ACM,* 4, 2, Apr., 151–71.

Metropolis, N., Howlett, J., and Rota, G.-C. (Eds.) (1980), *A History of Computing in the Twentieth Century,* Academic Press, New York.

Metropolis, N., and Worlton, J. (1980), "A Trilogy of Errors in the History of Computing," *Annals of the History of Computing,* 2, 1, 49–50.

Mill, J. S. (1843/1974), *A System of Logic: Ratiocinative and Inductive,* University of Toronto Press, Toronto.

Miller, A. I. (1986), *Imagery in Scientific Thought*, MIT Press, Cambridge, MA.

Milutinovic, V. (Ed.) (1989), *Microprogramming and Firmware Engineering*, IEEE Computer Society Press, Washington.

Minsky, M. (1967), *Computation: Finite and Infinite Machines*, Prentice-Hall, Englewood Cliffs, NJ.

Minsky, M. (1985), The *Society of Mind*, Simon & Schuster, New York.

Mitchell, W. J. (1990), *The Logic of Architecture*, MIT Press, Cambridge, MA.

Myers, G. J. (1980), *Digital System Design with LSI Bit-Slice Logic*, Wiley (Wiley-Interscience), New York.

Newell, A. (1982), "The Knowledge Level," *Artificial Intelligence*, 18, 87–127.

Newell, A. (1990), *Unified Theories of Cognition*, Harvard University Press, Cambridge, MA.

Newell, A., and Simon, H. A. (1972), *Human Problem Solving*, Prentice-Hall, Englewood Cliffs, NJ.

Newell, A., and Simon, H. A. (1976), "Computer Science as Empirical Inquiry: Symbols and Search," *Communications of the ACM*, 19, 113–26.

Newell, A., Rosenbloom, P. S. and Laird, J. E. (1989), "Symbolic Architectures for Cognition," in Posner (Ed.) (1989), 93–131.

Newell, A., Shaw, J. C., and Simon, H. A. (1962) "The Processes of Creative Thinking," in Gruber, Terrell, and Wertheimer (Eds.) (1962), 63–119.

Nickels, T. (Ed.) (1980a), *Scientific Discovery, Logic and Rationality*, Reidel, Boston.

Nickels, T. (1980b) "Introductory Essay: Scientific Discovery and the Future of Philosophy of Science," in Nickels (Ed.) (1980a), 1–60.

Nozick, R. (1989), *The Examined Life*, Simon & Schuster, New York.

Ortony, A. (Ed.) (1979), *Metaphor and Thought*, Cambridge University Press.

Osowski, J. V. (1989), "Ensembles of Metaphors in the Psychology of William James," in Wallace and Gruber (Eds.) (1989), 127–46.

Pacey, A. (1992), *The Maze of Ingenuity* (2d Edition), MIT Press, Cambridge, MA.

Papert, S. (1988), "One AI or Many," *Daedalus*, Winter 1–14; also in *Proceedings of the American Academy of Arts and Sciences*, 117, 1, 1–14.

Partington, J. R. (1960), *A Short History of Chemistry*, 3d Edition, Macmillan, London.

Patel, S., and Dasgupta, S. (1991), "Automatic Belief Revision in a Plausibility-Driven Design Environment," *IEEE Transactions on Systems, Man and Cybernetics*, Sept.–Oct., 21, 5, 933–51.

Pattee, H. H. (Ed.) (1973), *Hierarchy Theory*, Braziller, New York.

Peirce, C. S. (1931–1958), *Collected Papers* (8 Vols.), C. Harshorre, P. Weiss, and A. Burks (Eds.), Harvard University Press, Cambridge, MA.

Perkins, D. N. (1981), *The Mind's Best Work*, Harvard University Press, Cambridge, MA.

Petroski, H. (1985), *To Engineer is Human: The Role of Failure in Successful Design*, St. Martin's, New York.

Petroski, H. (1991) "Paradigms for Human Error in Design," *Proceedings of the 1991 NSF Design and Manufacturing Systems Conference*, Austin, TX, 1137–46.

Poincaré, H. (1913/1946), "Mathematical Creation," in *The Foundations of Science* (G. B. Halstead, Translator), Science Press, Lancaster, PA.

Popper, K. R. (1957), *The Poverty of Historicism*, Routledge & Kegan Paul, London.

Popper, K. R. (1965), *Conjecture and Refutation: The Growth of Scientific Knowledge*, Harper & Row, New York.

Popper, K. R. (1934/1968), *The Logic of Scientific Discovery*, Harper & Row, New York.

Popper, K. R. (1972), *Objective Knowledge: An Evolutionary Approach*, Oxford University Press.

Posner, M. I. (Ed.) (1989), *Foundations of Cognitive Science*, MIT Press, Cambridge, MA.

Pye, D. (1978), *The Nature and Aesthetics of Design*, Herbert Press, London.

Pylyshyn, Z. W. (1980), "Computation and Cognition: Issues in the Foundations of Cognitive Science," *Behavioral and Brain Sciences*, 3, 1, 154–69.

Pylyshyn, Z. W. (1984), *Computation and Cognition*, MIT Press, Cambridge, MA.

Pylyshyn, Z. W. (1989), "Computing in Cognitive Science," in Posner (Ed.) (1989), 49–92.

Qin, Y., and Simon, H. A. (1990), "Laboratory Replication of Scientific Discovery Processes," *Cognitive Science*, 14, 281–312.

Randell, B. (Ed.) (1975), *Origins of Digital Computers* (2d Edition), Springer-Verlag, New York.

Reichenbach, H. (1938), *Experience and Prediction*, University of Chicago Press, Chicago.

Reiter, R. (1987), "Nonmonotonic Reasoning," *Annual Review of Computer Science*, 2, 147–86.

Richards, I. A. (1936), *The Philosophy of Rhetoric*, Oxford University Press.

Rogers, G. F. C. (1983), *The Nature of Engineering: A Philosophy of Technology*, Macmillan, London.

Roller, D. (1950), *The Early Development of the Concepts of Temperature and Heat: The Rise and Decline of the Caloric Theory* (Harvard Case Histories in Experimental Science), Harvard University Press, Cambridge, MA.

Root-Bernstein, R. S. (1989), *Discovering*, Harvard University Press, Cambridge, MA.

Rosin, R. F. (1969), "Contemporary Concepts of Microprogramming and Emulation," *ACM Computing Surveys*, 1, 6, Dec., 197–212.

Rowe, P. G. (1987), *Design Thinking*, MIT Press, Cambridge, MA.

Rumelhart, D. E., and McClelland, J. L. (1986), *Parallel Distributed Processing, Vol. 1: Foundations*, MIT Press, Cambridge, MA.

Ruse, M. (1986), *Taking Darwin Seriously*, Blackwell, Oxford.

Schön, D. A. (1983), *The Reflective Practitioner*, Basic, New York.

Scriven, M. (1959), "Explanation and Prediction in Evolutionary Theory," *Science*, 477–82.

Searle, J. R. (1983), *Intentionality*, Cambridge University Press.

Searle, J. R. (1984), *Mind, Brain and Science*, Harvard University Press, Cambridge, MA.

Shapere, D. (1964), "The Structure of Scientific Revolutions," *Philosophical Review*, 73, 383–94.

Shrager, J., and Langley, P. (Eds.) (1990), *Computational Models of Scientific Discovery and Theory Formation*, Morgan Kaufman, San Mateo, CA.

Siewiorek, D. P., Bell, C. G., and Newell, A. (1982), *Computational Structures: Principles and Examples*, McGraw-Hill, New York.

Simon, H. A. (1962), "The Architecture of Complexity," *Proceedings of the American Philosophy Society*, 106, Dec., 467–82.

Simon, H. A. (1973), "The Structure of Ill-Structured Problems," *Artificial Intelligence*, 4, 181–200.

Simon, H. A. (1975), "Style in Design," in C. M. Eastman (Ed.), *Spatial Synthesis in Computer-Aided Building Design*, Wiley, New York.

Simon, H. A. (1976), *Administrative Behavior*, 3d Edition, Free Press, New York.

Simon, H. A. (1981), *The Sciences of the Artificial*, 2d Edition, MIT Press, Cambridge, MA.

Simon, H. A. (1982), *Models of Bounded Rationality*, Vol. 2, MIT Press, Cambridge, MA.

Simon, H. A. (1983), *Reason in Human Affairs*, Blackwell, Oxford.

Simon, H. A. (1989), *Models of Thought*, Vol. 2, Yale University Press, New Haven, CT.

Simon, H. A., and Kaplan, C. A. (1989), "Foundations of Cognitive Science," in Posner (Ed.) (1989), 1–48.

Smith, C. S. (1981), *A Search for Structure*, MIT Press, Cambridge, MA.

Snow, C. P. (1967), "Foreword" to G. H. Hardy, *A Mathematician's Apology*, Cambridge University Press.

Stern, N. (1980), "John von Neumann's Influence on Electronic Digital Computing, 1944–1946," *Annals of the History of Computing*, 2, 4, 349–62.

Stern, N. (1981), *From ENIAC to EDVAC: A Case Study in the History of Technology*, Digital Press, Bedford, MA.

Sternberg, R. J. (Ed.) (1988a), *The Nature of Creativity*, Cambridge University Press.

Sternberg, R. J. (1988b), "A Three-Facet Model of Creativity," in Sternberg (Ed.) (1988a), 125–47.

Stone, H. S. (1990), *High Performance Computer Architecture*, Addison-Wesley, Reading, MA.

Storr, A. (1972), *The Dynamics of Creation*, Secker & Warburg, London.

Suppe, F. (Ed.) (1977a), *The Structure of Scientific Theories*, University of Illinois Press, Urbana.

Suppe, F. (1977b), "The Search for Philosophic Understanding of Scientific Theories," in Suppe (Ed.) (1977a), 3–241.

Tanenbaum, A. S. (1984), *Structured Computer Organization*, 2d Edition, Prentice-Hall, Englewood Cliffs, NJ.

Taylor,. C. W. (1988), "Various Approaches to and Definitions of Creativity," in Sternberg (Ed.) (1988a), 99–124.

Thagard, P. (1988), *Computational Philosophy of Science*, MIT Press, Cambridge, MA.

Thagard, P. (1989), "Explanatory Coherence," *Behavioral and Brain Sciences*, 12, 435–502.

Thagard, P. (1990), "The Conceptual Structure of the Chemical Revolution," *Philosophy of Science*, 57, 183–209.

Thagard, P., and Nowak, G. (1990), "The Conceptual Structure of the Geological Revolution," in Shrager and Langley (Eds.) (1990), 27–72.

Turing, A. M. (1950), "Computing Machinery and Intelligence," *Mind*, 59, 236.

Vernon, P. E. (Ed.) (1970), *Creativity: Selected Readings*, Penguin, Harmondsworth.

Vincenti, W. G. (1990), *What Engineers Know and How They Know It*, Johns Hopkins University Press, Baltimore.

von Neumann, J. (1945), "First Draft of a Report on the EDVAC," Moore School of Electrical Engineering, University of Pennsylvania, June 30.

Wallace, D. B., and Gruber, H. E. (Eds.) (1989), *Creative People at Work*, Oxford University Press.

Wallas, G. (1926), *The Art of Thought*, Jonathan Cape, London.

Wechsler, J. (Ed.) (1978), *On Aesthetics in Science*, MIT Press, Cambridge, MA.

Weisberg, R. W. (1986), *Creativity*, Freeman, New York.

Weizenbaum, J. (1976), *Computer Power and Human Reason*, Freeman, San Francisco.

Wheeler, D. J. (1949), "Planning the Use of a Paper Library," *"Report of the Conference on High Speed Automatic Calculating Machines,"* June 22–5, University Mathematical Laboratory, Cambridge.

Wheeler, D. J. (1950), "Programme Organisation and Initial Orders for the EDSAC," *Proceedings of the Royal Society,* A, vol. 202, 573.

Whewell, W. (1847/1967), *The Philosophy of the Inductive Sciences,* Frank Cass, London.

Whyte, L. L., Wilson, A. G., and Wilson, D. (Eds.) (1969), *Hierarchical Structures,* Elsevier, New York.

Wilkes, M. V. (1951), "The Best Way to Design an Automatic Calculating Machine," *Report of the Manchester University Computer Inaugural Conference,* Manchester, July. Reprinted in Wilkes (1986), 118–21.

Wilkes, M. V. (1956), *Automatic Digital Computers,* Methuen, London/Wiley, New York.

Wilkes, M. V. (1968), "Computers Then and Now," ACM Turing Award Lecture, *Journal ACM,* 15, 1, 1–7.

Wilkes, M. V. (1969), "The Growth of Interest in Microprogramming: A Literature Survey," *ACM Computing Surveys,* 1, 3, 139–45.

Wilkes, M. V. (1981), "The Design of a Control Unit – Reflections on Reading Babbage's Notebooks," *Annals of the History of Computing,* 3, 2, Apr. 116–20.

Wilkes, M. V. (1984), "The Origins and Development of Microprogramming," Inaguration (Videotaped) Lecture, International Repository on Microprogramming, Dupré Library, University of Southwestern Louisiana, Oct. 29.

Wilkes, M. V. (1985), *Memoirs of a Computer Pioneer,* MIT Press, Cambridge, MA.

Wilkes, M. V. (1986), "The Genesis of Microprogramming," *Annals of the History of Computing* 8, 2, Apr. 116–26.

Wilkes, M. V. (1991), "EDSAC 2," Draft Manuscript, Olivetti Research Laboratory, Cambridge.

Wilkes, M. V., and Renwick, W. (1949), "The EDSAC," *Report of the Conference on High Speed Automatic Calculating Machines,* June 22–5, University Mathematical Laboratory, Cambridge.

Wilkes, M. V., and Stringer, J. B. (1953), "Microprogramming and the Design of the Control Circuits in an Electronic Digital Computer," *Proceedings of the Cambridge Philosophical Society,* Pt. 2, 49, Apr., 230–8. Reprinted in Wilkes (1986), pp. 121–6.

Wilkes, M. V., Renwick, W., and Wheeler, D. J. (1958), "The Design of a Control Unit of an Electronic Digital Computer," *Proceedings of the Institution of Electrical Engineers,* 105, 13–21.

Wilkes, M. V., Wheeler, D. J., and Gill, S. (1951), *The Preparation of Programs for an Electronic Digital Computer,* Addison-Wesley, Reading, MA.

Williams, F. C., and Kilburn, T. (1948), "Electronic Digital Computers," *Nature,* 162, Sept., 487. Reprinted in Randell (Ed.) (1975), 387–88.

Winograd, T. and Flores, F. (1987), *Understanding Computers and Cognition,* Addison-Wesley, Reading, MA.

Worsley, B. H. (1949), "The EDSAC Demonstration," *Report of the Conference on High Speed Automatic Calculating Machines,* June 22–5, University Mathematical Laboratory, Cambridge. Reprinted in Randell (Ed.) (1975), 395–401.

Index

abduction, 6, 44, 57, 64, 102, 111, 201
ACT, 56
Act of Creation, The, 4, 33, 46, 196
action: examples of, 97, 98, 107, 108, 110,
    115, 116, 121, 129, 135, 148, 152, 167,
    178; nature of, 56, 58–59, 102
activation network, 101, 108, 109, 143
acoustic storage, *see* ltrasonic memory
Addis, W. R., 44, 45, 64, 233
aesthetics, 7, 46
agent, cognitive, 17
Aiken, H., 124
AI paradigm, 39, 56
Alexander, C., 45, 233
algorithms, 10
analogical reasoning, *see* inference, by
    analogy
Anderson, J. R., 37, 56, 87, 100, 216, 233
Archimedes, 193
Archimedes' principle, 212
architecture of computers, 13, 15
Aristotle, 212
arithmetic unit, 85, 86, 132, 145, 176
Arnheim, R., 37, 50, 214, 233
Arrenius, Svante, 214
artifact, 7, 9, 126
artificial intelligence, xi, 10, 37, 39, 49
artificial sciences, 6–9, 11, 25, 38, 43, 45,
    46, 47, 61, 64, 91, 182, 209, 210
artificial selection, 31, 195
artistic traits in scientists and engineers, 46
Ashenhurst, R. L., 26, 233
Aspray, W., 45, 233
association, 100
associative network, 71, 207
Atanasoff, J. V., 45, 233
Atanasoff–Berry computer, 45
Autobiography of Charles Darwin, The, 211
Automatic Computing Engine (ACE), 86
Automatic Sequence Controller Calculator,
    124

BACON, 183, 197–9, 209, 212
Bacon, Francis, 211
Bacon, Roger, 212
Balachandran, M., 234
Ballistics Research Laboratory (U.S.), 67
Barlow, Nora, 211
Barr, A., 71, 86, 233
Basalla, G., 123, 233
Bell, C. G., 45, 63, 233, 239
benzene, ring structure of, 4, 28
Bernard, Claude, 214
Berthollet, Claude, 214
Berry, C., 45
Berry, J. R., 45, 233
Bigelow, J., 68, 69
Billington, D. P., 45, 233
biological level, 55, 100
bisociation, 33–4, 36, 44, 194–6
bit-slice devices, 83, 87
Black, M., 29, 32, 33, 49, 233
Black's specific heat law, 212
Blockley, D. I., 45, 233
Boden, M., 10, 18, 20, 22, 25, 37, 46, 49,
    106, 213, 233
Bohr, N., 11, 17, 44, 214
Boltzmann, Ludwig, 11, 214
Boole, George, 181
Boolean equation, 130, 181
bounded rationality, principle of, 31, 48–9,
    57, 59, 60, 61, 93, 100, 206
Boyle's law, 212, 216
Brachman, R., 71, 86, 234
Bradshaw, G. L., 237
Briggs, F. A., 45, 236
Brown, D. C., 44, 45, 234
Bruner, J. S., 25, 234
Bugliarello, G., 45, 234
Burks, A. R., 45, 234
Burks, A. W., 12, 13, 45, 130, 132, 145, 154,
    158, 160, 234
Burt, Cyril, 46

Butterfield, E. C., 100, 216, 237
Butterfield, H., 50, 234

caloric, 48
Cambridge Philosophical Society, 83
Cambridge University Mathematical Laboratory, 14, 45, 65, 83, 84
carbonic acid, 48
Carnap, Rudolph, 6, 44, 50, 234
Carr, E. H., 102, 234
case study approach, xi, 6, 11–15, 43, 50, 213, 214
cathode ray tube, *see* electrostatic storage tube
Cavendish Laboratory, Cambridge, 181
Chandrasekaran, B., 44, 45, 234
Chandrasekhar, S., 46, 234
charbon, 48
chemical revolution, the, 4, 45
Chomsky, Noam, 87, 234
circuit level of description, 53, 63
citation index, 25
Clark, R., 211, 234
cognitive process, 10, 16, 17, 19, 22, 27, 38, 39, 216
cognitive science, xi, 37
cognitive system, 55
Cohen, I. B., 24, 47, 50, 234
Coleridge, Samuel Taylor, 4, 36, 44, 193, 211, 214
Collins, A. R., 100, 234
complexity of designs, 14, 45, 65, 66, 68, 70, 71, 80, 103
complexity of systems, 10, 45, 52, 63
computation as metaphor, xi, 12, 35–9, 43, 51, 215
computational artifacts, 9–10
computational explanations, 10, 12, 35–9, 43, 62
computational philosophy of science, 39
computational process, xi, 37, 38, 43
computational theory of scientific creativity (CTSC), 39, 43, 50, 51, 56, 60–63, 91, 102, 190, 206, 210–11, 215
computer architecture, 13, 26, 52, 63, 127, 140
computer science, 9, 12, 36, 91
computers as intelligent entities, 37
Conant, J. B., 3, 4, 50, 234
conceptual fact, 104, 123, 202
conceptual matrices, 33, 34, 36, 44, 195
conceptual network, 71, 72, 73, 94, 96, 99, 100
conceptual rule, 125, 126, 129
connectionism, 63
conservation of momentum principle, 212
context of discovery, 5–6, 23, 44, 210
context of justification, 5, 23, 44, 210

control matrix, *see* diode matrix
control step, *see* micro-operation
control store, 82
control unit, xi, 13, 15, 25, 65, 66–9, 78, 79, 115, 134, 136, 142, 158, 168, 170, 175, 190
control unit, as a stored programmed device, 81, 91; function of the, 127
control units, designability of, 70, 71, 74, 192; functional flexibility of, 117; maintainability of, 70, 71, 74, 192; regularity of, 71, 80, 115, 192; reliability of, 70, 71, 74, 86; reparability of, 70, 71, 192; simplicity of, 80, 115, 192
corroboration of theories, 42, 63, 116, 123
Coulomb's law, 212
coupled diode matrix, *see* dual diode matrix
Coyne, R. D., 234
creative act, instantaneousness of, 46
creative process, illumination stage in, 34, 36, 44, 106, 193; incubation stage in, 34; nature of the, xi, xii, 4, 12, 18, 20, 25, 33–5, 37, 38, 39, 40, 43; preparation stage in, 34
Creative Process, The, xi
creative process, verification stage in, 34
creativity, xi, 3, 6, 8, 10, 13, 15–22, 33, 35–9, 46, 213, 214; as the combination of ideas, 36, 38, 194–6, 209; contingent nature of, 40, 43, 62, 92, 189; definition of, 18; Eureka moments in, 192–3; evolving systems theory of, 23; gradualistic nature of, 38, 44, 192–4, 208; HN-, 18, 19, 22; HO-, 18, 19, 22, 24, 25, 26, 47, 60; in art and literature, 49; in the invention of microprogramming, 24–6; indeterminacy in, 40; nonpsychological factors in, 22–24; opportunism in, 208; PN-, 18, 19, 20, 21, 22; PO-, 18, 19, 20, 21, 22, 24, 47, 60; purposiveness in, 191, 208; role of consciousness in, 34, 192; role of knowledge in, 38, 201–6, 208; role of logic and reasoning in, 196–201, 208; role of revision of ideas in, 38, 50; role of the unconscious in, 34, 36, 106, 192, 211; testability of theory of, 39–43, 62–3, 195; the central hypothesis, 210–11, 216; the four-stage model of, 34, 106, 193; the processing of symbolic structures in, 36, 61; types of, 16–17
Cross, N., 44, 234
Csikzentmihalyi, M., 23, 24, 234
Curie, Marie, 44

Daedalus, 63
Darwin on Man, 11
Darwin, Charles, 27, 31, 35, 44, 48, 191, 193, 211, 214

Darwinian evolution, 31, 32, 191, 193, 195
Dasgupta, S., 26, 31, 44, 45, 46, 47, 48, 49, 50, 61, 63, 64, 87, 123, 183, 184, 210, 234, 235, 238
data-driven discovery, 197
Dead, The, 3
decoder, 75, 76, 77, 81, 82, 85–6
deduction, 6
deductive logic, 6
Dennett, D., 63, 235
description levels, 52, 54, 55, 63, 64
design and its connection with science, 210–11
design as an act of creation, 8, 11
design as an evolutionary process, 31–2, 49, 184
design as scientific discovery, the hypothesis, 210
design as the initiation of change, 123
design, the nature of, 44, 61; the logic of, 201
designs as theories, 64
determinacy, Einstein's belief in, 17
determinacy, principle of, 58, 61
digital computer, 74
digital systems, 53
diode matrix, 75, 77, 78, 79, 80, 81, 82, 83, 91, 92, 111–17, 125–8, 132, 134, 136–52, 150, 154, 155, 156, 157–61, 166, 181, 183, 192, 196, 212
directed graph, 211
Doner, D. B., 45, 234
Dreyfus, H. S., 49, 235
dual diode matrix, 158, 167, 172, 179
Duheim, Pierre, 50, 235

Eckert, Presper, 12, 13, 45, 86
EDSAC, 14, 45, 65–9, 71, 74, 75–7, 80, 84–5, 86, 87, 91, 93, 111, 115, 145, 151, 158, 160, 170, 175, 181, 183
EDSAC-2, 15, 84, 87, 181, 183
EDVAC, 13, 66, 86
Einstein, Albert, 11, 17, 44, 214
electronic computer, origins of, 45
electrostatic storage tube, 145–6, 151, 154, 160
Eliot, T. S., 49, 214
Ellman, Richard, 3, 38, 49, 214, 235
empirical fact, 104, 123, 202
encoder, 75, 76, 77, 80
endoarchitecture, 53, 54, 64
ENIAC, 12–13, 45, 124
Essay on the Principles of Population, An, 193
evolving systems theory, 23
exoarchitecture, 52, 53, 54, 64
Experience and Prediction, 5
explanandum, 33, 38

explanation, xii, 7, 10, 11, 27, 33, 35–9, 42, 61, 91, 92, 93, 102, 189, 190

Facts, classes of, 202–3; examples of, 95, 104, 111, 112, 113, 116, 125, 128, 136, 141, 143, 176, 202, 203, 207, 219–22
Faraday, Michael, 11
Feigenbaum, E., 71, 86, 233
Ferranti Mark I, 83
Fetzer, J. H., 37, 44, 49, 235
Feyerabend, P., 6, 50, 235
Findlay, A., 28, 235
Findler, N. V., 71, 235
fixed air, 48
Flores, F., 45, 49, 241
Floyd, R. W., 87
Fodor, J. A., 235
forgery in science, 46
Forrester, Jay, 124
Fuchsian functions, 28
functional autonomy, 52, 53, 54
functional capability, 176
functional entity, 127, 129, 130, 131
functional flexibility, 117, 124
functional similarity, 141, 142, 144, 147, 149, 150

Galileo's law, 212
Gardiner, P., 102, 235
gate, 154
gate level, *see* logic level
Gero, J. S., 45, 234
gestalt, 6, 11, 36
Ghiselin, B., xi, 4, 211, 235
Gill, S., 87, 158, 170, 183, 241
goal graph, 122, 136, 144, 145, 151, 153, 156, 157, 169, 173, 174, 180, 190
goal in science, 61
goal-directedness, 190–1, 208
goals in the creative process, 36, 38, 102
goals, examples of, 94, 98, 104, 110, 119, 122, 132, 134, 138, 139, 150, 156, 163, 165, 168, 169, 171, 176, 177, 192, 230–2; nature of, 56, 58, 102
Goldstine, H. H., 13, 130, 132, 145, 154, 158, 160, 234, 235
Gould, Stephen Jay, 40, 46, 92, 235
Graham, S., 26, 233
Gries, D., 35, 235
Gruber, H., 11, 13, 23, 27, 35, 36, 38, 44, 46, 48, 191, 193, 194, 214, 235
Guernica, 37, 50, 214
Gutenberg press, 195

Habib, S., 46, 48, 235
Hadamard, J., 34, 36, 38, 44, 106, 193, 194, 195, 213, 235
Hanson, N. R., 5, 6, 50, 111, 201, 210, 235

Hardy G. H., 21, 22, 25, 235
Harre, R., 44, 50, 212, 235
Hartree, D. R., 124
Hayes, J. P., 86, 87, 235
Heisenberg, Werner, 214
Hempel, C. G., 33, 50, 236
Henderson, J. R., 45, 233
Hershel, John, 212
Hesse, M., 161, 183, 236
heuristic problem solving, 87
heuristics, 38
hierarchical organization, 52, 53, 54, 63
hierarchy, 7, 10, 45
high level programming languages, 63
high Speed Automatic Calculating Machines
    Conference, 86
historical evidence, 6, 91, 214
historical explanation, *see* explanation
history of science, 40, 50
history of technology, 9, 123
Hoare, C. A. R., 35, 45, 236
Hodges, A., 86, 236
Hofstadter, D. R., 49, 236
Holland, J. R., 100, 113, 161, 183, 236
Holmes, F. L., 4, 11, 28, 30, 35, 36, 38, 44,
    48, 193, 214, 236
Holton, G., 35, 46, 50, 236
Holyak, K. J., 236
Hopper, Grace Murray, 124
Howlett, J., 237
Hume, David, 5, 236
Husson, S. S., 15, 182, 236
Hwang, K., 45, 236
hypotheses, xii, 191–2
hypotheses about invention, 208–11
hypothesis law of design, 184

IBM Hursley Laboratory (U.K.), 87
IBM System/360 series of computers, 15, 87
Ideal gas law, 212
Ihde, D., 45, 236
imagery in scientific thought, 11, 28–9, 214
induction, 5
inductivism, 211–12
inference, abductive, 6, 97, 110–11, 116,
    118, 200; by analogy, 145, 159, 161–2,
    183; by generalization, 112, 113, 114,
    118, 137, 143, 145, 200; by instantiation,
    97, 104, 109, 115, 118, 119, 120, 128,
    133, 134, 139, 140, 165, 170, 178, 200;
    by modus ponens, 120, 121, 127, 128,
    131, 134, 135, 139, 140, 144, 150, 151,
    153, 154, 159, 165, 168, 171, 173, 177,
    179, 200; deductive, 6, 155; rules of, 200,
    217–18
Institute of Advanced Study, Princeton, 68,
    160
intentional stance, 63

intentionality, 64
International Archive on Microprogramming,
    49
introspection, 28
invention, xii, 8, 10, 11, 24, 43, 190–2, 201,
    208–11, 213
invention, its connection with science, 210–
    211
Iowa State University, 45
Italian Renaissance, 23, 24

James, William, 11, 28, 29, 49
Jaynes, J., 27, 236
Jeffrey, L., 38, 50, 214, 236
Johnson-Laird, P. N., 20, 22, 37, 194, 213,
    236
Jones, J. C., 123, 236
Joule's law, 183
Joyce, James, 3, 28, 214

Kaplan, C. A., 37, 216, 240
Keats, John, 17
KEKADA program, 209
Kekule, Friedrich August, 4, 28, 29, 33, 313
Kepler's laws, 6, 195, 197, 199, 216
Kilburn, T., 14, 130, 236, 241
kinetic theory of gases, 35
knowledge, conceptual structure of, 24, 25,
    38, 47, 72, 73; domain-specific, 203–4;
    engineering-related, 206; hierarchical
    nature of, 203–4; logic of, 5; personal,
    17, 21; psychology of, 5; public, 17; qual-
    itative, 206; types of, 56, 57, 203–6
knowledge body, 17, 19, 25, 33, 34, 46, 59,
    61, 71, 72, 73, 102, 111, 142, 170, 175,
    181, 201–6
knowledge level, 38, 52, 55–60, 63, 64, 92,
    93, 189
knowledge level action, *see* action
knowledge level agent, 56, 94
knowledge-level computation, 38, 39, 51, 59–
    60, 61, 62, 93, 94–100, 98, 99, 101, 106,
    126, 189, 196, 199
knowledge level explanation, *see* knowledge
    level computation
knowledge level goals, *see* goals, examples
    of
knowledge level process, *see* knowledge level
    computation
knowledge level theory of creativity, *see*
    computational theory of scientific
    creativity
knowledge representation, 71–5, 86, 94
knowledge token, 17, 93, 202
knowledge tokens, examples of, 74, 94, 96,
    171, 205
Koestler, Arthur, 4, 25, 33, 36, 38, 44, 46, 48,
    194, 195, 196, 236

Krebs, H., 4, 11, 210, 214
Kubla Khan, 4, 193, 211, 214
Kuhn, Thomas S., 6, 7, 8, 11, 22, 24, 35, 44, 46, 47, 49, 50, 63, 210, 212, 215, 236, 237
Kulkarni, D., 43, 44, 51, 56, 199, 209, 216, 237

Lachman, J. L., 100, 216, 237
Lachman, R., 100, 216, 237
Laird, J. E., 55, 237, 238
Lakatos, I., 6, 46, 49, 50, 210, 215, 237
Langley, P., 43, 45, 56, 183, 197, 209, 216, 237
Laudan, L., 6, 11, 42, 44, 46, 47, 49, 50, 210, 215, 237
Lavoisier, Antoine, 3, 4, 11, 28, 29, 30, 35, 36, 44, 48, 193, 214
laws, artificial, 7
laws, natural, 7
Lawson, B., 45, 237
Lenat, D. B., 199, 237
Levesque, H., 71, 86, 234
links, component type, 73; goal type, 95; instance-of type, 73; kind-of type, 72; property type, 73; rule type, 74, 95
Loftus, E. F., 100, 234
logic level, 53, 63
Logic of Scientific Discovery, The, 5, 6
Losee, J., 44, 50, 212, 237
Lowes, J. L., 36, 44, 194, 211, 214

Mallach, E., 48, 237
Malthus, Robert, 193, 195
Manchester Mark I, 14, 45, 71, 130, 160
Manchester University, 14
Manchester University Computer Inaugural Conference, 83
March, L., 45, 201, 237
Massachusetts Institute of Technology, 78, 84
Masterman, M., 49, 237
Mathematical Tripos (Cambridge), 181
Mathematician's Apology, A, 25
Mauchley, John, 12, 13, 45, 86
Mayr, E., 40, 44, 50, 237
McClelland, J. L., 56, 239
McCluskey, E. J., 237
means–ends analysis heuristic, 164–5, 184–5, 201
Medawar, Peter, 34, 194, 196, 237
Mercer, R. J., 183, 237
metaphier, 27, 30, 31, 32, 33, 38
metaphor, xi, 12, 27, 28, 32, 35, 49, 215
metaphor, as comparison, 29; as explanatory model, 27–33, 35–9, 44; as scaffolding, 30; as thought, 48; consciousness as stream, 28, 29, 32; design as an evolutionary process, 31–2; interaction view

of, 29; programs as formal entities, 35; respiration as candle burning, 28, 29–30, 32, 35; substitution view of, 29
metaphorical model, 32–3, 35, 38
metaphrand, 27, 30, 31, 32, 33, 38
metaphysics, role in science of, 46
Metropolis, N., 13, 237
micro-architecture, 53
micro-operation, 81, 82, 142, 150, 154, 155, 156, 181, 182, 183
micro-order, 81, 134, 138, 139, 144, 150, 155, 170, 181, 182
micro-order address, 81, 82, 87, 127, 131, 134, 140, 156, 160–2, 171, 173–81
microinstruction, 81, 82, 87, 183
microprogram, 53, 81, 83, 124, 134, 136, 138, 139, 150, 156, 181
microprogrammed control unit, 15, 81, 82, 84, 87, 170, 181, 182, 196
microprogramming, as a case study of creativity, 12–15; commercial adoption of, 87; idea of, xii, 15, 40, 80, 83, 119–23, 132, 196, 216; invention of, xii, 10, 12–15, 22, 24, 25–6, 42, 65, 68, 92, 190, 196, 214; its influence on computer design, 15, 26, 47; its origins, 14, 80–3, 214
Mill, John Stuart, 113, 212, 237
Miller, A. I., 11, 214, 234
Milutinovic, V., 46, 48, 238
misfit identification and elimination heuristic, 168–9, 173, 184, 201
Mitchell, W. J., 45
Moore School of Electrical Engineering, 12, 86, 124
Mozart, Wolfgang Amadeus, 4
multiple description levels, 51–5
Musgrave, A., 49, 237
Myers, G. J., 87, 238

National Academy of Engineering (U.S.), 48
National Academy of Sciences (U.S.), 48
National Physical Laboratory (U.K.), 86
natural sciences, 7, 8, 11, 43, 46, 61, 209, 210
natural selection, 193
neural network, 55
Newell, A., 37, 38, 39, 45, 51, 55, 56, 63, 64, 87, 164, 191, 233, 237, 238, 239
Newton, Isaac, 44
Newton's law of gravitation, 212
Newton's laws of motion, 212
Nickels, T., 6, 44, 238
nonmonotonic reasoning, 42, 50
nonrational actions, 59, 60, 106, 192, 211
normal science, 8, 11, 22, 44
novelty, historical, 18, 20, 22; psychological, 18

Nowak, G., 24, 51, 56, 216, 240
Nozick, R., 20, 22, 238

Ohm's law, 212
Olivetti Research Laboratory, 86, 87, 212
ontology of science, 50
order code, 71
order interpreter, 66, 80, 91, 93, 112, 116, 151
order tank, 159
Origin of Species, The, 31
originality, historical, 18, 19, 20, 22, 60, 61; psychological, 18, 19, 21, 60, 61
ornithine cycle for urea synthesis, 4, 11, 210
Ortony, A., 48, 238
Osowski, J. V., 28, 29, 238
Ostwald, Wilhelm, 214

Pacey, A., 9, 206, 238
paper tape reader, 145, 160
Papert, S., 63, 238
paradigm, 8, 11, 25, 35, 39, 44, 46, 47, 49, 63, 212, 215
paradigm shift, 24, 44, 47, 216
paradigms in the artificial sciences, 47
parallel distributed processing, 56
parallel processing, 45
Partington, J. R., 48, 238
Pasteur, Louis, 214
Patel, S., 50, 238
Pattee, H. H., 45, 63, 238
Patterns of Discovery, 5
Peirce, C. S., 44, 238
Perkins, D. N., 22, 38, 44, 191, 194, 196, 211, 213, 238
Petroski, H., 45, 238
philosophical issues in science, 50
philosophy of natural and artificial sciences, 216
philosophy of science, indifference of scientists to, 40; its significance to invention, 6–9, 213; its significance to scientific discovery, 4–6, 44, 213
philosophy of technology, 45
phlogiston theory, 4
physical artifacts, 126, 127
physical entity, 125, 126, 129, 130, 131
PI system, 183, 210
Picasso, Pablo, 37, 50, 214
plausible explanations, xii, 10, 27, 43, 92, 102, 126, 199, 216
Poincare, Henri, 4, 28, 33, 34, 44, 106, 193, 195, 213, 238
Popper, Karl, 5, 6, 11, 50, 102, 123, 184, 196, 199, 210, 238, 239
Popper's theory of science, 184

Posner, M. I., 239
Post, Emil, 87
Pound, Ezra, 49
Prelude, The, 50, 214
Principles of Psychology, 28, 49
problems, conceptual, 14, 45, 46, 69, 71, 103; empirical, 14, 45, 46; recognition of, 14, 103–6, 211
process, concept of, 46
production rules, *see* rules
protocol analysis, 199
purposiveness in creativity, 38, 191
Pye, D., 44, 239
Pylyshyn, Z., 55, 56, 63, 235, 239

Qin, Y., 197, 199, 213, 239
qualitative reasoning, 206
Queen Mary, 81

Rachman, J., 160
radar, 181
Radford, A. D., 234
Ramanujan, Srinivasan, 21, 22, 35
Randall, B., 12, 67, 86, 239
random logic, 80
rational actions, 59, 111, 192
rationality, principle of, 7, 56–7, 61, 93, 99, 206
recursion, 26, 47
register, 86
regularity of designs, 14, 26, 65, 66, 68, 71, 75, 103
Reichenbach, Hans, 5, 6, 210, 239
Reiter, R., 50, 239
relativism in science, 215
reliability, 70
Renwick, W., 15, 65, 83, 84, 145, 183, 241
research program, 45, 215
research tradition, 11, 46, 215
retroduction, *see* abduction
Revolution in Science, 47
revolutionary science, 4, 8, 24, 44, 47
Richards, I. A., 27, 239
Rime of the Ancient Mariner, The, 24
Rogers, G. F. C., 44, 64, 239
Roller, D., 50, 239
Root-Bernstein, R., 38, 46, 103, 214, 234
Rosenbloom, P. S., 55, 237, 238
Rosenman, A., 234
Rosin, R. F., 239
Rota, G-C., 237
Rowe, P. G., 45, 239
Royal Society, 48
rules: classes of, 126, 129, 130, 199–200; examples of, 74, 95, 98, 104, 109, 110, 112, 114, 119, 125, 128, 132, 133, 137, 138, 140, 141, 150, 152, 154, 155, 159, 171,

173, 176, 178, 197–8, 200, 207, 222–9;
  origins of, 87
Rumelhart, D. E., 56, 239
Ruse, M., 6, 50, 239
Rutherford, Lord, 181

Schon, D., 45, 239
science, its connection with invention, 210–
  11
sciences of the artificial, *see* artificial
  sciences
Sciences of the Artificial, The, 7, 9
scientific discovery, 4, 5, 6, 8, 16, 197, 210–
  11
Scientific Discovery, 197
Scotus, John Duns, 212
Scriven, M., 50, 239
search, 38
Searle, J. R., 49, 64, 239
semantic network, 71
sequence control tank, 158, 159
Shapere, D., 49, 239
Shaw, Cliff, 37, 38, 39, 57, 191, 238
Shrager, J., 239
Shriver, B. D., 26, 46, 48, 235
Siewiorek, D. P., 45, 239
Simon, H. A., 7, 9, 37, 38, 39, 43, 44, 45, 48,
  51, 57, 63, 87, 123, 164, 191, 197, 199,
  209, 213, 216, 237, 238, 239, 240
Smith, Adam, 28
Smith, C. S., 45, 63, 240
Snell's law of refraction, 212
Snow, C. P., 240
SOAR, 56
solution space, 38
Sondak, N., 48, 237
Special Interest Group on Microprogram-
  ming, 48
spreading activation, 100–1, 106, 142, 154,
  207–8
Stern, N., 240
Sternberg, R. J., 103, 260
Stone, H. S., 45, 240
stored program computer, 12–13, 14, 45, 65,
  67, 84, 117, 119, 124, 142, 159, 168, 169,
  175, 182, 196
Storr, A., 46, 240
stream of consciousness, 28, 29, 32
Stringer, J. B., 70, 83, 86, 183, 241
structural similarity, 140, 141, 145, 147, 149
Structure of Scientific Revolutions, The, 6, 7,
  212
structured set of actions, 58, 59
subaction, 97
subgoal, 122
Suppe, F., 49, 50, 240
symbol, formal, 57; physical, 58

symbol level, 55, 56, 64, 100, 189
symbol processing actions, 57–8
symbol system hypothesis, 39, 51
symbolic artifacts, 7
symbolic entity, 125, 126, 127
symbolic structures, 36, 38, 39, 57–8, 61, 64,
  126

Tanenbaum, A. S., 63, 240
Taylor, C. W., 16, 240
Tchaikovsky, Piotr, 4
Technical Committee on Microprogramming,
  48
telegraphy, 145
teleology, 191
teletype printer, 145
Terrell, G., 235
Thagard, P., 24, 39, 43, 44, 45, 51, 56, 71,
  87, 100, 113, 183, 199, 210, 216, 240
theories, empirical, 42; explanatory, 50, 62;
  predictive, 50, 62
theory of creativity, nature of, 39, 40–3; testability of, 39–43
theory of evolution, 28, 35, 191, 195
truth table, 130, 131, 181
Turing, Alan, 37, 47, 83, 240
Turing Award Lecture, 26

University of Southwestern Louisiana, 48
ultrasonic memory, 84–5, 126, 127, 133, 151,
  154
ultrasonic storage devices, *see* ultrasonic
  memory

Van't Hoff, Jacobus, 214
Vernon, P. E., 49, 240
Vincenti, W. G., 45, 240
Visitors' A-Z London Map, 54
von Helmoltz, Herman, 34, 49, 193, 195, 213
von Neumann, John, 12, 13, 66, 86, 130, 132,
  145, 158, 160, 234, 240

Wallace, D. B., 11, 44, 240
Wallas, G., 34, 44, 49, 106, 193, 195, 240
Waste Land, The, 49, 214
wave theory of sound, 210, 216
Wechsler, J., 46, 240
Weisberg, R. W., 240
Weizenbaum, J., 49, 240
well-structured problem, 45
Wertheimer, Max, 11
Wertheimer, Michael, 235
Wheeler, D. J., 15, 87, 158, 170, 183, 241
Whewell, William, 50, 212, 241
Whirlwind I, 78–9, 80, 84, 91, 111, 112, 117,
  136, 137, 143, 160, 182
Whyte, L. L., 45, 63, 241

Wilkes, Maurice V., xi, xii, xiv, 13, 14, 15, 22, 24, 25, 26, 27, 40, 42, 43, 45, 48, 65, 68, 69, 70, 71, 75, 77, 80, 83, 84, 85, 86, 87, 91, 101, 102, 108, 111, 124, 130, 140, 142, 145, 158, 159, 161, 170, 175, 181, 182, 183, 189, 199, 212, 214, 216, 241
William of Occam, 212
Williams, F. C., 14, 130, 241
Williams tube, 130

Wilson, A. G., 45, 63, 241
Wilson, D., 45, 63, 241
Winograd, T., 45, 241
Woolf, Virginia, 28
Wordsworth, William, 11, 50
Worlton, J., 13, 237
Worsley, B. H., 241

Zytkow, J. M., 237